Believers Church
Bible Commentary

Elmer A. Martens and Howard H. Charles, Editors

Believers Church
Bible Commentary

Genesis

Eugene F. Roop

HERALD PRESS
Scottdale, Pennsylvania
Kitchener, Ontario
1987

Library of Congress Cataloging-in-Publication Data

Roop, Eugene F., 1942-
    Genesis.

    (Believers church Bible commentary)
    Bibliography: p.
        1. Bible.   O.T. Genesis—Commentaries.
I. Title.   II. Series.
BS1235.3.R56   1987   222'.1107   87-10969
ISBN 0-8361-3443-5 (pbk.)

BELIEVERS CHURCH BIBLE COMMENTARY: GENESIS
Copyright © 1987 by Herald Press, Scottdale, Pa. 15683
    Published simultaneously in Canada by Herald Press,
    Kitchener, Ont. N2G 4M5. All rights reserved.
Library of Congress Catalog Card Number: 87-10969
International Standard Book Number: 0-8361-3443-5
Printed in the United States of America

93 92 91 90 89 88 87 10 9 8 7 6 5 4 3 2 1

To my family:
Delora, Tanya, Fred Roop

Contents

*For a more comprehensive outline of Genesis, see pages 296-310.

Series Foreword

The Believers Church Bible Commentary Series makes available a new tool for basic Bible study. It is published for all who seek to understand more fully the original message of Scripture and its meaning for today—Sunday school teachers, members of Bible study groups, students, pastors, or other seekers. The series is based on the conviction that God is still speaking to all who will hear him, and that the Holy Spirit makes the Word a living and authoritative guide for all who want to know and do God's will.

The desire to be of help to as wide a range of readers as possible has determined the approach of the writers. No printed biblical text has been provided in order that readers might continue to use the translation with which they are most familiar. The writers of the series have used the *Revised Standard Version*, the *New International Version*, and the *New American Standard Bible* on a comparative basis and indicate which of these texts they have followed most closely, as well as where they have made their own translations. The writers have not worked alone, but in consultation with select counselors, the series' editors, and with the Editorial Council.

To further encourage use of the series by a wide range of readers the focus has been centered on illumination of the text, providing historical and cultural background, sharing necessary theological, sociological, and ethical meanings and, in general, making "the rough places plain." Critical issues have not been avoided, but neither have they been moved into the foreground as a debate among scholars. The series will aid in the interpretive process, but not attempt to provide the final meaning as authority above Word and Spirit.

The term "believers church" has often been used in the history of the church. Since the sixteenth century it has frequently been applied to the Anabaptists and later the Mennonites, as well as to the Church of the Brethren and similar groups. As a descriptive term it now includes more than Mennonites and Brethren. It represents specific theological understandings such as believers baptism, commitment to the Rule of Christ in Matthew 18:15-18 as part of the meaning of church membership, belief in the power of love in all relationships, and a willingness to follow the way of the cross of Christ. The writers chosen for the series stand in this tradition.

Believers church people have always been known for their emphasis on obedience to the simple, literal meaning of Scripture. Because of this, they do not have a long history of deep historical-critical biblical scholarship. This series attempts to be faithful to the Scriptures while also taking archaeology and current biblical studies seriously. Doing this means that at many points the writers will not differ greatly from interpretations which can be found in many other good commentaries. But basic presuppositions about Christ, the church and its mission, God and history, human nature, the Christian life, and other doctrines do determine a writer's interpretation of Scripture. Thus this series, like all other commentaries, stands within a specific historical church tradition. A felt need for help on the part of many is, therefore, understandable and justification enough to attempt its production.

The Holy Spirit is not bound to any tradition. May this series be an instrument in breaking down walls between Christians in North America and around the world, bringing new joy in obedience through a fuller understanding of the Word.

The Editorial Council

thor's Preface

oups in the Believers Church tradition have long been reluctant to
ommentary on the Bible. A number of factors have contributed to
esitancy. Some of the problem relates to one purpose of com-
ry. In part Bible commentary arose out of a desire to provide au-
tive interpretation of the Bible for the church (Grant, 1984: 73-
he church leaders wanted to be sure the laity and pastors in-
ed the Bible correctly.

ennonites, Brethren, and Baptists, among others, often found
elves persecuted because they did not follow "authorized" under-
ngs of the Bible. Certainly we expect to witness passionately to
ve believe. We do not accept every proposed interpretation of the
Nevertheless, we become uneasy when we hear that a primary
on of commentary is to set forth what is "legitimately normative"
cripture (cf. Kaiser, 1981).

any times what seems "legitimately normative" has been used by
urch to define heresy. Certainly the possibility of physical torture
ical heresy seems remote in our day in North America. However,
t so in other places. The problem of psychological coercion arising
laims of authoritative interpretation continues to plague us even in
America.

he believers church tradition has never advocated Bible study in
Christians merely do what is right in their own eyes. Such sim-
individualism is not the only alternative to control by church or
mic authorities. Instead our tradition encourages the community
dy the Bible together. The task of leaders is to promote such study
ster responsible interpretation of the texts. Hence a commentary

11

in the believers church tradition must promote regular and careful study of the Bible in the community of faith. Obviously the one who writes a commentary does not need to shy away from his or her own best interpretations of the text. This would reduce the commentary to an academic explanation of words, phrases, and historical backgrounds. But neither will the believers church tradition permit a claim of authority which does not at the same time invite ongoing discussion and discovery in the church.

I do not claim this perspective on commentary writing to be the unique contribution of the believers church tradition. Nor is it the only distinctive element we bring to the task. Nevertheless, this commentary grew out of the study of Genesis in the congregational and seminary community, and it is intended to promote and enhance study in those settings.

Though my name appears as author, this book belongs to the church, and the church must receive credit for any contribution it makes to the ongoing study of Genesis. To be sure, someone must accept responsibility for the inadequacies and problems of this book. It is for that purpose that my name appears as author.

Because of the abundance of English translations and the limited space available, one translation of the Hebrew functions as the common thread in this commentary. For that thread I have used the RSV. That text appears in italics. Other translations (e.g., NASB, NIV), as well as my own translations of the Hebrew text, appear in quotation marks rather than italics.

Since the full text of Genesis is not included, this commentary will need to be read alongside an open Bible. In any case, it would hardly do to have a believers church commentary that did not require the reader to open the Bible.

The names of those who have contributed indirectly to this commentary are too numerous to remember, let alone list. They must, like Abraham's friend in Genesis 24, be simply called *the servants*. Some others contributed directly to the production and improvement of the book. My wife, Delora Roop, typed the manuscript on computer disks. That skill, which I do not have, allowed the text to be revised with an ease that I find unbelievable.

However much computers may help, errors do not find and correct themselves. Much of the finding and revising on the computer was done by Dorothy Ritchey with additional proofreading by David Leiter. The manuscript was read and substantially improved by Dwight Beery, Walter Brueggemann, Kiyo Mori, Robert Neff, Donna Ritchey Martin, and the Old Testament editor of this series, Elmer Martens.

I want also to thank the faculty and staff of Bethany Theological Seminary, who provided encouragement, opportunity, and the impetus to write. And, of course, I cannot forget the students who taught me Genesis. It is to them that this book is especially dedicated. It belongs to them.

> *Gene Roop*
> *Bethany Theological Seminary*
> *Oak Brook, Illinois*
>
> *August 1986*

Genesis

A Look at the Whole Story

The Parts and the Whole

We know the stories of Genesis, at least most of them. We read them in our worship and work with them in our study. We teach them to our children and allude to them in our songs. These texts as individual stories have found an important place in the life of the faith community.

Yet we can miss some of their richness when we see these texts only as individual stories without exploring their role in the larger drama of the whole book. The same thing happens with episodes in our own life. We often tell single episodes of our life to others. Those episodes have significance in and of themselves, but when set in the context of our whole life pilgrimage, the same stories can take on a different shape and new meaning. The individual stories of Genesis are part of a larger story also. The depth and richness of this biblical book becomes most visible when we gain some perspective on the whole narrative as well as immerse ourselves in these individual episodes. The whole drama of Genesis gives new shape, meaning, and significance to the individual moments.

Before we explore the individual texts, let us look briefly at the shape of the book as a whole. In the history of the church's study of Genesis, the most common division has been between chapters 11 and 12. In Genesis 1—11 the narrative focuses on all of humanity. Genesis 12:1ff. turns from this broader focus and directs the reader's attention to one family, that of Abraham and Sarah. Nevertheless we must be cautious about assuming a sharp division at that point. Abraham and Sarah have already been introduced in chapter 11. In fact, Sarah's barrenness, which is so central to the story, is stated first in 11:30. So while we can speak generally about Genesis 1—11 and 12—50, the text as we have received it does not sharply separate the story at that point.

As we move through Genesis, the individual narratives seem to divide themselves from each other naturally [*Genres of Hebrew Literature, p. 319.*] Any way we choose to outline the book, we will have to take into account its story form. In Genesis 12—50 these narratives group themselves around the life of particular families. We usually think of the family stories in terms of the father—Abraham or Jacob, for example. The tradition itself speaks of God as the *God of your father, the God of Abraham, the God of Isaac, and the God of Jacob* (Exod. 3:6, 15). But the stories of Genesis feature not only fathers, but also mothers, sisters and brothers. Hence the narratives ought to be called "family stories" rather than the more familiar term, "patriarchal stories" (Westermann, 1980: 59f.).

The general flow of the whole book divides the material this way:

Stories of all humanity (primeval story), Gen. 1—11

Story of the ancestral families, Gen. 12—50
    Abraham, Sarah, and family, Gen. 12—25
    Isaac, Rebekah, and family, Gen. 26—27
    Jacob, Leah, Rachel, and family, Gen. 28—36
    Joseph, Gen. 37—50

These divisions are approximate and as we look at the text more closely we will look for clues to a more precise division.

Some who study Genesis concentrate their work on the history of the book, exploring the historical process by which the independent collections of stories became the book of Genesis as we know it. A common explanation suggests that an old epic handed down through many generations was later supplemented by or joined with material collected by the priestly community of the Babylonian Exile to form the present text of Genesis. Some propose that this old epic was composed from two groups of material, one preserved in the Southern Kingdom, Judah, the other preserved first in the Northern Kingdom, Ephraim-Israel. For many those traditions and/or literary sources have provided an important way to develop an interpretation of the book. [*Historical Study of Genesis, p. 320.*]

While this continues to be an important way to arrange and interpret the material, some students of the Bible feel uncomfortable with this approach to Genesis. A few reject the historical-analytical (critical) approach altogether, insisting that it is harmful. But other scholars seek not to reject but supplement historical analysis with other methods that give attention to the final form of Genesis. While remaining sensitive to the history of the composition of the book, that is not the primary focus in this commentary. Whether looking at the large units of the book or the individual stories, the focus is less on historical analysis and more on the book as it lies before us.

These Are the Generations

In the text of Genesis as we have it, the phrase *these are the generations* ("this is the account," NASB, NIV) marks important divisions in the book. This phrase consistently signals the beginning of a new unit (cf. 5:1; 10:1; 37:2). Sometimes the phrase seems to come in the middle of the story as we have traditionally read it (6:9), or does not mark the beginning of the new unit quite as we have been accustomed to dividing the material (2:4; 11:27). Nevertheless, this formula does designate important divisions. We will pay attention to this phrase as a primary marker as we explore Genesis.

Recognizing that story line, history of composition, and the formula "these are the generations" all have a contribution to make in looking at the book of Genesis as a whole, we will use the following major divisions:

> The stories of all humanity, 1:1—11:26
> > Creation, 1:1—2:3
> > The heavens and the earth 2:4—4:26
> > Adam's family, 5:1—6:8
> > Noah's family, 6:9—9:29
> > Sons of Noah, 10:1—11:9
> > Shem's family, 11:10—11:26
>
> The stories of Israel's early families, 11:27—50:26
> > Terah's family: Abraham, 11:27—25:18
> > Isaac's family: Jacob and Esau, 25:19—36:43
> > Jacob's family: Joseph, 37:1—50:26

For the most part, this outline follows the formula "these are the generations." I have not broken chapter 25 into as many separate genealogical lists as the formula would indicate. Nor have I separated chapter 36 from 35, even though chapter 36 uses the "generations" formula not once but twice (vv. 1, 9). Furthermore, Genesis 37:1 might be taken as the introduction to the Joseph story as we have usually done. Or it might be seen as the concluding statement of the previous unit, similar to 25:18 and 35:29. In the outline earlier, Isaac and Rebekah appear as main characters. However, the text preserves very little of the family story of Isaac and Rebekah. The material we do have has been incorporated into the sagas of Abraham and Jacob.

Just as our lives are a part of a larger drama, so each of these nine divisions appears as a part of a great "story of the generations." *[Reading Genealogies, p. 326.]* In considering this "family story," we will explore the individual stories, but also watch for guiding theological motifs such as creation, disaster and re-creation, promise and fulfillment, infertility and blessing. That is part of telling the family story.

Even as the sagas of Genesis cannot be treated simply as isolated stories, so also the book of Genesis belongs as a part of the whole Bible. As the word "genesis" signals, this is but the beginning. The beginning cannot be ignored as if it is past. Beginnings do not disappear; they form the ground from which all subsequent moments arise. Indeed Genesis intends to portray the formative shape of humanity and the community of faith in "these generations." All subsequent generations are tied to these as "descendants." Clearly, subsequent generations can take the heritage of the ancestors in many different ways, as Islam, Judaism, and Christianity display. But they remain by public confession descendants of these generations. The confessional shape of that tie is expressed in the ancient creedal-like formula, *the God of your father, the God of Abraham, the God of Isaac, and the God of Jacob* (Exod. 3:6). As descendants of these generations we turn to the beginning.

Part 1

The Saga
of All Humanity

Genesis 1:1 – 2:3

Creation

PREVIEW

The remarkable symmetry of this unit strikes the reader immediately.
The whole unit follows a regular pattern of organization:

Word: "God said."
Result: "It was so."
Assessment: "God saw that it was good."
Action: "God separated/made."
Name: "God called."
Time: "There was evening and morning."

Through a six-day sequence this flow repeats itself with variations.

The structure appears not rigid and inflexible, but as a steady, ordering element. No two days are exact duplicates either in outline or
content. The action is not always the same (*separating*, 1:4, 7; *making*,
vv. 7, 16, 25; *creating*, vv. 21, 27). Sometimes one of the regular elements drops out only to reemerge in the next sequence (e.g., v. 6 lacks
the "result" and v. 8 the "assessment"). Some of the elements appear in
the Greek text but not in the standard Hebrew text. These differences
will show up in the various English translations. Occasionally a distinctive
element will emerge in one of the "day" sections. For example, the very
extensive statement about the function of the *two lights* in the heavens
(vv. 14-18) appears in *day three* and then we find no other elaborate
description of function until *day six*—the function of humanity. Clearly

this unit is not ordered rigidly, but we do find a persistent sequence and careful symmetry.

A similar repetitive and symmetrical arrangement of material occurs in other genres or types of literature with which we are familiar. Children's literature frequently employs a repetitive style (McEvenue, 1971: 10ff.). Adults sometimes find the repetition in the story of "the little red hen" monotonous, but just this symmetry enables the youngster to absorb the material step by step. We encounter the same repetitive style in some songs, especially folk songs. The repetition of a single phrase can carry the singers along as the story line is developed through several verses.

Genealogical tables provide an example of a biblical genre which displays a rigid pattern of organization. Although Genesis 1 does not have the strict pattern of some of the genealogies, the presentation is more in the form of a "list" than a narrative (Westermann, 1984: 81ff.). Order is one of the unit's most obvious characteristics.

Finally, this chapter has been likened to a liturgy (Brueggemann, 1982: 29ff.). Liturgy again connotes a sense of careful ordering of the material, but liturgy also emphasizes movement along with repetition, song as well as list. Calling Genesis 1 liturgy reminds us that these words reflect the language that is found in the hymns and doxologies of the Psalter.

All of these comparisons help us see certain aspects of the unit. No other unit in the Old Testament is exactly like Genesis 1:1—2:3 nor, so far as we know, can we find a duplicate in the literature of Israel's neighbors. They, too, had collections of material about creation. We can learn much by comparing this passage with the literature of the ancient Near East. But we have found no other narrative or poem organized like this "hymn" about God, the Creator, with its symmetrical rhythm that flows from chaos to work to rest.

When we encounter this list/liturgy of creation, the regularity and symmetry of the text gives us a sense of order and stability. The language of praise has compelling power. Such a combination of hymnic praise and ordered structure speak deeply to the faith community when it experiences the world as dangerous and chaotic. Hence it is not surprising that during the Babylonian Exile this presentation of creation grounded Israel's experience of God and provided the community a way into God's future.

Certainly the message of this text cannot be reduced to its orderly structure and psalmlike language. But we tend to focus so much on the content that we miss the power of this presentation of creation. We may not experience the art of this passage when things are going well. We know life has order to it, and take it for granted. But the matter is different when our individual lives or our community's life is falling apart. To read this text then produces a different impact. The impact comes not so much in terms of data as drama, the drama of creation that grounds our hope. [Creation and evolution, p. 317.]

OUTLINE

Introduction: Creation and Chaos, 1:1-2

List of Creation, 1:3-31

1:3-5	Day One: Light
1:6-8	Day Two: Firmament
1:9-13	Day Three: Dry Land; Vegetation
1:14-19	Day Four: The Two Lights
1:20-23	Day Five: Water and Air Animals
1:24-31	Day Six: Land Animals; Humanity

Conclusion: The Seventh Day—Rest, 2:1-3

EXPLANATORY NOTES

Introduction: Creation and Chaos 1:1-2

The unit begins with a concern central throughout Genesis 1—11, the creating God and chaos. We commonly translate these two verses as two complete sentences (RSV, NASB, and NIV). The Hebrew words allow either this familiar translation or a translation similar to that found in the footnote of the RSV: *When God began to create.* . . . Neither Hebrew syntax nor historical investigation can clearly decide for one translation over the other.

While we might like certainty in translation, the presence of two possibilities may free us to focus on the central affirmation of the text, God creating a livable world. Sometimes in studying Genesis 1:1 we become sidetracked with the philosophical issue of "first cause." (If there must be a "cause" for everything, is there a "first cause" for God?) But the translation is not precise enough to use the text in that debate. Genesis 1:1-2 shows less concern with philosophical speculation than with theological confession: the creating God provides us with a livable world.

The earth could be different. Notice the poetic description of the nonlivable world.

> The earth, an empty wasteland,
> Darkness, over the surface of the great deep,
> Mighty wind moving over the surface of the waters.
>   (Gen. 1:2, translation mine)

We usually translate 1:2 with past tense, but the Hebrew poetry here has no defined verb tense. The prophets used the same word picture to say that the world could again become unlivable (Jer. 4:23-26).

God is not missing from even this poetic description of the unlivable world. To translate the phrase in the third line of the poetry "mighty wind" intensifies the feel of the unlivable world. But more commonly the Hebrew phrase is rendered "the Spirit [or wind] of God was moving over the surface of the waters" (NASB). The direction of those two different translations mirrors the human experience of the unlivable world: empty, bleak, dark, and windy. But God does not abandon that world. In the midst of that darkness and wind we can find the power of God.

The power of God creates a livable world. Indeed, the word *create* (Hebrew, *bara'*) in the Old Testament allows only God as the subject. God never ceases to create, bringing a livable world out of one too dark, too wet, or too dry.

> The afflicted and needy are seeking water,
>   But there is none,
> And their tongue is parched with thirst.
> I, the Lord, will answer them myself,
>   As the God of Israel, I will not forsake them.
> I will open rivers on the barren hills,
>   and the springs in the midst of the valleys . . .
> That they may see and recognize,
>   May consider and perceive
> That the hand of the Lord has done this,
>   The Holy One of Israel has *created* it.
>   (Isa. 41:17-20, translation mine)

Genesis begins with this affirmation. Whatever else the narratives of Jesus say, they affirm that the power of God continues to create a livable world:

> He has sent me
>   to proclaim release to the captives,
>   and recovering of sight to the blind,
>   to set at liberty those who are oppressed,
>   to proclaim the acceptable year of the Lord.
>   (Luke 4:18-19)

List of Creation 1:3-31

God creates the world through speech: *And God said*. . . . Speech in the biblical tradition is not a monologue but a bonding between two persons. The use of *word* to describe the creating work does not emphasize the separation between God and creation. Nor does the use of divine speech constitute a dramatic demonstration of magical power, as it does in some other ancient Near East stories. Rather, as the prophetic tradition of the Old Testament and the prologue to the Gospel of John recognize (John 1:1ff.), the *word* establishes and expresses a bond between God and the world. When God speaks and the livable world comes to be, God is not more distant or less involved than when God "acts" by making, separating, placing, or forming (Gen. 2).

This text uses many different words to describe God's relationship to the world which God brings into existence: speaking, making, separating, blessing, creating, and so forth. All of these words express the Creator's bond to the creature.

1:3-5 Day One: Light

God speaks with power, but not the power of an autocratic monarch. One must be careful not to draw too many conclusions from particular Hebrew verb forms. Even so, the form of a verb does give us some interpretive clues. Grammatically, the verb form throughout this section is jussive, not imperative. *Let* there be, not *Be*. Imperative command is a verb form we understand from our own language. The jussive has no exact counterpart in English. Jussive verb forms in Hebrew describe a broad range of declarations from the very strong (almost a command) to the very soft (almost a wish). Whether hard or gentle, the jussive always possesses a voluntary element. Our English translations try to pick up this voluntary element with the phrase *Let there be* . . . Perhaps to say that God gave permission for light and it happened would underplay the strength of the jussive. But making it God's command eliminates the gentleness of the jussive. Creation comes by divine direction, not by a dictator's demand.

God's speaking/acting established a cycle of day and night. We describe that cycle in terms of "natural law." Ancient Israel did not hear through those ears. God's speaking and acting continues to be the reason why day follows night.

A world of endless night would not be a livable world. We might describe this in strictly natural terms—without the sun, life as we know it would be impossible. But natural science does not exhaust our fear of dark without end. That fear, mostly buried in adults, continues to be

voiced by children. This text responds to such anxiety, not with a statement about natural law, but with an affirmation about the creating God.
Darkness will not have the last say. The night will end and the day will
come, always.

1:6-8 Day Two: Firmament

A second separation brings the waters under control. A great dome,
the *firmament* ("expanse" NASB, NIV), keeps the waters in their place.
Under control, the waters above the earth bring rain and fertility.
Unleashed, these same waters bring flood (7:11). A livable world needs
water under control as well as a limit to darkness.

In the Bible, control of the waters remained in God's hands (1 Kings
17—18; Mark 4:35-41). God did not install an automated water system
but acted out of a bond between Creator and creature that brings water
on the just and the unjust (Matt. 5:45). As the community of faith knows,
God is more impartial in the distribution of water than is humankind
when in control of its distribution.

By separating the ground water into its assigned place, God brought
the dangerous elements, darkness and water, under control. While
recent interest in the creation has centered on the first moment in which
matter came into existence, our biblical ancestors wondered about a different question: Is the earth a dangerous place? This text affirms that the
dangerous elements were and are in God's control. We can trust God's
world. [*Creation and Evolution, p. 317.*]

1:9-13 Day Three: Dry Land; Vegetation

The earth brings forth the plants in response to God's speech. This
affirmation addressed a critical issue in the precarious agrarian society of
ancient Palestine: when the farmer planted corn seed, would corn grow?
Two problems hide in this question. The first we know well: the problem
of crop failure. But the second, we have almost lost in the maze of detail
which attends our technical knowledge of plant reproduction: when we
plant corn seed, will we get corn and not some other vegetable? Do we
have to do something special to make sure that corn seed produces corn
rather than beans? Genesis 1:1-13 declares the trustworthy regularity of
the seasonal crops and the wonder of the reproductive process as God's
continuing gift toward a livable world.

1:14-19 Day Four: The Two Lights

We have observed the symmetry of this unit in the flow of each of
the six-day sections. We can see it again as we compare days one to

three with days four through six. Days one through three moved from lights to plants with four creative words (two on day three): light, firmament, dry land, and plants. Days four through six have a parallel movement from "great lights" to humanity. Again there are four creative words with two on day six: lights, animals of the waters and air, dry land animals, and humankind.

Day One	light	two great lights	*Day Four*
Day Two	waters controlled by firmament	water and air animals	*Day Five*
Day Three	dry land	land animals	*Day Six*
	plants	humanity (who eats plants)	

Even the structure of the text affirms the consonance and symmetry, the harmony and balance in God's world.

Looking at the content of day four, the lights in the dome have specific functions: separating day and night, marking seasons and special times, and giving light to the earth. The stars shine, but they have no significant role. Considerable care was taken to avoid misunderstanding the functions of the lights. These lights are not divine beings capable of controlling or revealing human destiny. The two great lights have no names in this text, perhaps because those names designated divine beings among Israel's neighbors. Not naming the two lights helped avoid a misunderstanding which might ascribe independent personality and power to the heavenly lights.

One word, however, proves troublesome. These two lights are said to *rule* (Hebrew, *mashal*) over day and night. Westermann (1966: 183) and Cassuto (1964: 45-46) remind us that this phrase comes from the psalms of praise (Ps. 136:7-9). As hymnic language the word *rule* evokes the feelings of grandeur and awe one experiences when looking at the "sky lights." But problems arise if that same word is interpreted as a concrete description of the power possessed by the sun and moon. The sun and moon might then be understood as royal beings who control life on earth. The thrust of this unit goes in exactly the opposite direction.

1:20-23 Day Five: Water and Air Animals

Yet another form of life thrives in God's world, *living creatures* (Hebrew, *nephesh ḥayyah*). In this narrative *living creatures* distinguish the world of animals from that of plants. All animals are living creatures

(1:20, 24, 30); plants are not. (The term *image of God* distinguishes human life from animal life, vv. 26-27.) We might wish to define *nephesh hayyah* precisely. But the text will yield only a little beyond the general observation that animals differ from plants (Wolff, 1974: 21ff.; Pedersen: 99-180). We need only to remember that *living creatures* belong here too, in the waters and the air.

The animals are *blessed (barak) [Blessing in Genesis, p. 312.]* Blessing constitutes the power of life: fertility and vitality, health and success (Westermann, 1978: 15-29). In connection with the animals, blessing brings the power to generate life. The animals have been given fertility to fill the earth. The blessing on humanity also brings fertility (1:28). But in addition, blessing empowers humankind to act as steward/ manager of God's good creation. Blessing appears a third time in connection with the seventh day. That day has been given the power to refresh, to reenliven all living creatures (Exod. 23:12; 31:17).

We often experience the world as unblessed with no power of life, even as ancient Israel did in the Babylonian Exile (597/586-538 B.C.). Sometimes we even see the world as cursed, possessing only the power of death and sterility. Genesis 1 knows that blessing is not alien to our world nor an occasional intruder in our drama. Our prayer at the table knows whereof it speaks. Blessing is present each day: a baby is born, food and rest bring new energy, a touch elicits a smile. God's blessing empowers today, not just yesterday, not only tomorrow.

1:24-31 Day Six: Land Animals; Humanity

Corresponding to the dry land of day three, on day six the earth is summoned to bring forth the land animals. Three categories symbolize and organize all land animals in this narrative: (1) domesticated animals *(cattle)*, (2) wild animals, and (3) creeping, crawling creatures. Certainly this represents some element of classification, but these expressions are also poetic. They call to mind pictures of animals, not just abstract categories. To obtain the greatest possible technical precision in classification, we use zoological terminology unintelligible except to one whose vocation or at least avocation is zoology. The lists of clean and unclean animals (e.g., Lev. 11) show that ancient Israel could work with complex classification systems. But such complexity is absent here. Domesticated animals, wild animals, and creeping/crawling creatures represent ordering by an artist as much as by a systematician.

The major focus of day six falls on the creation of humankind. This distinctive "moment" represents the peak of the six-day pattern. In addition this passage has occasioned the most discussion of the whole unit, especially over the phrases *God said, Let us . . .* and *the image of God.* [*Image of God, p. 321.*]

Christian interpreters of the past often interpreted the plural of God's address here to be a reference to the Trinity (John Wesley: 7). Present scholars are more cautious about reading the Old Testament texts as if they contain New Testament perspectives.

A second interpretation understands *Let us* as a rhetorical device. The plural of majesty or the royal plural represents one possible rhetorical interpretation. However, we have little evidence that this particular rhetorical device was used in biblical Hebrew.

A third interpretation proposes that the words *Let us . . .* refer to other divine beings such as angels. This interpretation also has a long history (cf. B. Jacob: 9). The phrase *Let us . . .* relates to the many pictures in the Old Testament of God as the Head of the divine court (e.g., 1 Kings 22; Isa. 6; Job 1; and Ps. 82) (P. Miller: 9ff.).

Vawter cautions that this phrase should not be overemphasized or overinterpreted (1977: 54). Karl Barth observes that this phrase wants at least to indicate "intra-divine unanimity of intention and decision" (1958: 182). In other words, the creating of humanity by God happened by a clear, intentional, and unanimous divine decision, whatever "unanimous" means in this case. Humanity cannot be responded to simply as an accident of history. Meaning, purpose, and intention characterize humanity's presence in God's world.

In this text, *image of God* relates at least in part to verse 28. [*Image of God, p. 321.*] God has put humanity in charge of the world. Royal and powerful words describe this responsibility: *have dominion, rule, subdue.* So the psalmist echoes,

> You have given them dominion over
> the work of your hands,
> You have put everything under their control.
> (Ps. 8:6, translation mine)

The language is uncompromising. Humanity does not have a weak and powerless role in the world, for God has entrusted us with control over creation (Bonhoeffer: 39). We are placed here to make decisions. Those decisions affect life on earth.

What does it mean to exercise *dominion?* (v. 26). The text says little more than that we are to manage the creation as ones created in the image of God. How then does God manage, rule, control? The psalmist, picturing Israel's king as one who rules as God rules (Ps. 72), uses words like justice, righteousness, compassion, and peace. The New Testament, by affirming and celebrating Jesus' connection with the royal tradition, declares that this one from Nazareth models how one rules in the image of God. Hence to be given domination over the earth does not license humanity's destruction of the world, but authorizes care for the world, care like that which comes from God.

This section concludes on a peaceful note. Plants provide unlimited food for humankind and animals (v. 29). The vision which informs this text is the same vision of the world that we find in Isaiah 11:6-9 (Vawter, 1977: 60f.). We find no strife in the world God is creating, no antagonism among the living creatures. In this picture of the peaceable kingdom, living creatures do not kill and eat other living creatures. Other texts describe differently the relationship between plants, animals, and people (e.g., Gen. 9). Nevertheless, this text affirms straightforwardly: God is creating a world without violence. Hence the concluding statement of assessment also serves as a benediction: *And God saw all that he made, and behold, it was very good (v. 31).*

Conclusion: The Seventh Day; Rest 2:1-3

The unit ends with the affirmation that God rested on the seventh day. God blessed and set aside the seventh as different from the other six. *[Blessing in Genesis, p. 312.]* The Sabbath tradition has stirred a great deal of discussion. Is the Sabbath firmly set in the "order" of creation? If so, how shall we keep it? What about Jesus' disregard of the Sabbath? Does the Sabbath have any importance for Christians who observe the first rather than the seventh day of the week?

These questions could easily lead to a broad discussion of Sabbath in the Old and New Testaments. Here we will note just two interpretative directions related to the place of 2:2-3 in the whole unit of Genesis 1:1—2:3.

The creation drama does not flow on in ceaseless activity. Creation moves toward rest. This "rest" is not the rest of one who is exhausted (Exod. 5:5; Matt. 11:28), although that may be included. Creation rest describes the rest of one who is satisfied, one who looks at the world saying, *Behold, it is very good.* Karl Barth reminds us that to talk about God at rest is to talk about a loving God (1958: 215). Never ceasing, never satisfied, never finding time for any creature does not characterize a loving God.

In the seven-day week, time for work will return. But the Sabbath day is a moment to enjoy, to love what is, to look at the world not in terms of what needs to be done, but of delight in what has been done.

We recognize the importance of the Sabbath for us when we realize how hard it is to look at the world around us without concentrating on what needs to be done. Part of our preoccupation with production comes because we see only what is wrong: the grass needs to be cut, the people need to be more faithful, almost everyone needs to lose weight—endless doing, improving, correcting, without end. But that is not the goal of creating. In Sabbath we receive the world as God gives it and experience the Word, *Behold, it is very good.*

THE TEXT IN BIBLICAL CONTEXT

Let us go back to where we began. Early on we observed that this unit is put together with visible symmetry. We found an orderliness to this unit that reminds us of a list, similar in some respects to a genealogy. We will meet a much different style in the narrative which follows in the next unit (2:4ff.). Claus Westermann (1972: 7) has called attention to the fact that the whole of Genesis 1—11 is made up of basically two genres of literature: narratives and lists. The narratives involve disobedience and disaster in the human family. They portray splits in the family: man from woman, sibling rivalry, children against parents, some groups alienated from others.

The "lists" are different. Woven in and around the narratives of disaster, they represent the rhythm and flow of God's blessing that cannot be destroyed by human disobedience. This blessing is not reducible to an order which runs on its own, but pictures the presence of the creating God that makes life possible. We experience disaster and discord as a part of our existence, but also regularity and generativity. Day follows night, one generation comes from the next, seeds produce expected plants, and animals reproduce their own. The narratives in Genesis 1—11 know the dark side of life as we experience it. But the lists proclaim another reality, the trustworthy regularity of God's creation, which continues despite the historical disasters.

Genesis 1:1—2:3, as noted above (p. 5ff.), has more the character of a "list" than a narrative. *[Characteristics of Hebrew Narrative, p. 313.]* But this account goes beyond many list genres in that it uses the praise language of hymns similar to that of Psalm 104. *[Genres of Hebrew Literature, p. 319.]* This connection with doxological language makes one reluctant to speak of creation only in the past tense. The "list" character of the unit indicates that creation has a past element. We experience an aspect of completion to the created "order" represented by the seven-day structure (Steck, 1980: 89-113). God has provided the design and framework of a livable world. But the Creator continues to bless. Theologically, we may distinguish between God's action in creating and ongoing blessing by the titles "creator" and "sustainer." The biblical creation tradition does not know a sharp distinction between the two. Some texts may emphasize "to create" as a verb in the past tense, while others emphasize the present and even future.

Isaiah 40—55, speaking expressly to the disaster of the Babylonian Exile, uses the same hymnic creation language to announce God's intervention in behalf of that community (cf., for example, Isa. 40:17-20). The letter to the Colossians again turns to creation language to help the early Christian community understand God's action in Jesus Christ (Col. 1:15-17). We experience God, the Creator, not only as the one who gave us a livable world, but as one who brings fertility, prosperity, and community to each new day and new age, one generation after another—plants, animals, and humans—reproducing each according to its own kind.

THE TEXT IN THE LIFE OF THE CHURCH

The community of faith regularly celebrates our dependence on the constancy of the world in which we live. We take a moment at the dinner table. We set aside special days of thanksgiving. Even so, as the center of life for our culture has moved from rural to urban, we may lose touch with our dependency on the creating, blessing God. We may forget the rhythm and symmetry of the world that undergirds our life. Such constancy supports the way we live, however much that reality is reorganized through artificial grass, light, and heat. God has given and is giving to us a predictable and trustworthy world.

Sometimes reawakening an awareness of the predictability of God's created world becomes especially important. In times when our historical life has collapsed as individuals or as a community, the dependable rhythm of creation may provide an experience of God's presence that will serve as an avenue of hope. Though all else changes, even disintegrates, the sun shines on the next day and the moon appears the following night.

We may be tempted to reduce the constancy of God's creation to a closed and automatic order. In fact, lay folk seem often to think of the world in much more mechanistic ways than do many scientists. The physicist and biologist also anticipate novelty in their exploration of the natural world. By using our present experience of God's symmetrical and regular world, we occasionally dismiss new possibilities, limiting the future to whatever happens regularly. Genesis 1 and the creation tradition in the Bible expect us, even while celebrating the order of God's creation, to remain open to new experiences of God's order and even a genuinely new order, a new creation.

The creation of the world belongs to God. The rhythm of life which makes the world livable remains as trustworthy as God. We can count on day after night, one generation after the other. But God stands beyond even that rhythm. We dare not absolutize any single experience of that order. The cross and resurrection make that clear, if we have forgotten.

The creation of the world belongs to God. And the regularity of life which makes the world livable reminds us that God is trustworthy. We can count on day after night, one generation following another. In addition the world being created belongs to God. We can expect in the world the genuinely new, new expressions of God's blessing-fertility, prosperity and community, not just for some, but for all those made in the image of God. [*Blessings in Genesis*, p. 312; *Image of God*, p. 321; and *Creation and Evolution*, p. 317.]

Genesis 2:4 – 4:26

The Story of Heaven and Earth

PREVIEW

Genesis 2:4—4:26 reads much differently than the previous unit. We observed that Genesis 1:1—2:3 moved along in a very orderly way, repeating formulas such as *And there was evening and there was morning. . . .* We find little of that style of writing in this unit. Rather, the narratives move by story line, making them easy to remember and retell.

Indeed, in this unit we find characteristic Hebrew narrative. *[Characteristics of Hebrew Narrative, p. 313.]* Each story contains only a few actors, and often the focal point is the dialogue between these actors (Alter: 1981). Most often in Hebrew narrative the talk happens between only two people, not in a group with three or more people involved at the same time. Hence in Genesis 3 God talks with one person at a time even when other actors are presumably present. Attention to the speeches often provides the key to interpreting narrative texts.

Genesis 2:4—4:26 contains at least two major subdivisions: 1) The story of the man and woman in 2:4—3:24, and 2) the tale of two brothers, 4:1-16. The content of 4:1-16 connects the tale of two brothers with the paradise tale in 2:4—3:24. Not only are two principle actors the same, but also the narratives flow the same way: creation of persons, transgression and punishment. This similarity in the flow of the narrative warns us not to separate the two "tales" too sharply. But the unit does not even end at 4:16. We find a formula in 4:1, 16, 25 that ties the genealogy (4:17-26) to the narrative that preceeds it: *and Adam/Cain/*

Adam knew (his wife). Hence we must give attention to the whole unit
2:4—4:26 as well as the separate parts: 2:3—3:24; 4:1-16; 4:17-26.

We know chapter 3 as "the Fall." That title helps us recall the story,
but causes problems as well. The word "fall" does not appear in the text.
It comes to us from the tradition of the church as a theological interpretation. The narrative itself talks about a disobedience and its
punishment. As such Genesis 3 is similar to the tale of the two brothers
(4:1-16), the story of the sons of God and the daughters of humanity
(6:1-4), the tower of Babel (11:1-9), and perhaps also the curse of
Canaan (9:20-27).

The church has tended to think of the paradise story as *the* crucial
story about the origin of sin and evil. Neither the Old Testament nor
most of the New Testament speak of Genesis 3 in this way. Paul is most
often given credit (or blame) for this attention on Genesis 3 as the
source of all human problems (e.g., Rom. 5:12). However, Paul was
interested in proclaiming the gospel, salvation from the troubled life,
more than in defining exactly how life got to be that way (Brueggemann,
1982: 43). Genesis 1—11 narrates a whole cluster of stories about
transgressions which have consequences far beyond the immediate
people involved: toil, separation, sterility, even death. Neither the Gospels nor the Old Testament refer to Genesis 3 as the only story about
when life became permanently distorted (cf. Jude 6).

In Genesis 2:4—3:24 and 4:1-16 we find two such stories about
transgression and its consequences. To some degree these stories set
forth a growing problem from the transgression by the woman and man
to the revenge by Lamech. The evil in life builds throughout the unit. At
the same time the narrative does not assume that the murder of the
brother follows automatically from the action in the paradise garden.
Transgression is not inevitable, but people just keep doing it.

OUTLINE

As we outline this unit, we need to remember some of the difficulties
mentioned above. While we might include the Cain and Abel tale in the
following genealogies, the connections between that tale and the
paradise story encourage us to set them side by side in our outline.

Introductory Formula, 2:4a
A Tale of Paradise, 2:4b—3:24
A Story of Two Brothers, 4:1-16
Genealogies, 4:17-26

A Tale of Paradise

Genesis 2:4b – 3:24

PREVIEW

To call this unit a "tale" raises some questions. *[Genres of Hebrew Literature, p. 319.]* We may use the word "tale" in ways quite different from what is meant here. A person might use "tale" to refer to stories one person (often a child) tells which others realize are not true. Or we may speak of a "tattletale," someone who tells true stories, but in a way that creates hostility. Neither of those definitions fits here. Nevertheless, we can borrow one element from that popular use of the word "tale." A tale was, originally, an oral story (Coats, 1983: 7). In Israel, storytellers handed the tales on from community to community. This passing on might happen in worship, in the home, or in gatherings at the town square.

Perhaps because it was first told rather than written, a tale is a relatively simple story. It contains only a few main characters and an uncomplicated plot. A tale moves quickly from a problem in the story to its resolution. Genesis 2—3 has these characteristics, although the problem in the story and its resolution carry the reader in an unexpected direction. This tale moves from a good situation to a bad one rather than from bad to good. The flow from paradise provided to paradise lost has been a very important theological motif in the church. But the story cannot end with paradise lost. The poetry of John Milton (1608-1674) in *Paradise Lost* and *Paradise Regained* along with Paul in Romans 5:15 makes explicit what the rest of the Bible also knows: paradise lost does not describe the end of God's story.

OUTLINE

The Creation of Humanity, 2:4b-25
>   2:4b-7   A Living Being
>   2:8-25   Provisions for Existence
>   Garden, 2:8-15
>   Freedom, 2:16-17
>   Community, 2:18-25

Disobedience and It's Consequences, 3:1-24
>   3:1-6   Disobedience
>   3:7-24   Consequences

Changed Self-Perception, 3:7-8
Judgment, 3:9-19
    Trial, 3:9-13
    Announcement, 3:14-19
    Naming, 3:20
    Provision of Clothes, 3:21
    Expulsion, 3:22-24

EXPLANATORY NOTES

The Creation of Humanity 2:4b-25

2:4b-7 A Living Being

The narrative begins with a long dependent clause (RSV) leading up to the creation of the human creature (2:4b-6). [*'adam, p. 311.*] In this descriptive clause the earth lies barren: no rain to bring fertility to the fields and no one to care for cultivation. Only a flood of water (RSV footnote) or "stream" (NIV) washes over the land.

Finally, the focal point of this long sentence, the human creature is *formed*—formed *(yaṣar)* by God (v. 7). The image used here pictures God working as a potter, or at least an artist, forming a work of art. God, the artist, carefully crafts a model and then breathes into the figure the breath of life: behold, a person, *'adam,* a living being. Children and adults who form things with their hands can understand some of the relationship between God and the person expressed in these few words. The "forming" creates a bond between the artist and the work. Creator and creature—a bond that grows with the gentle process of making. The gentle hand of the Creator results in a royal creation. Elsewhere this language describes the raising up of a king (1 Kings 16:2).

The human being is related not only to the Creator, but also to the earth. God molds the person *('adam),* not out of some exotic material, but from the earth *('adamah),* or more precisely "dust" *('apar)* from the earth (v. 7). The human being is inescapably a creature of the earth (Trible: 77).

Yahweh forms the animals out of the earth as well (2:19). To be sure, the narrative does not say that God breathed the breath of life in the animals. However, we need to be careful about making too much of that, as other texts talk about animals and human beings both possessing *the same breath* (Eccles. 3:19).

The creature of the earth became a *nephesh* being, a "living being." The translation of *nephesh* as "soul" in the King James Version encouraged the church to think of the person as made up of separable parts, body and soul. This led to a picture of the *real* person as existing in the soul with the body as a temporary shelter. We now recognize that *nephesh* does not mean "soul" as we once understood it. Genesis 2:7 uses *nephesh* to refer to the whole living person. Indeed, the Bible understands the person as a unity. Of course parts exist: heart, bone, blood. Sometimes the essence of life is closely associated with one of the parts, most often "blood" (9:4). Nevertheless, personhood does not reside in one detachable part. God formed the person, breathed in the breath of life, and behold: a whole person, a *nephesh* being.

2:8-25 Provisions for Existence

A garden, 2:8-15. The narrative speaks of a God who provides for the human creature a marvelous environment in which to live, a "paradise garden." The text does not locate the garden geographically, but only states that it is *planted in Eden.* The direction, *in the east,* may point toward the Mesopotamian River Valley as the location of *Eden,* which may have come to the mind of the ancient readers. But we do not know. Isaiah 51:3 picks up the tradition of Eden and looks forward to God as provider of a garden like Eden in the future.

As with the garden, we cannot locate the four rivers geographically (vv. 10-14). Obviously, we can locate the *Tigris* and the *Euphrates* in Mesopotamia. But we do not know what bodies of water are meant by the *Pishon* and *Gihon.* Probably more important than the location is the purpose of the rivers: to "water" (v. 10). The rivers make fertile the garden and the land beyond it.

The flow of the story turns our attention especially to the two special trees growing in the garden: the tree of life and the tree of knowledge of good and evil (vv. 16-17). Unfortunately, our desire to learn about the trees exceeds the data the narrative provides us. The tree of life in Proverbs refers not to that which lengthens life but enhances life (Prov. 3:18; 11:30; 13:12; 15:4). However, the way this story uses the *tree of life* is similar to the way some epic poems in the ancient Near East use it. For example, in the Gilgamesh epic, the hero searches for a plant that will prolong his life (Pritchard, 1969: 72ff.). The tree of life in Genesis 2 is that plant. God did not create human beings immortal and then subsequently they became mortal. Rather, God set the person in the garden where there was provided a tree of life from which one could eat and live (2:16).

We know even less about *the tree of the knowledge of good and evil.* No such tree appears elsewhere in the Bible. The term "the knowledge of good and evil" may be used to describe comprehensive knowledge, meaning "everything" (von Rad, 1973: 81). On the other hand, the phrase can refer to a more specific kind of knowing. The language "to know/speak/discern good and evil" often occurs in a legal proceeding (W. M. Clark, 1969: 266-298). An official, often the king, is called on to "know" the difference between good and evil and render a decision that determines the future of himself and others (2 Sam. 14:17). In any case, *good and evil*, as used here, does not have the moral connotation which we tend to hear. Nor does it have to do primarily with one's conscience. The tree of the knowledge of good and evil may have provided unlimited knowledge or knowledge which enables a person or group to control the future.

Genesis 2:15 repeats and extends verse 8. Together they form a bracket describing God as provider of a garden. The human creature is put in charge of the garden—"to cultivate and to keep" (NASB). These words reflect the world of farmers and shepherds. The word *keep (shamar)* refers to shepherds who keep watch over the flocks (1 Sam. 17:20), as well as the farmer who cares for the garden. As in Genesis 1:28, in 2:15 humanity has been put in charge.

The words used in the two texts have a different ring to them—"to cultivate and to keep," "to dominate and control," although the actual intention may not be as different as the words sound (Coats, *Interpretation*, 1975: 227-239). God created human beings and invested them with the responsibility to enable the earth to bear fruit, whether that be said in the gentle terms of agrarian life or in the power terms of the royal world.

Freedom, 2:16-17. In addition to a garden, God provided the human being with freedom. Genesis 2:16 constitutes the first speech of the unit and declares the person free in the garden. The Hebrew places an exclamation point at the end of the phrase: "from any tree of the garden, eat!" God, the provider, grants freedom.

The freedom requires known boundaries. No freedom exists without limits. If we could only do one thing, e.g., eat from all the trees, that would not be freedom. Freedom must include genuine choice, choice that matters. If God had left the tree out of the garden, there would have been no disobedience, but also no freedom to choose. Hence the provision of freedom includes one tree from which the person may not eat, *the tree of the knowledge of good and evil.* This limitation may suggest that universal knowledge, the key to all knowledge, belongs to God, as expressed by the poet of Job 28:

> Whence then comes wisdom?
>> And where is the place of understanding? . . .
> God understands the way to it,
>> And he knows its place. (Job 28:20-23)

Or this boundary on freedom may be a reminder that finally the control of my life and the lives of others belongs only in God's hands, as the psalmist declares:

> The earth is the Lord's
>> And the fulness thereof,
> The world
>> and those who dwell therein. (Psalm 24:1)

The same God who provides defines the limits on that provision. God's speech does not give the reason for such a limitation. Only later, first from the serpent's speech (3:5), then from God's speech (3:22), do we learn the reason for the limitation. Certain "knowing" belongs to God and to possess it is to preempt God's role in the world. In this speech God does not force humanity to stay within the limits provided, but attempts to persuade by simply stating the consequences. The person apparently is not finally persuaded.

Community, 2:18-25. Besides a fertile environment and freedom, God provides community for the human creature. This section begins with a second speech from God: *It is not good that a person should be alone* (v. 18). Because in Genesis 1 we listened to the repeated refrain, *And God saw that it was good,* the *not good* of this speech stands out sharply. After providing a garden and granting freedom, still one problem must be solved—loneliness. [*'adam, p. 311, and Male and Female in Genesis 1—3, p. 323.*]

God forms animals. Perhaps they will solve the problem of human loneliness. The animals are brought to *'adam* for a response. The person names the animals, thereby giving them a place in the world. Although these creatures were made *of the earth* like the human creature, the animals cannot fulfill humanity's need for community (vv. 19-20).

The tale, using a series of verbs, slows down at this point: *caused a deep sleep . . . took . . . closed . . . made . . . brought* (v. 21). The tone is private and mysterious. Out of this mystery a surprise emerges: a woman alongside a man. Through poetry, covenantal language, and sexual imagery, the text gives voice to the joy of community: *This at last is bone of my bones . . .* (v. 23). The human community is formed (2:25).

With this surprise, this section of the drama ends. God has formed humanity and provided for its life: food, freedom, and now family. Whatever the history of this narrative as it was retold in the community, the story in the received text has a carefully crafted flow, moving from a barren landscape to a fertile garden filled with life: all this as a gift of the artistry of God.

Disobedience and Its Consequences 3:1-24

In this section we see again the careful balance typical of Hebrew narrative. Look, for instance, at the order in which we meet the characters in this drama. In the first scene (3:1-6) we are introduced first to the serpent, then to the woman, and finally briefly, to the man. In the trial (3:9-13) God questions first the man, then the woman. Naturally, the reader expects the serpent to be questioned next. However, the serpent, though implicated by the woman, is not questioned. The narrative moves immediately to the announcement of the consequences. That announcement (3:14-19) picks up the order of the first scene again: man, woman, serpent.

We need to be careful with Genesis 3 because we are often so sure about what it says. Perhaps we might begin by listing some of the things that the text does not say.

1. The word "fall" is not used, not here or any place in the chapter. The dialogue in 3:9-13 makes language like "disobedience" more appropriate than heavily theological language like "sin" and "fall."

2. We are told very little about the serpent. Hebrew narrative does not use extensive description. The reader must be attentive to the description as we find it, so as not to hear more than the text says. The only word used for snake is *'arum*. This word appears often in Proverbs. Proverbs 14:18 illustrates the word's use:

> The simple acquire folly,
> but the *prudent ('arum)* are crowned with knowledge.

While the word can be used negatively (Job 5:12), all through Proverbs *'arum* means the opposite of foolish or simple. The snake in Genesis 3:1 is a creature like other animals, just a bit more astute (Sarna: 26).

3. The narrative does not tell us why the confrontation happens between the serpent and the woman rather than the snake and the man. Tradition has suggested that the serpent came to the woman because of her weakness, perhaps because she was made second (1 Tim. 2:13-14), or because the woman was evil (Sirach 25:21-24). The narrative states

none of those. Nor does the narrative say that the woman's alertness to the danger in the situation caused her to step forward to confront the serpent (although this explanation remains as plausible as one blaming the woman's weakness). Hebrew narratives normally have only two actors "on stage" at one time (Vawter, 1977: 79). Here the woman and the snake are those two characters. We are told nothing more. We should likely assume that the man and the woman are free and responsible together.

3:1-6 Disobedience

Genesis 3:1-6 provides a short, but powerful narrative about how the disobedience happened. The woman and the snake discuss God as "provider" and "withholder." The snake asks whether God acts exclusively as withholder. The woman says, "No." God acts first of all as provider. But we notice that even the woman overemphasizes the withholding action of God: *neither shall you touch it* (v. 3). Apparently neither are persuaded that God wants most of all to provide. So the talk turns to the reason for the withholding. The serpent suggests that God's withholding is motivated not by the danger of death, but by the threat of people becoming like God, possessing knowledge which unlocks all the mysteries of the world or knowledge which controls human destiny.

The serpent, the woman, and the man have turned the content of chapter 2 completely around. The attention focuses now exclusively on a God who has withheld. This distortion of the drama of creation opens the door to disobedience: *she took of its fruit and ate; and she also gave some to her husband, and he ate* (v. 6).

3:7-24 Consequences of Disobedience

Changed self-perception, 3:7-8. This moment in the narrative draws the reader back to the earlier story. The woman and the man were naked and not ashamed (2:25). God could talk in the garden, bringing the animals and even the woman to the man (2:18-22). The interaction between God and the woman and the man was comfortable and without shame. Suddenly everything changes. The man and woman find themselves exposed and they cover up. They hear God and hide. Comfort and intimacy have been replaced by covering up and hiding. The brokenness has immediate impact on life in the garden.

Again we must be cautious not to let our imaginations run too fast before carefully reading the text. The narrative does not picture a man and woman seized with shame and guilt. Instead, we read simply that they *saw* and *made*, *heard* and *hid*. The flow of the narrative leaves no doubt that these actions came as a consequence of the disobedience. As is typical of Hebrew narratives, we learn little about what the woman and the man were feeling. Instead, we find actions or speech: thoughts and feelings are left to the imagination of the readers. *[Characteristics of Hebrew Narrative, p. 313.]*

Judgment 3:9-19. The narrative turns into a trial. The opening question, *Where are you?* sounds innocent enough. But like the opening question to Cain, "Where is your brother, Abel?" (4:9), this functions as an accusation. At first the man admits only to being afraid of God. In response to a direct question concerning the tree, the man and the woman confess—well, sort of. The man frames his confession as an accusation of the woman and perhaps God. The woman, while less directly implicating God, turns the attention to the snake. The serpent is not asked for an explanation. We do not know why. Hebrew narrative does not always tie up all the loose ends in a tale.

The announcement of judgment (3:14-19) turns first to the snake. A wordplay begins this announcement (Trible: 124). The snake was introduced to the listener as *'arum*, "smart," "clever." Now the serpent is *'arur*, "cursed." The defining characteristic of the snake had been a positive one (or at least ambiguous). Now that which distinguishes the snake from all the animals is manifestly negative. The snake is the only animal living under curse.

A second problem affects the snake, coming not as the result of the curse, but as a part of this disaster. Hostility will rage between the descendants of the snake and the offspring of the woman. Irenaeus (130-200) suggested that 3:15 referred to the hostility between Christ and Satan; others proposed Mary and Satan (cf. Vawter, 1977: 83). This messianic interpretation, although traditional in Roman Catholic and some Protestant circles, is not without problems, given the language of the text. Used in this way, the word *seed* consistently refers to "descendants" (a collective), rather than an individual (Mary or Jesus) (Westermann, 1984: 260). It seems best to lay aside the allegorical interpretation of the patristic medieval interpreters and go with the more literal understanding.

The announcement of judgment then addresses the woman (v. 16). Although the consequence for the woman does not directly involve a curse, "severe afflictions and terrible contradictions break" into the woman's life (von Rad, 1973: 93). In whatever way we today might define what it means to be a woman, we must remember that motherhood was basic for the definition to those who heard this text in ancient Israel. They observed that great pain and danger was part of motherhood. How could this be understood? Furthermore, the relationship between women and men clearly was distorted. What God intended to be a relationship of mutuality and companionship was characterized instead by domination. *[Male and Female in Genesis 1—3, p. 323.]* The woman's urge toward the man remains, but domination by the man, not companionship, results.

God addresses the lengthiest speech to the man (vv. 17-19). Like the previous speeches, this third speech appears in poetic form. The man is not cursed, but he must deal with a curse, a curse placed on the ground. The text understands the man's relationship to the soil as central to what it means to be a man, even as it had assumed motherhood as basic to the woman. Similarly, the man's experience with the soil turns out to be far different from what God intended. Grain and grapes have been invaded by thorns and thistles. The dust of the earth, the material out of which human life was formed, has the feel of death.

Names and clothes, 3:20-21. The disobedience has resulted in disruption and distortion of all life. The naming of the woman reflects that distortion (v. 20). The language reminds the reader of Genesis 2:20, where the person ordered and managed the animals by naming them. The man had already called her woman *('ishshah),* which corresponded to man *('ish)* (2:23). The woman's new name—Eve—does not express that correspondence. Even so the narrative understands the woman's new name as speaking of life. In the middle of distortion and disaster, Hebrew names often speak of death (1 Sam. 4:21; Ruth 1:20). But in the disrupted existence of human existence described here, the woman is called Eve *(hawwa), the mother of all living (hay).*

In the next statement of the consequences of the disobedience (3:21), God acts again as provider. While this action duplicates the couple's making of their own clothes, narratively, the verse is crucial. After the disaster of disobedience, God still provides for humanity.

Expulsion, 3:22-24. The speech in 3:22 presents some difficulties. God speaks to a group, stating that the man and woman have become "like one of us." The reference is likely the same here as in Genesis 1:26. Yahweh sits in the company of other divine beings, for example, angels. God's speech is addressed to that company.

Expulsion from the garden brings us the last of the consequences of the disobedience. Because sin has become universal, a new boundary has been given, one that cannot be crossed. Control has replaced freedom. Coercion has replaced persuasion. God's act to withhold the tree of life cannot be violated. Death, however delayed, will come (Coats, 1975). Von Rad points us to an element of grace in this withholding of the tree of life (1973: 97). Humanity cannot choose to eat from the tree of life and thus remain living indefinitely. In a distorted and disrupted world, interminable life would be unbearable. In expelling humanity from the garden we experience a God who withholds, but who also provides a tolerable life.

THE TEXT IN BIBLICAL CONTEXT

Christian interpretation of this text has been deeply imprinted by the late Jewish interpretation reflected in 2 Esdras 7:118: "Oh Adam, what have you done? Although you (alone) sinned, the fall was not yours alone, but ours too who descended from you" (Anchor Bible translation). In this statement we find Genesis 2—3 interpreted as the one event which determined the life of all generations. Paul seems to follow this traditional Jewish interpretation (Rom. 5:12-21), although Paul's precise meaning has been disputed (Käsemann: 139ff.). Even if Paul did interpret Genesis 2—3 as the decisive moment when sin entered the world, Paul's interest was not basically to inform readers about the origin of our problems. Paul wanted to proclaim that regardless of how life came to be dominated by sin, in Christ grace reigns instead of sin.

The Old Testament does not understand the story of the garden as the single event that determined all human destiny. No other explicit reference to this story exists in the Hebrew Bible, or, for that matter, in the Gospels either. Genesis 1—11 has not one, but several, narratives of disobedience, transgression, and sin (Westermann, 1980). All of these stories taken together portray the world as we find it: a world filled with pain and suffering, with separation and misunderstanding, with domination and destruction. The Old Testament, like Paul, knows that God does not want such a world. Rather, God wants all the peoples of the world to receive blessing (12:1-3).

As mentioned in the Explanatory Notes, Genesis 3:15 has been interpreted as a prophecy of Christ (and/or Mary). Patristic, medieval, and some modern interpreters assumed that her *seed* (the woman's) referred to one individual person (Christ) who crushed the head of *your seed* (the serpent's), again a single individual, Satan. [Of the sixteenth-century Reformers, Menno Simons (pp. 503, 734, 892) took that position; Calvin did not.] The collective meaning for seed makes the messianic interpretation improbable. The narratives in Genesis 1—11 describe a world distorted and nearly destroyed by human disobedience. The gospel proclaims that through Christ, God has reconciled the world to God (1 Cor. 5:16-21), and a new world comes, one that perfectly reflects the divine intention (Rev. 21:1-6). In this way, the narrative is tied to the gospel, not allegorically through a single verse, but as a whole in the divine drama of deliverance through Jesus Christ.

THE TEXT IN THE LIFE OF THE CHURCH

This narrative does not tell us all the details we might wish to find in such a story. But Genesis 2—3 is a portrayal, not a chronicle. As such it invites the listener to enter and understand, rather than remain outside analyzing or speculating. The narrative does not tell us the location of the garden or why the man sat on the sidelines while the discussion was going on about the fruit. We are not told why the snake came to the woman or what kind of fruit the two of them ate. Because much is left unsaid, we can allow our imaginations to help us enter the story. Not accidentally, the tale of the garden has been the vehicle through which poets and artists have talked about life and its problems.

We must continue to listen as the story is retold, taking care not to require that our retelling be the only one. One brother will insist that the story locates sin in the heart of the individual. A sister will use this narrative to talk about distortion arising in the interaction between the person and the world or in the dialogue between one person and another. Still another will talk about evil outside of us, evil that sneaks upon us, using Genesis 2—3 as an illustration. The narrative makes room for these and other understandings. The openness of the narrative helps us avoid the pitfall of reducing the problem of evil to just one cause. The locus of the problem is in us: pride, anxiety, seizing. But trouble also arises between us: conversation creates conflict as well as consensus, blaming as well as accepting responsibility. In addition, we experience sin as outside us and against us. Some talk about this external aspect of evil in terms of a demonic figure, others do not. But we all realize that evil cannot be reduced to an evil heart or distorted discussion; principalities and powers also confront us.

Genesis 2—3 encourages us to talk seriously about the *presence* of evil and not get lost in discussions about the *origin* of sin. The situation portrayed in the narrative is a very normal tension in life. We all live within boundaries, and at the same time we possess the power to cross those boundaries. Even though this drama comes to us as a story about a garden long ago, we know the tension created by "boundaries" very well. We hear God's call to exercise the freedom to stay within the limits. We remember our experiences of violating those limits. Not that we regularly set out to misuse our freedom—those decisions happen in very mysterious ways. Together we live with the consequences of such misuse of our power and freedom: thistles and thorns, pain and oppression. This narrative does not end on a happy note, but it does leave the future open—open to celebrate God's act to replace curse with blessing, judgment with grace.

A Story of Two Brothers

Genesis 4:1-16

PREVIEW

In this section, we have a second in the series of narratives about transgression and punishment, a simple story of two brothers. As a tale it shares the characteristics of that genre of literature (see preview to Genesis 2:4b—3:24). We find an uncomplicated plot involving three characters with only two of them "onstage" at a time. The story presents us with little descriptive material, leaving much to the participation of the listener. [Characteristics of Hebrew Narrative, p. 313.]

The story of two brothers stands alongside the story of the garden. The text does not tell us that the conflict between the two brothers is the result of the disobedience in the garden. Hence we must be careful lest we too easily assume that this murder is the inevitable result of what happened in the garden. The unit simply recounts the two stories side by side. One involves the man and woman who violate limits set in their life. The second concerns two brothers, their sons, who come into conflict over a worship service. The woman/man and sibling relationships represent the foundation of the community in Hebrew tradition. Disruption which strikes these relationships affects the very heart of the community.

While this is a story of two brothers, it portrays the sibling relationship, sisters as well as brothers (Brueggemann, 1982: 54). Certainly the society through which these texts were passed on to us was a society organized to favor men over women. Even so, as Genesis 1:26 and 2:23-24 show us, the vision and impulse of the faith move toward a social world of mutuality. God will not let the vision be swallowed up by specific social structures—structures that favor one group over another.

OUTLINE

Genealogical Introduction, 4:1-2

The Crime and Its Consequences, 4:3-16
    4:3-8 Crime
          The Circumstances, 4:3-5
          Speech of God, 4:6-7
          Murder, 4:8
    4:9-16 Consequences
          Trial, 4:9-15a
          Execution of Sentence, 4:15b-16

EXPLANATORY NOTES

Genealogical Introduction 4:1-2

These verses set the stage for the story of the brothers. Along with 4:16, they form the boundaries of the narrative. The speech of Eve is difficult to translate and understand. The Hebrew words translated, *I have gotten . . . with the help of the Lord* (RSV, NASB) can be understood in several different ways. The word *qanah* can be translated with the English words "get/acquire" or with the words "create/produce" (NIV). The preposition *'et* normally means "with" in the sense of "companionship." Many scholars feel that meaning is not adequate in Genesis 4:1; hence the common translation *with the help of.* The speech could be understood as Eve saying that she obtained this baby boy by God's gift of fertility. But Eve might also be rejoicing that like God (Gen. 2), she too has produced a human being.

In this introduction we learn only two things about Cain and Abel: they are brothers and they have different occupations. This signals to the listeners the possibility of conflict. Brothers are regulary at odds in the narratives of Genesis as well as elsewhere: Jacob and Esau, Joseph and his brothers, Moses and Aaron, the sons of David. However, in Genesis 4 occupational tension compounds the problem of sibling rivalry. Cain is a farmer and Abel a rancher. Perhaps in the early retelling of this story, the occupational tension played a more prominent role. In the text as we have it, the sibling rivalry is emphasized, and the tension between farmer and herder serves mostly to give depth to the conflict between two brothers.

The Crime and Its Consequences 4:3-16

4:3-8 The Crime

Worship provides the context in which the conflict erupts. Cain and Abel bring offerings from their respective worlds. God responds positively to Abel's, but not to Cain's. The narrative does not tell us why God made this choice. We can suggest many possible reasons for God's decision. For example, perhaps Abel brought a better quality offering: firstborn and best of the flock. Or maybe the narrative was passed down through shepherd families prejudiced against farmers. Others propose that God already knew Cain had a bad attitude (v. 5). Or maybe God just preferred the smell of animal offerings (Gen. 8:20-21). We are not given that information. We know only that God decides. Cain was crushed.

The Lord interrupts with a speech of warning (vv. 6-7). The specifics of the speech are uncertain, as one can see by comparing the translations. But the direction of the speech is clear. By choosing Abel's offering, God has created a crisis. Cain's future depends on how he responds to God's choice. The danger is described by picturing an animal or a demon lying in wait at the door. While the force of most translations insists that Cain is responsible to "master" the danger, Brueggemann calls attention to an ambiguity in the Hebrew verb, an ambiguity that is difficult to carry into English (1982: 59). The conclusion of 4:7 may be translated *you must master it, (RSV),* "you *can* be its master" (NAB), or even "you *shall* master it." Cain's future is open: promise and hope as well as responsibility and danger. The text does not assume that Cain's destiny is sealed either because of his own character or the sin of those who went before him.

A single sentence reports the murder (4:8). The Hebrew text does not even tell the listener what Cain says to Abel, simply that *Cain said to Abel his brother.* This way of describing the murder distances the reader from the crime, perhaps even depersonalizing the victim. On the other hand, ancient Greek texts do tell us Cain's speech: *Let us go out to the field* (RSV, NIV). This establishes the drama of the moment in a different way. Cain speaks to his brother and then strikes.

This murder drives to the heart of the community, tearing apart the relationship among brothers and sisters. Genesis 4 sits alongside the paradise tale (Gen. 2—3), where disobedience rent the community fabric by distorting the woman-man relationship. Together the two stories portray a community in disarray.

4:9-16   The Consequences

As in Genesis 3:9, God enters the narrative asking a question: "Where is Abel, your brother?" Cain answers with an excuse, much like the man in Genesis 3:10, only Cain's response has even more sting: *Am I my brother's keeper?* We have sometimes understood Cain's question as a refusal to accept normal family responsibility. We need to be cautious with that assumption. Shepherds keep sheep. In fact "to keep" used in this way normally refers to keeping such things as livestock (30:31), or money and goods (Exod. 22:7). A "keeper" of people refers to one who keeps others in custody (1 Kings 20:39). Although a bodyguard in 1 Samuel 28:2 is designated "keeper," people do not normally keep people. God keeps people (Ps. 121:3-8; Num. 6:24).

In this sense no one is his "brother's keeper." So Cain seeks to absolve himself of responsibility (Rieman, 1970: 482-491). Cain may even be passing the responsibility for Abel's absence to someone else, acting as the man and woman did in the garden. Since God is responsible to "keep" the people, Cain's question may imply that God has not acted as a competent keeper.

God, who declared the man and woman responsible for their own actions, declares Cain responsible for his (vv. 10-12). Cain will find himself alienated from the ground out of which humanity was taken. Life for Cain will have no task, no goal, no meaning. Cain will wander, not toward promise, just wander. Nevertheless, the murderer will not fall victim to the same crime (4:15). God grants Cain protection, acts as Cain's keeper. In the words of the priestly benediction: even though God will not bless Cain, God will keep him (Num. 6:24).

THE TEXT IN BIBLICAL CONTEXT

In later tradition Cain is used as a type of an evil person, and Abel of a good person. This perspective is reflected in the Jewish literature of the first century B.C. (Wisd. of Sol. 10:3-4) as well as the later literature of the New Testament (Heb. 11:4; 1 John 3:12; Jude 11). The Old Testament itself does not make further reference to Cain.

One can understand the inclination of the community of faith to use Cain as an example of evil. The opportunity would present itself particularly in times of persecution or when evil seemed overwhelmingly dangerous to the faithful community. But the danger of such interpretation is also clear. The Genesis 4 story does not talk of Cain as the personification of evil. The tendency to make him such and identify certain other people as "like Cain" has led the Christian to identify certain individuals or groups as evil while judging themselves as good. At the very least, this flirts with self-righteousness. Even more destructive, such judgments have been used to justify destroying the "evil ones" in God's name. It seems far better to understand Cain as this tale does. God's choice of Abel's offering creates tension in the relationship between Cain and his brother. Cain's response to that tension alienates him from God and from his brother. He acts out that anger so as to dramatically violate both relationships. Cain lives with the consequences of such action—consequences, bad though they may be—that are less severe than law and custom might dictate. Even as a murderer, Cain is not beyond God's mercy and protection.

THE TEXT IN THE LIFE OF THE CHURCH

Tensions which arise between brothers and sisters may in fact be the fault of no one person. The gifted and the less gifted, the blessed and the less blessed appear in any community. Frequently one child is favored over another or one group receives more attention than the next. This preferential treatment may be the result of unfair favoritism, but often it arises simply because of specific gifts or skills, gifts which enable one to stand above another. Particular circumstances often create recognition for one more than another, as the New Testament parable of the two brothers relates (Luke 15:11-32). These preferences, be they accidental or intentional, create dangerous tensions. The possibility "lurks at the door" that the less favored one will seek to resolve the tension by destroying the other.

In Genesis 2—3, a transgressable boundary created the tension, and in Genesis 4, an inexplicable preference precipitated the crisis. In both cases the tensions were resolved in life-destroying rather than life-enhancing ways. The tale of two brothers declares that the world we inherit has been rendered barren in significant ways by previous generations who have resolved these tensions in life-destroying ways. Meaningless wandering and alienation from God as well as our sisters and brothers exist as a part of the world we have been given. But this tale of two brothers is not the end of the story, a story which through Christ calls us to a ministry of reconciliation (2 Cor. 5:16-21).

Genealogies
Genesis 4:17-26

PREVIEW

This section forms the conclusion of the "Story of Heaven and Earth"; it begins in Genesis 2:4 and centers on two narratives of disobedience and transgression. The world becomes disrupted and distorted in the deepest part of its social fabric. God does not abandon this distorted world but remains actively present, not only in moments of judgment but also in gifts of "clothing" and protection. This genealogical conclusion reflects both the distortion and disruption so visible in the world and the creativity and faithfulness which will not be denied.

The statement *And Adam knew ... his wife ...* (Gen. 4:1-2) connects the tale of the two brothers with this genealogical conclusion. Also, the repetition of the phrases *Cain knew his wife* (v. 17) and *Adam knew his wife* (v. 25) divides 4:17-26 into two genealogical lists.

OUTLINE

The Kenites, 4:17-24
    4:17-22   Genealogy
    4:23-24   Revenge Song

The Sethites, 4:25-26
    4:25-26a   Genealogy
    4:26b   Statement about Worship

EXPLANATORY NOTES

The Kenites 4:17-24

4:17-22 Genealogy of the Kenites

A glance at different translations displays the difficulty we have in saying too much about these verses. We find a list of five generations following Cain set up as a strict linear genealogy, one parent - one child - one grandchild, and so forth. After that, the genealogy branches, or segments, listing four children of Lamech.

In 4:18 the genealogy branches out not only to include four children but also other kinds of information. Lamech had two wives and three sons and a daughter. The three sons represent different vocations: shepherds, musicians, and blacksmiths. There may or may not be some connection with the occupation of the later specific groups in and around Israel, but, consistent with one function of genealogies, this list groups together trades and arts. *[Reading Genealogies, p. 326.]* In 4:17, the presence of cities is also incorporated into the genealogy. We inherit a world with a rich diversity of occupations. This genealogy provides a vehicle for expressing differentiation in human culture, but also reminds us that all the groups belong together.

4:23-24 Revenge Song

An ancient poem concludes this section of the genealogy. The singer boasts to his wives of his power and prowess. In the context of this genealogy, the poem introduces a world of uncontrolled violence. This stands in an ambiguous relationship to the spread of culture portrayed in the sons of Lamech (vv. 19-22). The text does not tie violence and culture together in such a way as to make one dependent on the other. At the same time we know well that the same energy in the human community that builds up can also be used to destroy. Living in a distorted world means we see both. By placing side by side a genealogy of the rise of human culture with a violent poem of male boasting, the reader experiences both the drama and danger of life.

The Sethites 4:25-26

4:25-26a Genealogy of the Sethites

The formula which marked this genealogical series *And Adam knew his wife*—begins this new section. The genealogical line of Seth will replace that of Abel. While this text provides a hint of a "good" line (Seth) and a "bad" line (Cain) heading into the Flood, the long genealogy in Genesis 5 breaks that pattern. The human community cannot be divided up that neatly. As it stands, 4:25-26a reasserts the sibling relationship as a central factor in the human story. Cain again has a brother. No situation arises in which we do not have to take account of sisters and brothers.

4:26b Statement About Worship

This phrase is difficult to translate, as a comparison of the English translations demonstrates. Cryptic though it may be, this phrase establishes worship as a factor in this genealogical portrayal of life. *[Reading Genealogies, p. 326.]* In a world marked by music, work, and uncontrolled violence, people call on the name of Yahweh. While Exodus 3:15 and 6:2 trace the worship of the Lord in Israel to Moses, Genesis 4:26 recognizes that the confession of Yahweh as God goes back before Moses.

THE TEXT IN BIBLICAL CONTEXT

The names which are found in this genealogy recur in Genesis 5 with a different order and in some cases with slight variations in spelling. Whereas 4:17-26 uses the names for a segmented or branched genealogy, chapter 5 puts all the names in a linear or single-line genealogy. It is that single-line order that is picked up and used by 1 Chronicles 1:1-4 and Luke 3:36-38. The segmented genealogy of 4:17-26 is not taken up in other biblical texts. Indeed, the figure of Lamech only reemerges in extra-biblical writing and there in connection with glorification of Noah.

The saying of Jesus in Matthew 18:21-22 turns the conclusion of the song of Lamech completely around. The community of Jesus will be marked not by unlimited violence, but by unlimited forgiveness. Lamech kills a youngster for striking him, as the NASB correctly translates Genesis 4:23. Jesus invokes God's forgiveness even for those who execute him. Through Christ, God creates a community to replace Lamech's community of violence.

THE TEXT IN THE LIFE OF THE CHURCH

We are well aware that the world we inherit contains music and violence, worship and revenge. We know how those can be destructively mixed together: the music can support the urge to violence and the worship can celebrate revenge. The negative pole of human experience seems dangerously close to determining history. Lamech's boast may be the only song heard, but that music is loud. Nevertheless, both Testaments declare that power and prowess will not finally determine human destiny. Union and fertility prove still stronger: *And Adam knew his wife again, and she bore a son and called his name Seth* (4:25).

It would be tempting to understand the line of Seth as the good family and Cain's line as evil. We could then combine musical instruments, cities, and violence all together and call them all bad. Fortunately, the text also includes the development of trades—blacksmiths, and livestock farmers—with that segment of the genealogy, aspects of life that we are less inclined to dismiss as "worldly." As we shall see in the story of Noah, evil and violence cannot be isolated into certain segments of the human genealogy. If evil could be isolated to one segment of the human family, then destruction of that group would remove the problem of evil and violence.

Human experience suggests that the "isolate and destroy" approach to the problem of evil is simplistic, naive, and doomed to fail. Hitler identified "the Jews" as the locus of the problems of Nazi Germany, causing a monumental tragedy. But we too are tempted to identify certain leaders as "evil" or another nation as an "evil empire." The followers of the one from Nazareth live out of a different paradigm for dealing with evil, one that understands that no branch of the human family is free of sin, violence, and evil.

Genesis 5:1 — 6:8

The List of
Adam's Family

PREVIEW

The genealogy in 5:1-32 takes up most of this unit. It enumerates the generations from Adam through Noah. The genealogy is so distinct that we might choose to treat it independently of narrative which resumes in 6:1. But the formula that we have used as our key, "these are the generations" (Hebrew *'elleh toledot),* sections the material differently. We cannot insist that one way of dividing the material is correct and all others incorrect. Different patterns of organization in the material emerge as we follow different literary "keys." Through consistent attention to the text, we can explore various ways of grouping the material and in the process find new facets to the texts and their message.

If we follow the "generations" formula, this unit includes the long genealogy followed by a short narrative concerning the sons of God and the daughters of humanity (6:1-4). The unit concludes with a paragraph that prepares the reader for the Flood (6:5-8). However, Genesis 5 has already anticipated the narrative of the Deluge. The genealogy breaks its repetitious pattern at verse 29 to call special attention to Noah. Both 5:29 and 6:8 set Noah before us as the key figure in the subsequent drama of the Deluge.

OUTLINE

Genealogy, 5:1-32
    5:1-2   Introduction
    5:3-32 Ten-Member List

A Narrative of Transgression
  and Consequence, 6:1-4

Divine Assessment, 6:5-8
    6:5-6   Situation
    6:7   Speech of Judgment
    6:8   Concerning Noah

EXPLANATORY NOTES

Genealogy 5:1-32

This text provides a clear example of a linear genealogy (Wilson, 1977). It does not branch out until the eleventh generation, i.e., the sons of Noah. *[Reading Genealogies, p. 326.]*Repetitiously, the list introduces us to the figures by giving
    1. The name.
    2. The age at the time of the birth of the son.
    3. The additional years after the birth of the son.
    4. A statement about other children.
    5. Total life span.

Ten generations are listed from Adam through Noah.

The dates concerning the life spans of the persons vary in different ancient texts. The Pentateuch preserved by the community at Samaria has different age spans from the Hebrew Bible on which our translations are based. The Greek Bible used by the early Christian communities contains still different numbers. The fluidity of the tradition concerning the numbers cautions us against spending too much time trying to discover number patterns or dating schemes. These age spans, which seem quite incredible to us, are smaller than those given in other lists of pre-Flood figures in the ancient Near East. These ancient Near East lists, which sometimes also contain ten figures, have life spans that stretch into the tens of thousands of years.

In several ways this genealogical list picks up the creation drama in Genesis 1. The repetitive character of the material reconnects us with the stability and symmetry of that presentation of creation. Indeed the strictness of this genealogy is significant. The reader is grounded anew in the underlying stability of creation. Following the grounding in Genesis 1, we have been led into an eruption of disorder. But that disorder has not destroyed the blessing in Genesis 1:28: the empowerment to be fruitful and fill the earth. Genesis 5 arises out of that blessing (Westermann, 1966: 488). God's blessing reasserts itself in the "boring" order of one generation after the next. *[Reading Genealogies, p. 326.]*

It is not only the structure that connects this section with Genesis 1. Chapter 5 begins with the language of chapter 1: image (of God), male and female, blessing. Adam became the father of one in his image (5:3) as all humanity is in the image of God (1:26). The position of chapter 5 after 2:4—4:32 gives additional impact to the reintroduction of this creation language. Disobedience cannot destroy the "image of God." Humanity's empowerment by God is not buried in the ground of the curse.

Breaks in the structure of the genealogy call attention to two names in the list, Enoch and Noah. Noah becomes the main character in the next unit, but Enoch remains a mysterious figure, found in the Hebrew Bible only in 5:21-24 (and the genealogical list in 1 Chron. 1). Out of these few phrases grew a large body of stories about Enoch. The tradition developed that this unusual man was taken into heaven and given access to the great mysteries of the universe. The text in 5:21-24 says that Enoch was unusual. Repetition of the phrase *Enoch walked with God* underlines "walk" as the difference between Enoch and others in the list. The phrase *walked with God* appears elsewhere only with Noah (6:9), and in Micah 6:8 ("humbly walk with your God"), but with a different preposition. Some texts take the phrase in the direction of moral uprightness (Jude 14-15) or faith (Heb. 11:5-6). A Hebraic context would suggest that the phrase "walk with God" talks more generally about the quality of the relationship between God and Enoch than about any specific element in that relationship, such as faith or obedience (Delitzsch, 1899: 217).

Noah is the figure this unit wants us to remember. The explanation of Noah's name in verse 29 calls the reader back to the disobedience in the garden in Genesis 3 and pushes us forward to the conclusion of the Flood (8:21-22). God's blessing that generates human genealogy brings the one through whom God will work toward a different world from the one created by the disobedience in the garden (3:1-6), the killing of a brother (4:8), and a song of revenge (4:23-24). Verse 29 relates the name Noah to the Hebrew word *niham,* "comfort." Through Noah, God, whose blessing brings fertility to all life, will bring comfort to those whose task has become meaningless toil.

A Narrative of Transgression and Consequence 6:1-4

Genesis 6:1-4 presents us with a puzzling narrative about the sons of God and the daughters of humanity. The phrase *sons of God* refers to the divine beings which we have met elsewhere in God's address to a plural audience (1:26; 3:22; 11:7, cf. Ps. 82). The phrase *daughters of men* refers to human women. There is no assumption of good or bad in those designations. These two groups form the tension from which the narrative departs. The designations present two antitheses which could create tension: divine beings - human beings, male - female.

The action consists of two verbs: *saw* and *took*. The divine beings *saw* that the women were beautiful and they *took* as wives whomever they chose.

Westermann reminds us of other narratives that operate out of this tension, male attraction to female beauty: Abraham and Sarah in Egypt (12:10ff.), and David and Bathsheba in Jerusalem (1 Sam. 11). In those stories after the action of "seeing" and "taking," God intervenes. This narrative also follows with God's intervention (v. 3) (Westermann, 1966: 495-497).

The parallel between Genesis 6:1-4 and other narratives must not be pushed far. Yet one can suggest that Genesis 6:1-4 follows a similar pattern to the one in Genesis 3 and Genesis 4. As in those stories, again we find a normal tension in life resolved in a destructive way. The garden story spoke of the common tension of freedom and boundary (Gen. 3); in the Cain and Abel story tension arose between siblings and those with different occupations (4:1-6). The destructive resolution of those tensions brought disaster. In the narrative of Genesis 6:1-4, the danger involves the breakdown of the separation between human and divine. That men see the beauty of women and take wives presents no problem in itself. The mixing of the divine and human does. Therein lie the seeds of disaster.

Many parts of 6:1-4 remain a puzzle (Childs, 1962a: 50-59). The intervention of God is directed against humankind. The *sons of God* are not judged. Moreover, 6:4 does not follow logically from verse 3. Perhaps Genesis 6:4 came from a time when a similar story was told to explain the presence of *giants* on earth. The explanation of giants seems less central to the function of 6:1-4 in the received text.

Instead of trying to explain the existence of giants, the story is now joined with the Adam-Eve and Cain-Abel narratives, forming a third story of human violation and divine intervention. Like the problem of freedom and limits (Gen. 3) and sibling rivalry (Gen. 4), the tension created by the boundary between divine and human has been resolved in such a way as to further distort creation (v. 2). The blurring of that boundary threatened to create an unmanageably distorted population. Some would have measured life spans; some would not.

God's intervention (v. 3) appears to fall as a one-sided judgment on humanity, even though the problem was caused by the divine beings. However, we remember that the expulsion from the garden had an element of grace. Humanity would not be permitted to live forever in a "distorted" world (cf. notes on Gen. 3:22-24). We recall that God also protected Cain from being completely destroyed by the consequences of his actions (4:15). So here too we find an element of grace in this limitation of life span. No *giants* can terrorize and oppress the land forever. The high and the mighty cannot control the low and powerless without end. Life span limits all of us, not just some.

Divine Assessment 6:5-8

After the narratives of disruption in chapters 3, 4, and 6, the creation vision portrayed in Genesis 1 and 2 lies in ruins. The language used here to express that disaster has the ring of deepest pathos. Wickedness has invaded the very heart of human response (v. 5). In Hebrew, "heart" is the center of human intentionality and action. This disaster affects the individual heart of course, but not just the individual. The problem goes beyond any individual, driving to the center of the community's conscious living. The language could scarcely be more inclusive: "impulse," "thought," "action"; "always," "only," "every day." Each time the human community faces the tensions and problems of life—boundaries, rivalries, limitations—those are resolved in ways contrary to the creation vision. It does not matter whether persons involved are wife and husband, brothers or sisters, even divine and human beings, the story ends the same way.

The portrait of God in verse 6 shows us, not a God enraged over the violation of creation, but a God in tears (Brueggemann, 1982: 77). The Hebrew word translated *grieve* (RSV, NASB) is the same Hebrew word we met in Genesis 3:16 to describe the pain of the woman in childbirth (cf. NIV). God too lives with the pain of a world distorted and disrupted. The anguish of that pain causes God to wish that humanity had never been formed. We seldom speak of God using the language of grief. The Bible speaks often of God's grief. The texts portray divine anguish, whether it be in response to the violation of creation (vv. 5-8), the collapse of hope that surrounded Saul's anointing as king (1 Sam.

15:11), or the realization that Jerusalem does not know the things that make for peace (Luke 19:41). The biblical community knows God, not as one distant, but as one deeply involved, not as an analyst, but as a participant. In Genesis 6:6-7, God speaks a word of judgment. The speech proclaims not expulsion from the garden, or alienation from God and the earth, not a limitation on life expectancy, but the end of life on earth. Judgment here means annihilation. When God comes in judgment, can humanity survive? (Coats, 1983: 75). Genesis 5:1—6:8 does not answer the question, but the unit does end with a note of hope—*Noah*.

Noah is the person through whom a future might happen. However, both Genesis 5:29 and 6:8 declare that any hope is grounded, not in the character of Noah, but in the grace of God.

THE TEXT IN BIBLICAL CONTEXT

The brief mention of Enoch in Genesis 5 gave rise to extensive speculation concerning this figure in the large body of extra-biblical literature. The New Testament reflects acquaintance with some of the stories told about Enoch (Heb. 11:5; Jude 14). But the New Testament does not actively follow the conjecture that surrounded Enoch's name. The story of the sons of God in 6:1-4 also provided fertile ground for speculation. Extra-biblical literature traced the origin of evil (Enoch 14:1ff.; Damascus Doc. 2:17-21) and "fallen" divine beings (Enoch 69:4-5) to this brief narrative. While the New Testament refers to such speculation (perhaps Paul in 1 Cor. 11:10), again the New Testament writers made little use of these stories.

Both Matthew and Luke place Jesus into a linear genealogy. In fact, Luke incorporates Jesus into the genealogy of Genesis 5 (Luke 3:36-38). This emphasizes the continuity between Jesus and his Hebraic roots, but it accomplishes more than that. *[Reading Genealogies, p. 326.]* The geneaology merges God's dramatic art of deliverance through Jesus with God's constant work of blessing grounded in creation (Westermann, 1966:490). By ignoring the genealogies, we may neglect this merger of salvation and blessing. Genesis 5 and Luke 3 remind us that God's drama happens in the context of God's presence in the regular, the every day. While the linear genealogy wants the reader to notice the beginning (God) and the end (Noah or Jesus), this drama comes as one generation follows another.

THE TEXT IN THE LIFE OF THE CHURCH

Our life depends on Genesis 5 following Genesis 3—4. God's blessing expressed in the unbroken sequence of generations has not been destroyed by human actions that disrupt and distort life. The world which all generations have inherited displays the consequence of human disobedience and transgressions. But still one generation follows the next—the blessing of God continues in our midst.

Some have wondered whether it is prudent to bring children into a world endangered by nuclear disaster. Genesis 5 would suggest that the birth of yet another generation serves as a sign of God's presence even if all other signs seem to disappear. The drama of deliverance has always come because one generation followed upon another in spite of the crisis of the moment. We could, of course, end all genealogy in a nuclear holocaust, but in the meantime the repetitive character of a continuing genealogy grounds the knowledge that hope does not rest only in what God can accomplish with the current generation.

The church has often lifted from the Old Testament a portrait of an "angry God." We have used that picture of God either as a way to justify our own rage or to contrast with a "God of love" taken from the New Testament. The anger of God is certainly present in Scripture. That anger often expresses itself in divine judgment. But anger does not tell the whole story of God's judgment. In our text, judgment arises out of God's grief as much as anger. Pain-filled grief changes God's direction. God regrets ever having made humanity and determines to destroy all life. That God can change a decision provides the ground of human hope in other texts (e.g., Jonah 3:9-10), but in this text, it poses the gravest danger.

We know from the Flood story that God does not finally destroy all creation, but we must not let that blind us to God's tears shed because the vision of creation lies in ruin. The very ones who carry the image of God have set themselves over against that God always, every day.

Genesis 6:9 — 9:29

The Story of
Noah's Family

PREVIEW

Following the formula "these are the generations," this unit (6:9—9:29) relates the generations/story of Noah and his family. Each of the units we have examined so far has contained one extended section, either a narrative (Gen. 2—3) or a list (Gen. 5). Then other smaller sections have been included in the unit. Genesis 6:9—9:29 follows that pattern. The Flood story takes up most of the unit. But in addition, the unit includes a short anecdote about Noah's family. Three genealogical notes serve as dividers in the unit, marking the beginning (6:9-10), the end (9:28-29), and the separation between the Flood story and the anecdote material (9:18-19).

The Flood story dominates this unit in Genesis, and as such is positioned in the middle of the whole story (Gen. 1:1—11:26). Its role is so dominant that the end of the Flood story, 9:1-17, seems like the conclusion of the whole drama. We often skip from here over to the beginning of Abraham's story, just touching the tale of the Tower of Babel (11:1-9), treating that as an isolated narrative. Even while acknowledging the climactic character of the Deluge account, we want to remember that the unit does not end with 9:17 and thus overlook the curious anecdote of Noah's family.

The literature of many ancient peoples contain stories of an earth-covering flood. Differences in culture, religion, and organization of the society shaped the stories as they were passed along. Indeed, the story in Genesis 6—9 shows evidence of being told and retold, written and rewritten, through many generations. Certainly we should not be surprised if the story in the received text has incorporated within it different retellings of a story so central to the community of faith. Still we wonder when we read in 6:19-20 that God commands two of every kind of animal be taken on board, whereas in 7:2-3 the speech of God directs that seven pair of clean animals and one pair of unclean animals be taken on board.

Some want to harmonize those two speeches, suggesting that God first directed one and then added the other. Our desire for logical consistency in detail can cause us to lose touch with the character of Hebrew narrative. Central to this narrative is not exactly how many pairs of animals were on the ark or how many days the Flood lasted. Far more important for this narrative is to answer the question: "When God comes in judgment, can anyone survive?" The story wants to declare that even then some living beings, people and animals, will survive by God's grace.

The narrative itself ebbs and flows like a flood. The narrative wave rolls up to a crest in Genesis 8:1a: God remembered Noah and all the wild and domestic animals with him in the ark. Building up to that point we find the description of the situation in the earth (6:11-12), preparation for the Flood (6:13—7:9), and the coming of the waters (7:10-24). Flowing from that center comes the receding of the water (8:1-14), the departure from the ark (8:15-18), and God's commitment to the post-Flood world (8:20—9:17). Closer reading can illuminate the nuances and complexity of the narrative, but that should not blind us to the flow of the narrative, which almost has the feel of a wave that thunders down on a shore and then silently leaves.

Although the narrative cannot be reduced to a tight outline with exactly corresponding parts, it does admit of a symmetry rotating around 8:1a. A more detailed outline would show that the narrative as we have it uses repetition to emphasize certain parts. For example, the "preparations" for the Flood and the "commitment and promise" after the Flood each contains two speeches of God, one right after another. It was God who brought the Flood and reconstructed the world afterward.

OUTLINE

Introductory Genealogical Note, 6:9-10

The Narrative of the Flood, 6:11—9:17
  6:11—7:24 The Deluge and Destruction
    Reason for the Disaster, 6:11-12
    Preparations, 6:13—7:9
    Coming of the Waters, 7:10-24
  8:1—9:17 The Deliverance and Re-creation
    Receding of the Waters, 8:1-14
    Departure from the Ark, 8:15-19
    Commitment and Covenant, 8:20—9:17

A Genealogical Note, 9:18-19

An Anecdote About Noah and His Sons, 9:20-27
  9:20-21 Description of the Situation
  9:22   Violation by Ham
  9:23-27 Response
    By Shem and Japheth, 9:23
    By Noah, 9:24-27

Concluding Genealogical Note, 9:28-29

EXPLANATORY NOTES

Introductory Genealogical Note 6:9-10

Genesis 6:9 declares that God selected Noah because he was different from others. The words describing Noah pile up on each other, making it difficult to translate. We might understand the description of Noah as three poetic lines which paint a picture of the person:

> Noah was a righteous man,
> Blameless in his generation;
> Noah walked with God. (6:9)

By using three different expressions, the text deepens the description of Noah. All three lines want to be heard together, rather than dissected and analyzed for their precise meaning.

We are inclined to understand righteous (*saddiq*) and blameless (*tamim*) in moral terms. A person is judged righteous if his or her behavior conforms to a specific moral or ethical standard. For example, a person is blameless if she or he is truthful. By "truthful" we usually mean a person whose speech conforms to observable data. However, the Hebrew tradition does not generally turn to abstract moral and ethical rules to decide whether a person is righteous and blameless. Instead, these Hebrew words describe the character of relationships within the community. A righteous person is one who acts so as to enhance the relationships in the community and thus augments the life of the persons in the community. An unrighteous individual is one who violates relationships and destroys the community.

The two terms used here, *righteous* and *blameless,* come from two different contexts in the life of the Hebrew people. "Righteous" requires responsibility in family and wider social contexts. "Blameless" refers to the worship or cultic life. While there may have been times in the history of the Hebrew language that these two words functioned quite separately, that does not seem to be the case in this text. Rather, this text uses them as synonyms that enrich each other. Noah is declared one whose life was lived responsibly with God and his sisters and brothers (cf. Mark 12:29-31).

The Narrative of the Flood 6:11 – 9:17

6:11 – 7:24 The Deluge and Destruction

Reason for the disaster, 6:11-12. The story of a cataclysmic flood is a familiar one in the religious literature of the ancient Near East. None of these stories exactly duplicates another, but the Gilgamesh Epic from ancient Babylon has much in common with the biblical Flood story. Both accounts share the same basic story line. In both, God or the gods choose a flood to destroy life, but decide to save one family. God or the gods direct the building of a vessel and the loading with animals. Birds are used to verify the end of the flood and the vessel settles on a mountaintop. The major differences come at the beginning and end of these different flood stories. In the epic of Gilgamesh, no clear reason is given for the decision by the gods to bring a flood. Genesis 6:11-12 gives a very clear reason. The Gilgamesh Epic concludes with the granting of immortality to the main character, Utnapishti(m), whereas Genesis 9 reports Yahweh's covenantal bonding to *all* humanity. This comparison with the epic of Gilgamesh encourages us to pay special attention to the reasons for, and the results of, the Flood.

The harsh language used in 6:11-12 dramatizes the reason for the disaster. Violence and corruption have destroyed the life space of humanity. In the Old Testament the word "violence" *(hamas)* is used to describe a wide variety of violation of one person or group by another, including physical injury, institutional abuse, and even psychological enticement (49:5; Deut. 19:16; Prov. 16:29). The word translated *corrupt (šaḥat)* also has a broad range of meanings. But its use in 6:13 *(I will destroy)* following the three times in 6:11-12 suggests that the word portrays a general sense of annihilation (Westermann, 1966: 359). The earth had already been destroyed in God's sight. All flesh had destroyed life on the earth. So God determines to carry out the destruction which all flesh had generated (v. 13).

Preparations, 6:13— 7:9. Two speeches by God dominate this unit (6:13-21; 7:1-4). After each speech we find the statement of Noah's compliance: Noah did all that the Lord had commanded him (6:22; 7:5). The final verses in the section expand Noah's execution of the Lord's instructions. God's long speeches in preparation for the Flood put Noah narratively on the sideline. Quite likely the narrative wants us to realize that God took extraordinary measures to insure the survival of life. Even with the *destroyed* condition of the earth and *all flesh,* God carefully directs the survival of humans and of animals—good ones and bad.

The narrative does not give us precise information about the numbers and kinds of animals taken on the ark. Genesis 6:20 talks about *two of every sort,* whereas Genesis 7:2 speaks of *seven pairs of all clean animals . . . and a pair . . . that are not clean.* These redundant instructions preparing for the Flood serve to emphasize God's resolve that not all life shall perish in the Flood. That same resolve becomes a hallmark of God's relationship to the post-Flood world. Insofar as the key question of the Flood narrative is "can life survive God's coming in judgment?" the answer is clearly "Yes." God will see to it.

Coming of the waters, 7:10-24. Genesis 7:11 and 12 set side by side two pictures of the coming of the waters. As we retell the story to children, we usually picture a rain lasting 40 days and nights (v. 12). Verse 11 portrays the Flood in even more cataclysmic terms. The dome (firmament) of the heavens kept the waters above separate and in their place (1:6). Suddenly the windows in the dome were thrown open, destroying the separation between the water above and the earth below. The waters that had been confined *below* (1:9-10) also erupted. Everything went back to the water chaos before God's speaking and acting (1:2).

Genesis 7:21-23 confirms the accomplishment of judgment. The disaster seems complete. Everything in which there was the breath of life died—except for Noah and those with him. Even for Noah the future does not seem clear. Only God's deathly anger over *violence* and "destruction/corruption" is visible in the flood (cf. 6:11-12).

8:1—9:17 The Deliverance and Re-creation

Receding of the waters, 8:1-14. The Flood story turns with 8:1a: "God remembered Noah and all the animals . . . with him" (NAB). God's remembering involves a moving toward the object (Childs, 1962: 35). There is more action to remembering *(zakar)* than a simple "calling to mind." Of course God's remembering can bring judgment, so the psalmist asks that God not *remember* this sin of the past (Ps. 25:7; 79:8). But in the depth of disaster the deepest yearning of the soul is that God remember (1 Sam. 1:11). The one who remembers, delivers. God does remember, not just Noah, but Noah and all the animals with him. In our person-centered perspectives, we often assume God only remembers people. According to the text, the Flood affected everything in which there was the "breath of life." Remembering was similarly inclusive. The re-creating God acted to promote all life, not just human life.

As was common practice, the mariner released birds to see if dry land was near: the raven (v. 7) and the dove (vv. 8-12). The attention of this narrative rests on the dove. The first sending of the dove returned the information that the Flood still covered the earth (v. 9). The second sending brought back the dove of peace (v. 11): peace had replaced anger. On the third sending the dove left to make a new life (v. 12). On new year's day the earth was dry; new life could begin (v. 13).

Departure from the ark, 8:15-19. As in the preparation for the Flood, so also in the departure from the ark, God speaks and Noah complies. Noah is directed to *go forth* and *bring forth.* The speech completes the re-creation of the earth. The story has moved now from creation (by God), uncreation (by humanity and completed by God), and re-creation (by God). A key word *(Leitwort)* repeated throughout the account appears again at the end of the story—*earth [Characteristics of Hebrew Narrative, p. 313.]* God *created the earth* (1:1); violence and destruction filled the earth (6:11), the waters prevailed *upon the earth* (7:18-19), and a fruitful life begins anew *upon the earth* (8:17). The repeated word—*earth*—serves to hold the narrative together, a kind of glue that keeps the story intact.

Commitment and covenant, 8:20—9:17. Noah appears as an active agent in this concluding section of the Flood narrative only in 8:20. In response to deliverance, Noah worships and God speaks. God's speech is not to Noah but *in his heart* (v. 21). *In his heart* is a phrase that introduces a soliloquy. God speaks to no one. But God declares a commitment to the future irrespective of humanity's response. Cataclysmic judgment may not change humankind, but the Flood has changed God (Brueggemann, 1982: 81). Even though humanity's thoughts and actions remain as they were before the judgment (6:5), God declares the alienation between humanity (*'adam*) and the ground (*'adamah*) removed (v. 21). This has to do with thorns and thistles, but as the Hebrew wordplay suggests, there is more meant than just weeds in the garden. God will not participate in the alienation of humanity from its formation, its moorings, its ground. Alienation from that which grounds us may happen, but not as God's act of judgment.

The second declaration by God concerns cataclysmic disaster. If humanity does not survive, it will not be because God comes as judge/ destroyer (Coats, 1983: 83). God's commitment is to never again destroy. The words *as I have done* do not leave the door open to another divine cataclysm by a different agent, for example, fire, as some have suggested (Luther, 1958: 160, following 2 Peter 3:7). Those words simply reinforce God's *never again.*

This speech concludes with a poem (NIV, NASB). The poem further underscores the divine *never again.* Humanity can trust the constancy of nature (v. 22). Nature shall never again erupt in response to God's anger and grief so as to come so close to eliminating life on earth. God resolves to bear with humanity as we are (Rom. 3:25b).

The second divine speech is directed to Noah (9:1-7). This speech is framed (vv. 1 and 7) by the benediction found in Genesis 1:28: *Be fruitful and multiply. . . .* In the speech itself, God's blessing once again extends to humankind the responsibility of managing and controlling the world. However, the blessing acknowledges that the interaction between people and animals will not be as benevolent as once was envisioned: fear and dread (9:2-3) will replace what was intended to be a peaceful relationship between the two groups (Gen. 1:29-30).

Human control is not within limits. Sanctity of life marks the basic limit beyond which humanity must not go in its dominion. The text defines that limit with a prohibition against eating meat containing blood and shedding the blood of a person. Verse 5 reserves unconditionally to God the taking of human life. People and animals must not take it.

Genesis 9:6 seems to go another direction. Commonly, this poetic structure is understood to grant to the legal system the right of capital punishment. This interpretation would be consistent with the legal practice in ancient Israel reflected in Exodus 21 and Deuteronomy 17—19. However, even Deuteronomy spells out strong limitations on capital punishment, setting aside cities of refuge so that the accused can be protected against instant revenge (Deut. 19) and requiring two or three witnesses for guilt to be confirmed (Deut. 18:15). Obviously, Hebraic practice allowed capital punishment, however curtailed it may have been.

In spite of the history of its interpretation, Genesis 9:6 does not authorize and promote capital punishment (Coats, 1983: 78). Coats suggests the poem in 9:6 works through irony to reiterate, not to undermine the strong assertion in 9:5 that life-death decisions belong only to God. Verse 6 sets up a sphere of violence: person B sheds the blood of person A, so person C takes the blood of person B. But person C has now become guilty of shedding blood. So the violence continues in an unending chain, *unless* life and death is left in God's hands as verse 5 requires. Verse 6b ("for in the image of God has God made man," NIV) provides further reason why the giving and taking of life belongs to God alone.

However one may choose to understand Genesis 9:6, its primary thrust is not to give biblical support to legalize the taking of life. Fundamentally, 9:4-6 wants to affirm in the strongest way possible that control of life is the exception to human dominion of God's world. By command (9:4), by declaration (9:5), and by poetry (9:6), the text cries out against the taking of human life.

Rainbow and covenant appear in the third speech by God (9:8-17). God's *never again* (9:11) is engraved in covenant and secured by a sign. Covenant is a broad word in the Old Testament; it includes many kinds of relationships and carries different sorts of expectations. *[Covenant, p. 315.]* Therefore, it is more prudent to talk about covenant in each text than to treat covenant as a general concept. Covenant in this text signifies God's unconditional commitment. The unconditional words *never again (lo 'od;* vv. 11, 15), *all (kol;* 9:10-12, 15-17), *all/everlasting ('olam;* 9:12, 16) determine the direction of this speech.

God is unconditionally committed to the world and its inhabitants. We are inclined to include a "but if . . ." in covenant. This covenant contains no condition. Some might go to the previous speech in 9:4-6, suggesting that if humanity does not acknowledge divine sovereignty over life, then the covenant will be broken. To be sure, the sacredness of life requires accountability. But that accountability does not function as a condition of covenant. In this covenant God promises to stay in relationship with *all* future generations unconditionally.

God's commitment to the covenant is secured by a sign—a bow in the clouds. We cannot be sure whether this sign was understood to symbolize the discarded and undrawn warrior's bow or whether it represents nothing more than the end of the rain. Whichever the background, the *bow in the cloud* functions first of all to cause God to *remember.* When the bow appears in the clouds God will remember the *everlasting covenant* (9:15-16). God's remembering which turned the Flood around (8:1) insures the future as well. God takes no chance; this covenant is forever and for everyone.

A Genealogical Note 9:18-19

This genealogical note serves as the end bracket of the story of the Flood. It complements the beginning genealogical note (6:9-11). While serving as the end bracket of the Flood story, it functions also as the beginning bracket of the narrative about Noah and his sons (9:20-27). Nevertheless, the concluding phrase, *from these the whole earth was peopled*, shows that it has more than only a literary function. The resumption of genealogy signals the return of fertility. God's blessing is once again empowering the earth.

THE TEXT IN BIBLICAL CONTEXT

The so-called Noachian code, which was based on Genesis 9:4-6, has played an important role in Jewish and Christian ethics. In the Jewish heritage it has affected the way meat is prepared as food. It represented the minimum morality expected of all humanity. As the Jewish tradition expanded the interpretation of this text, the number of prohibitions given to Noah for all humankind was said to be seven: injustice, prohibition of blasphemy, idolatry, murder, incest, robbery, and eating an animal with its blood (B. Jacob: 64). The early church, as reflected in Acts 15:1-35, discussed this "code" and decided at the council of Jerusalem that while much particular Jewish law would not be required of Gentile Christians, the Noachian code remained obligatory. The code at that time prohibited four things: idolatry, sexual immorality, eating food with its blood, and food improperly butchered.

   Although the Bible seldom refers to the Flood story directly, the frequent motif of deliverance from dangerous water echoes this story. The narrative of Jonah and the story of Jesus calming the sea (Mark 4:35-41) come immediately to mind. But even beyond those, the Exodus crossing of the sea (Exod. 14) and Christian baptism echo the motif of God's deliverance through dangerous water (1 Pet. 3:18-22). Luther, commenting on the verses in 1 Peter, called them a "most beautiful allegory of the Flood story" *(Luther's Commentary:* 170). However, Luther's hesitancy about using allegory made him reluctant about pressing the Flood-baptism connection very far. Luther's counsel on that seems wise.

THE TEXT IN THE LIFE OF THE CHURCH

God did not intend the world to be as we find it. The destruction and distortion of life precipitates God's coming in judgment. Will anything survive that judgment? We might wonder how God could put survival in jeopardy at all. Will not the love of God override destructive anger? The narrative refuses to let the reader use an understanding of the love of God to avoid God's ache and anger at the human destruction of the world. The writer of the Flood story knows that the pain and grief of a world which violently destroys itself hurt the Creator so deeply that God can come in judgment, even to destroy life on earth.

The narrative signals from the beginning that God will not completely destroy—almost but not quite. God makes elaborate preparations so life can survive divine judgment. Nevertheless, in the midst of the judgment suddenly we find ourselves uncertain that even God's own preparations are sufficient. At that moment God remembers (8:1). Because of God's remembering, humankind and animals live. The story attributes to Noah unusual integrity in his relationship with God (6:9). Nevertheless in the end, survival depends on God's remembering, as the psalmist knows:

> How long,
> Lord, will you forget me forever?
> How long,
> Will you hide your face from me?
> (Ps. 13:1, translation mine)

> Arise, Lord, God,
> Lift up your hand.
> Do not forget the afflicted.
> (Ps. 10:12, translation mine)

Hannah's vow similarly expresses the anguished longing for the life-giving remembering of God.

> Lord, Sabaoth, if you will give attention to your servant—remember me, do not forget your servant—and give to your servant a baby boy, then I will give him to Yahweh all the days of his life. . . .
> (1 Sam. 1:11, translation mine)

God's remembering changes death to life, (Luke 23:42). In the Flood narrative, God's remembering leads beyond survival to covenant, God's unconditional promise never again to participate in the annihilation of all life. Sitting on the edge of nuclear disaster, we wonder whether the story promises that God will prevent the annihilation of life. The covenant does not answer that question. It only declares that God's patience will never run out. God will not bring such a disaster as punishment. God still allows humanity the freedom to destroy. That freedom has not been revoked even in the depths of God's grief over evil that controls the impulse of the human heart (8:21).

The story of the Flood assures us that God's action among us will always and only be toward creation and not destruction. No wonder we run excitedly toward the window to see the sign of God's covenant once again. Scientists as we are, we know that a rainbow is the special pattern of the sun's rays refracted and reflected by the drops of rain in the air. Children of faith as we are, we know that God can make the common special. Common water drops refracting and reflecting light or common bread and wine become symbols of God's everlasting love and unconditional *never again.*

Noah and His Sons

Genesis 9:18-29

PREVIEW

Most of us stop reading with the covenant in 9:8-17. However, the unit does not end there, even though we have made a separate section of 9:17-26 for the purpose of commentary. Instead, as illustrated by the outline above (p. 67), it goes on to narrate a curious anecdote about a violation of Noah by Ham. The incident leaves us with more questions than clarity.

As illustrated by the earlier outline (p. 67), the anecdote is bracketed by two notes with genealogical elements (9:18-19, 28-29). Genesis 9:18-19 serves as a transitional note referring to the Flood, "The sons of Noah who came out of the ark . . ." (v. 18a, NIV) and anticipates the role of Canaan in the next narrative, *Ham was the father of Canaan* (v. 18b). The concluding genealogical note (vv. 28-29) repeats the form of the long genealogy in chapter 5, completing the note on Noah left unfinished in 5:32.

Defining the genre of this narrative immediately thrusts us into the interpretation of the text. Historically speaking, the narrative is deeply related to the strife between the Israelites and Canaanites for religious, economic, and political dominance in Palestine. Hence it might be classified as a story about the origins of political conflict, an ethnological narrative. But its literary location places it as the conclusion of the Flood story, the deliverance of the Noah family. As such, it functions as a family story in association with the other family stories of Genesis 1—11—Adam and Eve, Cain and Abel. While acknowledging its role in Israel's internal political strife, we want to give primary attention to the role this anecdote plays as the conclusion of the Flood story.

OUTLINE

A Genealogical Note, 9:18-19

An Anecdote About Noah and His Sons, 9:20-27
    9:20-21 Description of the Situation
    9:22   Violation by Ham
    9:23-27 Response
        By Shem and Japheth, 9:23
        By Noah, 9:24-27

Concluding Genealogical Note, 9:28-29

EXPLANATORY NOTES

An Anecdote About Noah and His Sons 9:20-27

9:20-21 Description of the Situation

Genesis 9:20 is difficult to translate, as a comparison of the different versions illustrates. The RSV translation—*Noah was the first tiller of the soil*—seems grammatically less likely than the translation in the NIV: "Noah, a man of the soil, proceeded to plant a vineyard."

This text sets the stage of the anecdote by describing Noah's occupation, grape grower (v. 20), and his physical condition, drunk (v. 21). The narrative does not condemn or even censure Noah, but states that this condition makes him weak and vulnerable (v. 21). The biblical tradition is aware of the danger of alcohol and warns against its misuse, but accepts it as a common drink in that culture. Nevertheless, drinking the products of his vineyards had left Noah very vulnerable.

9:22 Violation by Ham

The text does not tell us exactly how Ham violated his father. "To uncover the nakedness" sometimes denotes sexual relations. To uncover the nakedness of one's father can refer to sexual relationship between a man and his father's wife (Lev. 18:6ff.). Some have suggested that homosexuality was Ham's transgression, although the phrase is not used in that way in other biblical texts. In fact the text as it has come to us

does not tell us what happened. Such "reticence" is a common characteristic of Hebrew narrative *[Characteristics of Hebrew Narrative, p.
313.]* All we are told is that Ham *saw* and *told.* Probably that "seeing"
and "telling" involved Noah's sexuality. Whatever the precise action, the
son saw the vulnerability of the parent and misused that. That misuse
deeply violated the relationship between parent and child.

9:23-27 Response by Shem, Japheth, and Noah

The narrative now moves ever so slowly. Emphasizing gentle care,
the other two sons respond by covering their father's vulnerability. In so
doing, they protect him from further abuse. Listen to the feel of verse 23
next to 22. In verse 22 the action is abrupt: *saw, told.* In verse 23 the
brothers take the blanket, lay it on their shoulders, and cover their father,
taking care not to add further injury to the situation. We can understand
the difficulty and delicacy of assisting one who has been violated, especially when that violation has involved the individual's sexuality.

Noah awakens and speaks (vv. 24-27). The text does not tell us how
Noah found out who had violated him. Nevertheless, the family must
now deal with the consequences of this violation. Those consequences
affect the following generation, *Canaan,* as much or more than the
present generation, *Ham.* Two speeches pronounce curse and blessing
(vv. 25 and 26-27). The emphasis in both speeches is on the enslavement of Canaan. Likely, this was used as a political statement in the conflict between various peoples living in Canaan. Shem represents the Israelites, and Japheth has been variously identified as the Philistines, or
perhaps the Ephraimites. But the lack of positive historical identification
makes it prudent for us to emphasize its function within Genesis 1—11
as a human family story. Just as in the family narratives of Genesis 3 and
4:1-16, so here the violation results in distorted human relationships:
one brother as slave to another. Enslavement distorts the vision of God's
creation as much as male/female relationships lived in domination and
subordination (3:16) and the murder of one brother by another (4:8).

THE TEXT IN BIBLICAL CONTEXT AND IN THE LIFE OF THE CHURCH

Whether it be by Calvin vilifying the pope *(Calvin's Commentaries:*
307-308) or white Americans justifying slavery, this text has been used to
serve social and political ends. Ancient Israel may have used the text in
its conflict with their enemy, the Canaanites. The danger remains that
this (and other) texts can be used to ratify political oppression and social

domination. Regretfully, we sometimes prove no wiser than our ancestors. For example, some of those who identify Ham's violation with one or another social problem are being inclined to use this text as support for oppressing others.

Luther was comforted by this story because it showed that even the greatest stumble on occasion *(Luther's Commentary:* 172). Although we no longer read the story assuming that it casts a shadow on Noah for his vineyard, Luther is right. The family that survived the Flood in part because of their unusual integrity in relationship with God and one another, stumbles just off the ark. The family rescued from the Flood has all the problems of those that created the disruption. Destroying the bad people does not annihilate the difficulties. Yet we continue to expect that if we can just eliminate the problem people, we will have a happy family.

Vulnerability is endemic in each family situation. We usually know where the other can be exposed. Violation of that vulnerability dramatically disrupts relationships. Both the violated and violator are victimized. Such violation may happen out of malice or indifference, perhaps even ignorance. This text does not call Ham an evil son. He simply *saw* and *told,* but the consequences are devastating: *a slave of slaves shall he be to his brothers* (9:25). Sometimes evil intention does lie behind such violation; other times it does not. But, even if ignorance explains a violation, it seldom removes the consequences of a crime against the soul. We did not know, we just saw and told, but as a result everything is changed. Very delicate, then, is the pastoral task in and by the community of faith: He has sent us to bind up "the hearts that are broken" (Isa. 61:1, JB). Very difficult also is the redemptive task in and by the community of faith to receive as sisters and brothers those whom we formerly treated as slaves (Philem. 16).

The List of the Sons of Noah

PREVIEW

If we follow the "generations" formula (RSV, NASB) through Genesis, the next unit runs from 10:1, *These are the generations of the sons of Noah,* through the story of the Tower of Babel (11:9). Commonly, the Tower of Babel is treated independently from the genealogy that precedes it. Certainly that story stands out as distinct. However, the "tale of the tower" does not stand alone in the text as we have it, but is related to the table of nations in Genesis 10 (Barth: 313).

The table itself is bracketed by the "generations" formula in 10:1 and a variation of that formula in 10:32. Inside these "bookends" we find the genealogy of Japheth (vv. 2-5), Ham (vv. 6-20), and Shem (vv. 21-31). Symmetry also exists in the beginning and ending formulas in each of these sections, but the formulas are not exact duplicates of one another. Internally in each section of the table, we find great variety, much more than is found in Genesis 5. *[Reading Genealogies, p. 326.]*

The tale of the Tower of Babel itself is enclosed in narrative brackets (11:1 and 9). The story begins with the action and speech of unnamed people (vv. 2-4). Providing balance, God responds to this by action and speech (vv. 5-8). We can also observe the same narrative flow from transgression to consequence that we have noted in several previous narratives in Genesis 1—11 (cf. Gen. 3; 4:1-16; 6:1-4; 9:20-27).

OUTLINE

Introductory Note, 10:1

EXPLANATORY NOTES

Genealogy of the Sons of Noah 10:2-31

10:2-5 Genealogy of Japheth

Even though Genesis 10 has the form of a genealogy, what we find is a list of people, political groups, stretching from the Black Sea on the north, south to the headwaters of the Nile, and from Greece in the west across to Persia in the east. Some are nations, others city-states. Some we know from other sources, others we do not.

In Genesis 5 we found a linear genealogy—one that moved from parent to one child without following the genealogy of other children. In Genesis 10, however, we have a genealogy with some branching (also known as segmenting). It follows all three sons of Noah, not just one. But the list does not deal with all branches of each "family." For example, Genesis 10:3-4 does not follow all the branches of Japheth found in verse 2, only Gomer and Javan. *[Reading Genealogies, p. 326.]*

Some of the names in the Japheth list can be identified with known groups. The identified groups include Gomer in the Black Sea area, Javan in the Greece/Cyprus area, and Madai in the area of Persia. These are located to Israel's north (including northeast and northwest) in the far reaches of the world known to the ancient Hebrews.

10:6-20 Genealogy of Ham

The descendants of Ham whose location we can fix with some certainty point to an area south of Palestine, including the northeast quarter of Africa. The groups are not defined here by racial, ethnic, or even precise territorial designations. For example, Cush was most probably a nation south of Egypt. But the names of the *sons of Cush* point to Arabian place names far to the east of Egypt.

The list gathers together diverse groups without specifying sharp geographical or cultural separation. This genealogical list does not reckon the peoples as a collection of divinely established political enclaves, but as the family of God's blessing spread without preferential treatment throughout the world. By understanding this variety of nations as an expression of God's blessing rather than as divinely established political entities, we cannot establish any political map as a particularistic expression of manifest destiny, as if God gave one group a particular land and all other groups must move aside.

The list changes format, with 10:8 giving major attention first to one of the sons of Cush, Nimrod, and then one of the brothers of Cush, Canaan. The text does not designate the Cushite, Nimrod, as a Southerner, but as the founder of the several Mesopotamian empires. An identification of Cush with a northeastern group, the Kassites, rather than the African nation, may explain this geographic jump.

Along with Canaan (vv. 15-20), the "genealogy" uses familiar biblical names such as the town of Sidon and names of people spread throughout Palestine such as Jebusites and Amorites. Although Israel found itself in regular conflict with both the Mesopotamian nations and the Canaanites, this genealogy accepts their presence without prejudice. [*Reading Genealogies, p. 326.*]

10:21-31 Genealogy of Shem

This list also contains some names that can be identified and others that cannot. Aram, Asshur, and Elam were nations that figured in Israel's formation and history: Aram, an inclusive term for northwest Semitic city-states in Syria; Asshur, Assyria, and Elam, a group located east of the Mesopotamian river valley. The credo-like recitation of Israel's story found in Deuteronomy 26 traces its ancestor to Aram: *A wandering Aramean was my father* (Deut. 26:5).

The list emphasizes the name of Eber by mentioning Eber out of order in 10:21, and by repeating the name again as son of Shelah in 10:24, and yet again as father in 10:25. Eber is here designated the ancestor of the Hebrews. However prominent the name in this section of the list, no unusual character is attached to Eber. He is simply the fourth generation in one branch of the Shemite genealogy. The tradition does not trace Israel's specialness to genes generating an extra good or powerful people (Vawter, 1977: 151). Israel sometimes succumbed to a very nationalistic understanding of its chosenness and its land as "promised." But this genealogy warns the Hebrews against distinguishing themselves from all people in such a way as to make themselves the only or best expression of God's blessing in the world. *[Reading Genealogies, p. 326.]*

The spreading abroad (10:18) of all peoples, which becomes a problem in "the tale of the tower" (11:1-9), appears here as a positive expression of God's blessing to *be fruitful and multiply, and fill the earth* (Gen. 1:28; 9:1).

Tale of the Tower 11:1-9

11:1 Introduction

This verse introduces us to some of the key words that carry the narrative along: *the whole earth, language.* The phrase *the whole earth* or *all the earth (kol ha'ares)* occurs five times in the story, three of those times in the narrative's "bookends" (vv. 1, 9). The word *language/ speech* is also used five times, appearing in both verses 1 and 9. These words certainly do not carry the whole meaning of the unit, but they do function as signals to its meaning. Hence this narrative intends to be about everyone, i.e., *the whole earth.* Furthermore, the attention rests more on *language* than on buildings. That leads to one final connection between verses 1 and 9: verse 1 emphasizes "one" language/"common" speech (NIV). Verse 9 describes a people scattered with confused language. Hence the story moves from unity to disunity.

11:2-4 Action of the People

Two speeches by the people *to one another* define their intended action (vv. 3, 4). Both speeches begin with the imperative *come (yahav)* followed by the proposed action—*make* (bricks) and *build,* and *make* (a name). Even though we know this story as the Tower of Babel, it is as much about building a city and making a name as a tower. Taking our clue from the key words in 11:1 and 9, we should pay closest attention not to the actual proposed action (firing bricks and erecting buildings) but to the reason for the actions stated in 11:4. The people fear being *scattered* over the *whole earth.* Chapter 10 has already told us that being scattered and filling the earth is an expression of God's blessing (10:5, 18, 20, 31). But in the tale of the tower God's blessing is experienced as something to fear. The people seek to establish a unity, apparently set against God's blessing to *be scattered.*

Often in reading the tale we give most of our attention to bricks and buildings. We may picture the tower as a Babylonian temple atop a hill, a ziggurat. There is much which is Babylonian in the story: the brick building materials (in Palestine they used stone), a tower expected to reach the dwelling of the gods, and a possible play on Babylon as the name of the abandoned city, Babel. But the people and the tower are unnamed. There may be an anti-urban, anti-Babylonian flavor to the tale, but the story as we have received it is not centered in a polemic against building cities or even Babylon. The city and tower are not an end in themselves, but a means to "prevent scattering" the people. The whole earth works to create by human effort a unity that is opposed to the intent of God's blessing.

11:5-8 Response of God

The section also centers in a speech, this time a speech given by God (vv. 6-7). The speech begins by stating that unity has already been given, *they are one people, and they have all one language* (v. 6). The people propose to use their unity to secure themselves, as protection against being scattered (Brueggemann, 1982: 98ff.). So in response to the *come, let us* speech of the people, the Lord speaks in the divine council, *Come, let us....* (v. 7). And God's action is similar to the expulsion from the garden (3:22-24); God acts to prevent further problems (Coats, 1983: 95). In trying to save their unity, the people have lost it.

11:9 Conclusion

The whole earth is filled with people. But no unity is experienced in this scattering, only confusion. The name of the abandoned city, Babel (*babel*), signals this confusion (*balel*). Indeed, "confusion" is the only proper name used in the tale. The people remain as they were at the beginning, without name. But what began in unity ends in confusion.

The genealogy in chapter 10 declared that the peoples had been spread abroad possessing different languages. The tale of the tower begins with the people together, speaking one language. Efforts to make chapters 10 and 11 work in chronological sequence seem misdirected. Whatever the explanation of the history of the material, the text as we receive it does not seek to establish a chronology for the existence of distinct people with diverse languages. Rather, "scattering" and "language," which were to be an expression of God's blessing, instead become a serious problem. We can no longer hear and understand each other (v. 8).

THE TEXT IN BIBLICAL CONTEXT

The Christian commentary tradition has regularly connected the narrative of the Tower of Babel with the experience of the church on Pentecost (Acts 2). Martin Luther observes,

> In view of this [scattering] we must regard it as a great blessing that on Pentecost the Holy Spirit united by various tongues peoples of many lands into the one body whose Head is Christ.
> *(Luther's Commentary:* ¡194)

At Pentecost the diversity of language does not prevent hearing and understanding.

The command to "go" to all the nations at the end of the gospel of Matthew changes the experience of being scattered. Once again scattering becomes an expression of God's blessing. In fact, the command to scatter in Matthew 28:19 is framed as a benediction. The newly scattered go, not out of punishment, but out of blessing.

Only occasionally in the history of Israel was scattering considered a working out of God's blessing. More often it was understood as a problem or even a punishment. Especially with the Babylonian Exile, the anticipation of blessing looked toward a time of "gathering"; scattering was a problem.

> Fear not, for I am with you;
>   I will bring you offspring from the east
>   and from the west I will gather you;
> I will say to the north, Give up,
>   and to the south, Do not withhold;
> bring my sons from afar
>   and my daughters from the end of the earth.
>   (Isa. 43:5-6)

For those who have experienced only forced "scattering," gathering presents a picture of hope. But for those sent by God's benediction, scattering is a fulfillment of blessing.

THE TEXT IN THE LIFE OF THE CHURCH

The tale of the Tower of Babel speaks to us of unity. Deep peace comes to a community where the sisters and brothers are at one, speaking the same language, sharing the same history, understanding the faith in the same way. Community as God's gift brings that peace. But that peace can neither be secured nor protected. Oneness as gift is elusive. It cannot be controlled or managed. Yet precisely the preciousness of this oneness creates the impetus for managing, securing, and even advertising the unity: let us form bricks, let us build a community, let us make a name. The attempt to establish the unity on a basis other than gift, thereby securing unity against scattering, is doomed. Scattering cannot be prevented. The church will experience it either as blessing or bane.

We know how important language is for unity. It can create or confuse a people. Language can construct or constrict a community. To speak about one people requires a common set of symbols to talk about that oneness. However, Brueggemann reminds us that language involves more than speaking (1982: 102-104). Language also incorporates hearing and listening. Crucial to the end of this story is that people could not hear/understand each other. Acts 2 restores the possibility of hearing one another, regardless of the language spoken: *How is it that we hear, each of us in his own native language* (Acts 2:8). The unity of the body depends on hearing. Speaking only one language, as do most North American Christians, severely limits our hearing and probably the breadth of our Pentecost. All of us have trouble hearing some words regardless of the tongue in which it is spoken. The cry of the oppressed is very difficult to hear. Sometimes only God hears that language (Exod. 2:23-25).

Genesis 11:10-26

Shem's Family

PREVIEW

Genesis 11:10-26 is a linear genealogy structured in much the same way as Genesis 5. Like Genesis 5, we find here nine or ten generations branching out at the end to include three sons: Abram, Nahor, and Haran. While the branching or segmented genealogical form used in chapter 10 incorporated the three sons of Noah, chapter 11 follows just one post-Flood line, Shem. Hence we find a progressive narrowing of focus: Genesis 10 involved the whole earth, the universal. Genesis 11 picks up one family, the particular. The next unit will narrow the focus even more to one of these three sons, Abraham (11:27ff.). [Reading Genealogies, p. 326.]

OUTLINE

Introduction, 11:10a

Genealogy of Shem, 11:10b-26
- 11:10b-11   Shem
- 11:12-13   Arpachshad
- 11:14-15   Shelah
- 11:16-17   Eber
- 11:18-19   Peleg
- 11:20-21   Reu
- 11:22-23   Serug
- 11:24-25   Nahor
- 11:26   Terah

EXPLANATORY NOTES

Genealogy of Shem 11:10-26

Like the names in Genesis 10, some names in this unit we recognize as places in the ancient Near East. Serug, Nahor, and Terah are towns or regions in northern Mesopotamia. The city in this region best known to us is Haran. A problem arises in this unit with Haran used both as a place and as a personal name. The Hebrew spelling of the name Haran as a person (haran, v. 26) is different from the spelling of Haran as a place name (ḥaran, v. 31). We do not know whether these are to be treated as two distinct names or the same name with a slight variation in the spelling. The correspondence between the personal name and place name happens frequently in the lists of Genesis 10 and 11. However, we cannot be sure such correspondence exists with Haran.

The genealogy of Shem encompasses the broad group in the ancient Near East known to us as the Semites. Semitic people were the dominant group in the area running from the Tigris and Euphrates rivers (Mesopotamian river valley) northwest to Syria and south through Canaan to Egypt. These people were not racially different from their neighbors. In fact the Semitic groups were likely as ethnically diverse among themselves as they were different from other surrounding groups. But they were folk who shared a common language "family." To say they shared the same language family is not to say they spoke the same language, but that language subgroupings shared many common features, including vocabulary. For example, we are best acquainted with two language families in Western Europe: the Romance languages (Latin, Italian, French, and Spanish) and the Germanic languages (German, Dutch, English, and Scandinavian). Much of Eastern Europe belongs to the Slavic language family. Biblical Hebrew and Aramaic (parts of Daniel and Ezra) are two of the Semitic languages. The most widespread Semitic language today is Arabic. In the time of Israel's ancestral families, Akkadian was the dominant Semitic language.

This unit uses a linear genealogy to describe Israel's origins in the world of the Semites. The effect of this presentation is to direct our attention to one Semitic family. The next unit takes up the story of one member of that Semitic family, Abraham. [Reading Genealogies, p. 326.]

THE TEXT IN BIBLICAL CONTEXT

This narrative quickly shifts our attention from the universal to the particular. The stories in Genesis 1—11 have been about all people, even though they have been cast often in the form of family stories. But with this linear genealogy the focus has narrowed to one family. While the linear genealogy draws our attention to just one family, it also anchors the one family in the many. The one family is not an isolated unit but a part of the larger world of families. What happens to this one Semite family will impact other families and vice versa.

The linear genealogy of Jesus (Matt. 1; Luke 3) moves in the same two directions. Jesus was not without genealogy. The Gospel of Luke explicitly ties Jesus to the whole human family rooted in the lists of Genesis 11, and chapters 10 and 5. In an effort to understand the distinctiveness of Jesus, the church has sometimes cut him off from all family. The most extreme example in the early church of such cutting off Jesus from his genealogical roots occurred in the Gnostic Christian communities (Koester, 1982, I: 388). Gnosticism so emphasized Jesus as the divine Redeemer that it lost Jesus' roots in and connection to human history. The Gospel writers avoided such a mistake. Clearly the actions of those around him affected Jesus and even defined the manner of his death. On the other hand, because he carried the whole human family with him, what happened to Jesus affected all humanity (1 Cor. 15:22).

THE TEXT IN THE LIFE OF THE CHURCH

The genealogy of Shem introduces the transition in Genesis from the stories of all humanity to stories of Israel's early families. As we look back on the unit which began in Genesis 1, we have found two different genre of literature: narratives and lists.

At the risk of oversimplification, we can describe the narratives as tales of disruption and distortion. The human family facing a tension or limitation had to decide how to respond to the problem: e.g., prohibition in the midst of permission (Gen. 2), inexplicable choice of one person instead of another (Gen. 4), sexual attraction (Gen. 6), vulnerability within the family (Gen. 9), and preserving and protecting unity (Gen. 11). Humankind commonly meets and resolves these problems in ways that distort and destroy God's creation. In most of the narratives God intervened to preserve justice and to keep the consequences of disruption within tolerable limits. In the Flood narrative God responded by joining the destruction in what appeared would be an unlimited way. But God placed limits even on that destruction, promising never to take that road again. The disruption in the human family continued as God knew it would.

The second kind of literature in Genesis 1—11 has been lists, genealogies mostly, but we have seen that even Genesis 1 is more list than story. The lists have held life together, witnessing to the presence of God's blessing beneath and in the midst of the drama of the stories. No amount of anguish or anger can destroy God's blessing: spring follows every winter, seeds spring up from deep in the ground, pregnancy happens side by side with death. This sustaining blessing carries out the vision of creation which God saw, saying, "Behold, it is very good."

Now attention turns to one family. This family has inherited a world of narrative and genealogy. The world is violation, oppression, and murder, but not only that. The world is also children, flowers, and rainbows.

Part 2

The Saga of
Abraham and Sarah

Genesis 11:27–25:18

The Saga of Abraham
and Sarah

PREVIEW

Most of us have studied the saga of Abraham and Sarah more as a series of episodes than as a single narrative. In the saga we find stories of conflict and occasions of reconciliation, times of faithfulness and moments of doubt. Perhaps the best known "episodes" concern the near sacrifice of Isaac (Gen. 22), the laughter of an old and barren Sarah (Gen. 18), and the mob action by the men of Sodom (Gen. 19). Only a few of us remember the warfare that made Lot hostage (Gen. 14) or the conflict over water rights for which Beersheba was named (Gen. 21). Very few of us could tell the saga of Abraham and Sarah as a single story as we might the stories of Joseph, Jonah, or Ruth. The episodic character of this narrative is characteristic of saga in Israel and also the literature of other cultures (Coats, 1983: 5). [Characteristics of Hebrew Narrative, p. 313.]

Nevertheless, the episodic character of the literature does not mean that a family saga such as Abraham's completely lacks coherence and flow. The flow of a family saga often follows the normal life cycle of a family: birth, marriage, children, death. We find some of that life cycle flow in the saga of Abraham. The saga begins with a genealogy of Abraham's father, Terah, and includes a note about his marriage to Sarah (11:27-29). The saga concludes with the death of Sarah and Abraham (23:25). However, this saga has a theological perspective which also

93

guides its flow. We find the promise of blessing placed in the center of the first section (11:27—12:9) so prominently that we can hardly miss it. The promise of blessing in the Abraham saga is expressed in very old promises, such as land and offspring. But distinctive to the ancestral stories is the promise that through the family of Abraham all the families of the earth will receive blessing.

As the saga moves along, the promise of land drops into the background—after Genesis 15—and the promise of descendants dominates. Although the promise of multiple descendants reappears throughout the saga (25:1-6), the controlling tension concerns the birth of one son, the son who is to carry the divine promise into the second generation. This son, by God's decision, must be born to Sarah, who, unfortunately, remains barren all through her "child-bearing" years (11:30; 18:12). In spite of the odds against any birth to the elderly Sarah and complications created by family efforts to deal with Sarah's sterility, the promise persists. Finally the promised son is born (Gen. 21), only to have his life threatened not by disease, accident, or war, but by God. Unexpected deliverance from this danger resolves the primary tension in the saga. The final section of the narrative brings to conclusion the life of Sarah and Abraham and prepares the family for the next generation. At the end of the Saga the narrator can return to the promise of blessing and say, *Now Abraham was old, well advanced in years; and the Lord had blessed Abraham in all things* (24:1).

By definition, a family saga focuses attention on the life of a family. Abraham plays the central role in the family saga. However, at times Sarah is the central figure, either in the foreground or background. For example in Genesis 12:10—13:1, Sarah is very much in the background, but all the action depends on her presence, as Abraham and Pharaoh clash over her role in the drama—sister or wife. On the other hand, in Genesis 16 Sarah functions as the active agent in the effort to obtain an heir through Hagar. The other main character in this family saga is Isaac, even though he arrives on the scene when the story is almost over, utters only one line (22:7), and is nearly removed permanently. Nevertheless, the promise of his presence is never far below the surface.

As we encounter the members of the family, we will find them presented as genuine people. They have become heroes of the faith and as such we have tended to idealize them, using the virtues we most admire—faithfulness, obedience, trust, honesty. To be sure, the family members act out those virtues at some moments. But Hebrew narrative seldom gives way to the urge to idealize God's people, not for long anyway. The stories show what God certainly knows, namely, that the faith has always been carried in the hands of people who stumble, grow weary, act incompetently, and disobey at some moments, while at other times they surprise us with their trust, perseverance, perceptiveness, and faithfulness. In the whole Abraham saga only Isaac does not run astray, perhaps because this presents him with little opportunity. On the other hand the saga evokes empathy, sometimes even admiration, for every person, save the mob of men living in Sodom. The story will disappoint those of us who wish for unblemished heroes. But insofar as we know the people of God in other generations, we will understand the people in this saga and perhaps even recognize ourselves where we least expect it.

The place to begin study of the Abraham saga is with the whole story as we have received it, not with only the well-known episodes. Read the saga as the story of a family, not primarily as a sourcebook for theological dogma or ethical virtues. Pay attention to the people, letting yourself laugh and cry, anguish and celebrate. In some episodes you will be proud of them, in others, ashamed. The "reasonable theology" of adulthood has robbed many Christians of the ability to hear biblical stories. We are inclined to be listening for examples of ethical virtue or theological propositions. This "adult" approach to the faith helps us organize our thoughts and manage our lives, but it can also anesthetize us, allowing us to block out anything new. It was that anesthetic quality of reasonable faith that Jesus found so frightfully troublesome (Brueggemann, 1978). We cannot ignore the fact that we are adults, but perhaps if we listen to these narratives as the saga of a family, we can regain some of the feeling for the stories many of us had as children (Mark 10:13-16).

With these introductory comments, let us move through the saga following this outline.

OUTLINE

Introduction: God's promise, 11:27—12:9

Episodes After the Promise, 12:10—14:24

Dialogue About the Promise, 15:1-21

A Story About an Heir, 16:1—21:34

The Story of a Test, 22:1-19

Conclusion: Testamentary
   Activities and Death, 22:20—25:18

Genesis 11:27 – 12:9

God's Promise

PREVIEW

Genesis 11:27—12:9 moves quickly from the more inclusive story of the world family to the saga of one family. Following the formula "these are the generations" (11:27a), we find a genealogy of Terah (11:27b-32). This genealogy connects with the previous unit: verse 27 reiterates data given in verse 26. But the genealogy moves on to introduce three of the characters who will play a central role in the following saga: Abraham, Sarah, and Lot. [Reading Genealogies, p. 326.]

This genealogy does not prepare the reader for what follows: a speech of God to Abraham (12:1-3). However, unexpected and important elements do tie the genealogy and the speech together, as we shall see below. In the concluding section of this unit, Abraham responds to God's speech by traveling to and within Canaan (12:4-9).

Even this quick glance shows that God's speech constitutes the center of this unit. The genealogy and report of Abraham's journey provide the framework for this speech whose importance for the family stories extends far beyond this unit (Wolff, 1966: 131-158).

In the biblical text the names of the two main characters are spelled Abram and Sarai until chapter 19. With the covenant in Genesis 17 the spelling is changed to the ones with which we are most familiar. Because of our familiarity with the spelling "Abraham" and "Sarah," the commentary will use that spelling throughout. The different spellings are variations on the same names. Hence the change in Genesis 17 does not represent a name change in the same way we later find a name change from Jacob to Israel (Gen. 32 and 35).

OUTLINE
Introductory Formula, 11:27

Genealogy of Terah, 11:27b-32

The Lord's Speech, 12:1-3
    12:1   Instruction
    12:2-3 Promise

Abraham's Response: Journey, 12:4-9

EXPLANATORY NOTES
Genealogy of Terah 11:27-32
The genealogy begins and ends with information about Terah. *[Reading Genealogies, p. 326.]* He fathered three sons (v. 27b) and he died at age 225 (v. 32). Between those two brackets the focus is on the three sons and a journey of Terah. Haran fathered children but then died early—*before his father,* vv. 27-28. Abraham and Nahor were married: Abraham to Sarah and Nahor to his niece, Milcah, one of Haran's daughters (vv. 29-30). With no explanatory comment, the genealogy reports that Terah took part of his family and moved (v. 31).

In terms of the larger unit, indeed the whole saga of Abraham, two elements stand out in this genealogy. Both elements are unexpected information in the midst of such a list. The first surprise element we meet concerns Sarah: she was barren. Lest we miss it, the statement is repeated: *Sarai was barren; she had no child* (v. 30). Sarah's barrenness becomes the unresolved problem that carries the Abraham saga to its most tense moment, the near sacrifice of Isaac (Gen. 22). No explanation accompanies the statement of Sarah's infertility. The abruptness and repetition of the comment serves to highlight the tragedy. *[Characteristics of Hebrew Narrative, p. 313.]* If Abraham and Sarah are to have a future, something new will have to happen—a blessing, a healing, another wife.

A second crucial element in the genealogy follows immediately after the statement of Sarah's barrenness. Terah begins a journey. He takes from the family only the persons who are to figure in the Abraham saga: Abraham, Sarah, and Lot. Terah sets out to go to Canaan, but he does not make it. The family gets no further than Haran. We are not told why Terah moved or why he did not complete his journey. We know only that Terah's journey stopped short of its goal. There Terah died.

Haran may or may not be a city associated with Terah's son, Haran.

In English the two names are the same. In Hebrew they begin with two different "h" letters, a soft "h" for the man's name and a hard "h" for the name of the city.

The genealogy presents us with no future—only a barren wife, an incomplete journey, and a father's death.

The Lord's Speech 12:1-3

God's speech promises a future where none existed before. Beginning with instruction, the Lord directs Abraham to journey on. The move terminated by Terah's death begins again by God's command.

This speech has been traditionally named the "call of Abraham." That designation runs into difficulties when we relate this text to other call narratives (e.g., Exod. 3 and Judg. 6). The usual narrative concerning the call and commissioning of an agent or servant of God differs from this text. This speech promises a future for Abraham and for others. God instructs—"calls"—Abraham to move toward that future.

The speech consists of both instruction (v. 1) and promise (vv. 2-3). God instructs Abraham to journey. Although the speech itself does not name the destination, in the context of this unit God's instruction directs Abraham to complete the journey Terah started (11:31 and 12:5-7). The land which God shows them (12:7) is the land toward which Abraham's father had moved, the land of Canaan.

Quite obviously, *blessing* figures as the key word in God's promise. The repetition of blessing five times in this short speech requires that we give attention to the word.

Unfortunately, difficulties of translation cloud several of the occurrences of *blessing* in this speech, as the variety of translations illustrates. Nevertheless, this much can be said. God promises life—enhancing power to Abraham and those after him. Blessing brings the power for life, the enhancement of life, and the increase of life (F. Horst: 194). Specifically in this speech, the promise of blessing leads us to expect that Abraham and Sarah's life story will produce a great people, well known and well respected (v. 12), with a place to call home (v. 1).

The promise of blessing is not exhausted on Abraham and his family. Instead, this family will be the occasion of blessing for all the peoples of the earth. The text does not explain how this will happen. Perhaps Abraham's family will be an agent of blessing for others, or a model of the blessed way. Be that as it may, God initiates a new future not only for Abraham and Sarah, who were homeless and barren, but for all peoples who are in whatever way living without blessing, if not under

a curse (Zimmerli, 1978: 172). *[Blessing in Genesis, p. 312.]*
        The first half of 12:3 remains difficult to interpret. It uses the plural when talking of blessing, *I will bless those who bless you,"* and singular for curse, *"and the one who curses you, I will curse. . . ."* Perhaps just that use of the plural *blessing* and singular *curse* suggests what the rest of the speech declares: God's blessing will determine humanity's future (von Rad, 1973: 161).

Abraham's Response: Journey 12:4-9

Traditional interpretation often suggests that Abraham set out on the journey only at great cost—leaving land, family, and home. The text does not tell us that explicitly. The story, with its long, slow narration of the departure, might suggest Abraham's reluctance, but not necessarily. Canaan, not Haran, had been Terah's original destination. In addition, the narration tells only about the death of Abraham's father and Sarah's barrenness. None of those factors would keep the couple in Haran. Not unexpectedly, perhaps, Abraham and Sarah, together with Lot, do step toward a better future, one promising blessing.
        Verses 4-9 provide us with elements we might too quickly read over. The family departs and arrives—promise and fulfillment (vv. 4-5). Yet arrival at Canaan does not end the journey. Their travel continues through the land (vv. 6, 8-9). Nor does their arrival exhaust God's promise. Even the promise of the land looks to a still different future (v. 7).
        With the mention of the Canaanites and local sanctuaries, the narrator signals some other possibilities and problems in the family's future. Shechem and Bethel, among other sanctuaries, become centers of worship and covenant (Gen. 28; Josh. 24), but also of violation and apostasy (Judg. 9; 1 Kings 12—13; Amos 7). Association with Canaanites will enable Abraham's group to move from family to nation, but will at the same time threaten to destroy their faith.
        Genesis 12:4-9 tells about fulfillment and further promise, celebration along with danger. Sarah and Abraham with Lot respond to God's promise of a future where as yet there was only barrenness. They arrive, but much of the blessing still lies ahead. The future will happen in this place, but not yet and not without problems.

THE TEXT IN BIBLICAL CONTEXT

The writer of Hebrews recalls the "unfinished" dimension of Abraham's journey (Heb. 11:8-12). Abraham and Sarah would not live to see the completion of their pilgrimage. The speech of Stephen connects with the same tradition, emphasizing that this family remained aliens in the midst of the land (Acts 7:2-5). The understanding of Abraham and Sarah as sojourners on the way toward blessing and aliens living in a hostile land spoke powerfully to the earliest Christians. Although they experienced in Christ the blessing of God's new world, these Christians often found blessing more a future promise than a bestowal on their present. The unfinished journey of Sarah and Abraham has continued to provide a powerful metaphor for the community of faith. Through this perspective Christians could celebrate elements of fulfillment in their own experience, while reaching beyond their present for a fuller realization of God's promise (cf. *Martyrs Mirror*: 528). For those who expect all to be realized in their generation, the unfinished journey reminds them that we cannot demand of the present all that the future promises.

Paul reminded the early church that the promise to Abraham was not for the benefit of his family alone (Gal. 3:8). God's promise of blessing extends to all the families of the earth. Just as the promise is not exhausted in one generation, neither is the blessing expended on just one group. Moving from the story of the whole human family (Gen. 1—11) to focus on one family (Gen. 12—50) has not narrowed the arena of God's concern. God's blessing intends to empower and enhance life for all the world. Israel will run into trouble when it tries to claim that blessing as its exclusive inheritance.

THE TEXT IN THE LIFE OF THE CHURCH

Geographically, this unit moves from Mesopotamia to Canaan. Theologically, the direction of God's instructions leads Sarah and Abraham from barrenness toward fertility. We need not presume any unique faith on the part of Abraham or Sarah to assume that they would step toward the promise. Everyone longs to move from barrenness to blessing. Furthermore, as Calvin observes, God's speech gives permission for Abraham to complete what his father had begun (1948: 350). It may serve to distance us from Abraham and Sarah when we ascribe to them superhuman faith. The saga does not begin assuming that Sarah and Abraham are far more faithful than anyone else can hope to be. Instead, the narrative portrays a family with the trust needed to travel from barrenness toward blessing, the faith necessary to choose a possible future over no future, the courage required to follow the promises of God over other options. We need not look for the extraordinary people to find trust, faith, and courage similar to that of Abraham and Sarah. Such faith lives in our congregations and family and perhaps in us.

Genesis 12:10 – 14:24

Episodes After the Promise

PREVIEW

This unit consists of three narratives portraying life for Abraham and Sarah after the promise. Genesis 13—14 involves Abraham and Lot, picking up a thread of the saga which was introduced earlier (11:31; 12:4), and is completed with the Sodom story (Gen. 19). However, the first story in this unit (12:10—13:1) features Sarah and Abraham rather than Abraham and Lot. Like the Abraham and Lot material, this story also connects with other parts of the ancestral sagas. It is one of three Genesis narratives in which the ancestral wife is placed in danger by her husband as they sojourn in a foreign land (20:1-18; 26:1-16). Possibly the Abraham and Lot material and the story of the endangered ancestral wife passed from generation to generation and village to village long before they joined to form part of the saga of Abraham.

Genesis 12:10—13:1 is framed by two corresponding journey statements: Abraham (Abram) *went down to Egypt* and *went up from Egypt* (12:10; 13:1). In terms of the flow of a journey, Abraham and Sarah (with Lot) end up in Genesis 13:1 exactly where they were in 12:9, the Negev area in southern Canaan. The tale itself flows from danger to deportation. The mother of the promised *great nation* has been taken into the Egyptian court. Abraham grows rich in 12:10-16 and God rescues Sarah from danger, but Abraham's actions cause them all to be deported (12:17-20).

Genesis 13:2-18 is similarly bracketed by the movement of the Abra-

ham family. Genesis 13:2-4 takes Abraham up to Bethel and 13:18
brings him back into the South, Hebron. Included in this framework is
mention of ancestral sanctuaries in both places. This narrative also
begins with danger. The flocks of Abraham and Lot had grown sufficiently that conflict had developed between the herdsmen of Abraham
and of Lot (13:5-7). Abraham and Lot resolve the conflict by dividing the
land between them (13:8-17).

The final story appears out of place. Certainly the Abraham-Lot
thread provides its connection with the ongoing saga, but the story itself
presents a surprising picture of Abraham. The unit consists of the annals
of a military invasion (14:1-16) followed by the disposition of the spoils
by the victors (14:17-24) (Coats, 1983:118-121). We find movement from
danger to its resolution in this story also. But the danger threatens Abraham, the bearer of the promise, only indirectly. Lot is the one captured
by the invading army.

These three episodes deal most directly with the promise of land announced by God in the introductory unit (12:1, 7). In these episodes the
gift of land is threatened in turn by famine, family strife, and international
conflict. Nevertheless, the gift holds fairly secure (13:14-17). Lost in this
attention to the promise of land is the major problem in the Abraham
saga, the birth of the son. Abraham will bring the promise of a son back
to center stage in his confrontation with God in Genesis 15.

OUTLINE

A Tale of the Ancestral Wife in Danger, 12:10—13:1
- 12:10   Introduction
- 12:11-16   Danger
- 12:17-20   Outcome: Deportation
- 13:1   Conclusion

A Tale of Conflict in the Family, 13:2-18
- 13:2-4   Introduction
- 13:5-7   Conflict
- 13:8-13   Outcome: Separation
- 13:14-17   Reiteration of Divine Promise
- 13:18   Conclusion

Annals of War in the Land, 14:1-24
- 14:1-16   Report of the Battles
- 14:17-24   Disposition of the Spoils

EXPLANATORY NOTES

A Tale of the Ancestral Wife in Danger 12:10 – 13:1

Famine, usually caused by a shortage of water, creates the complications in several biblical stories (e.g., Joseph, Gen. 41:54; Ruth 1:1). Archaeology shows us that water has been the key factor determining the occupancy of many villages in Palestine throughout the centuries. Those who live in areas of abundant water can only try to imagine how precious water has been and continues to be in many areas of the world. In some biblical texts, drought and famine are understood to be an act of God, perhaps in judgment (1 Kings 17:1; Jer. 14). But other texts give no reason for the drought. They simply state, "There was a famine in the land." In all such stories famine brings danger, dislocation, and often death.

12:11-16 Danger

The focus of many discussions of this tale has been the morality of Abraham. Some wish to salvage Abraham's honor by taking from Genesis 20 the statement that Sarah really was Abraham's half sister, using that information to excuse his action. However, this narrative assumes that Abraham wants Sarah to misrepresent the actual relationship between them. Luther suggests that God inspired Abraham to take this action (Luther's Commentary, I: 226). If so, the narrative does not tell us. Still others hint that the shrewdness of Abraham brought delight to Hebrew ears and the tale must not be judged by later norms of truth-telling. Again the narrative does not explicitly confirm this suggestion.

The only evaluation of Abraham's behavior comes from Pharaoh (12:18-19). The lack of any other evaluation invites the listener to participate in the drama, experiencing the threat Abraham felt and in the midst of that danger deciding about the action he took. Abraham comes to the land of promise, only to find famine. Uprooted by the famine, Sarah and Abraham move into another life-threatening situation.

Displaced by famine and confronted with danger, Abraham speaks for the first time in the entire saga. The beauty of Sarah becomes a threat to Abraham's life (cf. 6:1-2 and 2 Sam. 11). Abraham fears that he will die while Sarah is allowed to live. Therefore, he asks Sarah to place herself in Egyptian hands so that he will live because of her. Abraham repeats, so that it may go well with me and "I may live" "because of you" (12:13, NASB). Fearing Sarah as a threat to his life, Abraham asks her to be the agent of his well-being at her own expense.

The narrative does not give us Sarah's response or even her action.

In fact, Sarah loses her name at this point in the narrative. She becomes *the woman* (vv. 14-15). We have only a report of the actions of the Egyptians and the result for Abraham. Blessing happens: Abraham lives and becomes wealthy. But the mother of the promised descendants lives as a member of the Egyptian royal household.

12:17-20 Outcome: Deportation

The resolution of the crisis begins with a narration of God's action. By God's action *the woman* regains her name, *Sarai*, and her relationship, *Abram's wife*. Disaster strikes the Egyptian royal household, again *because of* Sarah. She may remain a backstage figure throughout the drama, but everything happens because of Sarah.

In the saga's first speech Abraham tells of being threatened through no fault of his own (12:11-13). The second speech (vv. 18-19) finds Pharaoh in danger in spite of doing nothing wrong. We are not told how Pharaoh connected the disaster in his house to Sarah or found out that Sarah was not Abraham's sister. We hear only Pharaoh's astonishment—*why* repeated three times (vv. 18-19). The question goes unanswered. The speech concludes with Pharaoh's deportation order.

This story remains fascinating and puzzling. A thread of constant danger touches Abraham first and then entangles others. Sarah apparently chooses to accept the danger; Pharaoh has no choice. The dark side of life, famine, elicits the fearful side of Abraham, the refugee, and even the inexplicable side of God who brings disease on ones not directly at fault. This first episode after the promise speaks not of security, rest, and joy, but of danger, deception, and disease. Yet unexpectedly in the middle of this disaster, Abraham becomes rich, certainly not because of his exemplary behavior.

This first tale "after the promise" revolves not around Abraham or Pharaoh but Sarah, the one who remains in the background, even for a time losing her name and her place in the family. Life after the promise will look puzzling both to those who think they understand the promise and to those who give up on God's blessing. *[Promise in the Family Stories, p. 325.]*

A Tale of Conflict in the Family 13:2-18

As in the first tale (12:10—13:1), so here again the introduction and conclusion of the story tell of Abraham's journey. In this introduction the movement is north to Bethel (13:3). In the conclusion the journey takes Abraham back south to Hebron (13:18). Bethel and Hebron were important religious and political centers for the North (Israel) and the South (Judah) before the establishment of Jerusalem. Even afterward, these two cities functioned almost as "capitals" for the South (2 Sam. 5:1; 15:7-10) and the North (1 Kings 12:29; Amos 7:13). Hence the journey framework of this episode ties Abraham to those two important sanctuaries.

13:5-7 Conflict

This introduction presents Abraham as one blessed with wealth. Lot too has prospered. But prosperity brings conflict—conflict over land for pasture. The conflict does not involve Abraham and Lot directly but those who herd their respective flocks.

The last half of verse 7 seems out of place. It has nothing to do directly with the narrative. Nevertheless, like a similar remark in 12:6, the phrase *at that time the Canaanites and the Perizzites dwelt in the land* reminds the reader that although the story concerns one family, they live in the context of many families. We are not told how the others relate to this episode, just that they exist. These "others" will become a factor in the family's future.

13:8-13 Outcome: Separation

Abraham's speech (13:8-9) calls for an end to strife between kinfolk and proposes a settlement: Abraham and Lot should separate, each occupying a specific territory for grazing their flocks. Abraham gives Lot the first choice. We do not have Lot's words, just a statement of his action. Lot chooses the best land, the well-watered Jordan Valley. This choice leaves Abraham with the rocky hill country. *Occupation: Keeper of Livestock, p. 324.]* Apparently the process of taking ownership of "all the land that the eyes could see" was not just an informal agreement between kinfolk. Such a procedure had the force of customary law (Daube, 1947: 24-39).

Seemingly, Abraham acts here as a model person, one interested in peace and willing to allow the other to choose first. The narrative from 13:2-12 at least suggests that. However, in terms of the larger context of this narrative, Abraham's proposal does not look as good. Abraham manages the conflict between the herdsmen, but at a high price. Lot may choose the land he wants, but that choice permanently separates him from the carrier of blessing (Coats, 1983: 117). Genesis 13:13 foreshadows what the next two narratives portray. The separation leaves Lot joined to another group, the people of Sodom. Such an association brings nothing but trouble. Abraham's suggestion of separation as a means to handle the conflict leaves Lot victimized. In the course of the history of Abraham's people this decision will create more conflict than it resolves (Deut. 2:9-19; 23:3-4).

Abraham offers to give away the land of the promise. The narrative does not tell us whether we are to evaluate that as a generous gesture or a problematic resolution to a family quarrel. The promised land is not lost, though perhaps only because it appeared to have the most rocks and the least water.

13:14-17 Reiteration of Divine Promise

The narrative concludes with a speech by God reiterating the promise: both land and descendants. [Promise in the Family Stories, p. 325.] The reiteration of this promise calls attention to the narrative time between promise and fulfillment. Some fulfillment has happened: Abraham's wealth. But much has not been fulfilled. The land, which he almost gave away, is shared with Canaanites and Perizzites. The ritual of walking and seeing may strengthen the promise of land with legal sanction, but it does not provide Abraham a home, not yet. Most distressing of all, Sarah and Abraham have no children.

However delayed, Abraham still carries the promise. Association with the promise and Abraham, its bearer, brings blessing. Hence this tale ends on a sad note, even if we should decide that Abraham acted wisely, perhaps even generously, toward his nephew. Separation from Abraham leaves Lot with no blessing.

Annals of War in the Land 14:1-24

14:1-16 Report of the Battles

This narrative differs so much from the other Abrahamic materials that many scholars have questioned whether this is authentic Abraham material, and most wonder about its function in the saga. The question of authenticity lies basically beyond the scope of this discussion (for contrasting conclusions see Vawter, 1977: 185-203 and Thompson, 1974: 187-195). Our attention will focus on the question of its function in the Abraham saga.

The narrative begins with an invasion by a coalition whose names are associated with the Mesopotamian river valley. The invading force seems to enter by way of the trade route east of the Jordan River, going down past the Dead Sea into the Negev Desert. The main interest for the Abraham saga comes with Lot's involvement. Lot gets caught in the war, is captured and carried off by a victorious invading army. The narrative then turns directly to Abraham, who is told by an escapee about Lot's capture. Taking 318 men, Abraham attacks the superior invading forces. Their "guerrilla action" routs the opposition and Abraham returns with the spoils of war.

The idea of Abraham leading an army, even as a small guerrilla operation, contrasts with the picture of the peaceful sojourner portrayed elsewhere in the saga. One is tempted to dismiss this battle report as uncharacterstic and unwanted. But in connection with the previous narrative of the separation between Lot and Abraham, we can at least ask about its place in the saga. Separation from the bearer of blessing renders Lot powerless. Abraham's intervention temporarily reverses the situation (Coats, 1983: 121). No foreign king can exercise power against the blessing of God, as Pharaoh discovered by accident (12:10-20; cf. also Num. 22—24).

14:17-24 Disposition of the Spoils

This text narrates Abraham's encounter with two kings concerning the disposition of the spoils. A meeting with the unnamed king of Sodom (vv. 17, 21-24) brackets a meeting with Melchizedek, king of Salem (vv. 18-20). Narrative position seems to point to the meeting with Melchizedek as the central one. Both Melchizedek and Salem are unknown to us outside of this text except for a couple of passages that refer directly to this narrative (Ps. 110:4; Heb. 5—7). It is likely that in the biblical tradition Melchizedek is understood as the king of Jerusalem. This "king-priest" pronounces benediction on Abraham using characteristic formulas from Canaanite religious tradition: *God Most High* and *maker of heaven and earth.* In meeting with the king of Sodom, Abraham's speech uses the same two phrases, but ascribes them to Yahweh (v. 22).

One dynamic to observe in the narrative of these two meetings involves the interaction between God and the religious traditions of the Canaanite population. On the one hand, Abraham's speech (vv. 22-24) asserts Yahweh's supremacy over the other gods (Ps. 82). Yahweh, not El, is the "God Most High," "Creator of heaven and earth" (NIV). But on the other hand, the use of these two Canaanite liturgical formulas unites the traditions of the indigenous population with the religion of this "new" family. The religion of the Abrahamic family, while uncompromising in some moments—as with the king of Sodom (vv. 22-24)—cannot be described solely with the words "exclusive" or "sectarian." Abraham receives ritual bread and blessing from the Canaanite priest and gives to this priest a "tithe" (Westermann, 1985:203-204). Whether or not this exchange is meant to call to the listener's mind the function of the later

Israelite priests in Jerusalem, in this context the priest is Canaanite. Collegiality, perhaps even covenant, characterizes the relationship between the Canaanite Melchizedek and the Hebrew Abraham. Distance, not collegiality, marks the interaction between Abraham and the king of Sodom (vv. 21-24). The king of Sodom makes a very generous offer: return the people but keep all of the goods won in the war (v. 21). Abraham, invoking an oath not mentioned previously in the narrative, refuses to keep anything for himself. Perhaps the proverbial character of Sodom, introduced in 13:13, accounts for the reaction of Abraham. The narrative does not explain to us why Abraham received the ministry of the king of Salem and would have nothing to do with the king of Sodom. The two scenes stand side by side. With one Canaanite king, Abraham will covenant, from another he will accept nothing.

THE TEXT IN BIBLICAL CONTEXT

The church's interpretation of the text has focused on the figure of Melchizedek perhaps more than any other aspect of these three stories. Elsewhere in the Bible only Psalm 110:4 and Hebrews 7—8 mention Melchizedek. In Psalm 110 the psalmist announces that the coming king will also be a priest, even as Melchizedek held both offices. The writer of Hebrews builds on the fact that Melchizedek mysteriously slips into and out of the saga of Abraham to talk about the wonder of Christ. Hebrews describes Melchizedek as being superior to all priests in the line of Aaron and Levi. Christ as the fulfillment of the Melchizedek priesthood is thereby elevated still further (Heb. 7:1-28). It is this affirmation of Christ as the fulfillment of all royal and priestly expectations, not commentary on Melchizedek, that concerns this New Testament writer.

The writer of Hebrews is not alone in appropriating the Melchizedek tradition. In the Qumran scrolls found near the Dead Sea, fragments of a manuscript (first or second century B.C.) have been found dealing with Melchizedek (11 Q-Melch). In the manuscript Melchizedek is portrayed as a heavenly figure functioning as both king and priest in the "last days." We can suspect that the tradition concerning this mysterious figure spread even further than our documents show. We know that the tradition concerning Melchizedek grew in the post-New Testament church, even relating the bread and wine of Genesis 14:18 to the sacrament of communion. In the third century Cyprian encouraged further use of the Melchizedek material, but Luther some 13 centuries later objected to such speculation. We know so little about Melchizedek that Luther appropriately warns us to err on the side of caution.

THE TEXT IN THE LIFE OF THE CHURCH

For Abraham in this saga, life after the promise proves to be surprising, to say the least. Narratively, these three stories delay the fulfillment of the central promise, the birth of a son/descendants. As we shall see, chapter 15 opens addressing just that problem. To be sure, there are elements of fulfillment in these three stories: Abraham grows wealthy, in part by deception; Sarah and Abraham find room in the land of Canaan. Even though not actually in possession of the land, Abraham has the promise of land secured by a legal title from God (13:14-17). Nevertheless, the tenor of the stories expresses not fulfillment but delay. Instead of fertility, Sarah and Abraham find famine, invading armies and quarrelsome herdsmen. Instead of a peaceful home Sarah finds temporary exile, with Abraham required to preside over family conflict and then take to the battlefield to rescue his nephew. Taken together in relationship to the promise in Genesis 12:1-3, these narratives present at best an ambivalent picture of life after the promise.

Abraham is similarly portrayed as an ambivalent carrier of God's promise. On the one hand, Abraham appears generous and concerned as he deals with his nephew (Gen. 13:2-13) and open yet wary in dealing with the non-Hebrew neighbors (Gen. 14:17-24). But on the other hand, Abraham protects himself at the expense of any other person, including Sarah. He solves conflict by legalizing division in the family, an act which supports institutionalized animosity between groups of people. In the flow of this saga one can guess that neither Abraham and Sarah nor God rest completely satisfied with life after the promise.

Most of us experience both Sarah and Abraham and the post-promise life they found as very familiar. We act like our ancestor: generous and open, but fiercely self-protective. We too find life a mixture of fulfillment and delay, success and disappointment. Noteworthy thus far in the saga: God has not given up on Abraham nor Abraham on God's promise.

Genesis 15:1-21

Dialogue About the Promise

PREVIEW

This dialogue between Abraham and God makes explicit the problem that the previous three episodes expressed quietly—the delay in the fulfillment of the promise. Abraham puts directly to God the pain of the family who carries the promise: "Lord, Yahweh, what will you give me" (15:2); "Lord, Yahweh, how shall I know" (15:8).

Chapter 15 stands by itself, distinct from the narrative episodes that precede it and the long narrative leading to the birth of the promised son which follows it. The phrase which opens Genesis 15:1, *after these things,* similarly marks off the beginning of the story about the near sacrifice of Isaac (22:1, 20). But more than the introductory phrase distinguishes Genesis 15 from the narratives around it. This unit has no story line. Genesis 15 consists of a series of speeches. In two sections of the chapter the speeches form a dialogue between God and Abraham (15:1-6, 7-11). In verses 12-21 only Yahweh speaks while Abraham in a deep sleep (15:12-16) experiences a mysterious ritual (15:17-21).

While distinct in themselves, these speeches use language that is quite traditional in the biblical world. In 15:1 we hear the way a prophet speaks to a king, and in 15:7 we find the language of a priest speaking in worship. The unusual ritual found in 15:9-11 uses the common language of an oath. Finally, 15:18 places the now familiar language of promise in the context of covenant. These different elements do not al-

110

ways fit together to make a smooth chapter. Rather, Genesis 15 sort of bumps along with shifts and turns. Nevertheless, as we have it before us, the unit can be divided into two main sections: the first centering on the promise of a son—descendants, the second on the promise of land.

OUTLINE

Dialogue Concerning the Promise of Descendants, 15:1-6
    15:1   Promise—God
    15:2-3 Complaint—Abraham
    15:4-5 Assurance—God
    15:6   Conclusion

Dialogue Concerning the Promise of Land, 15:7-21
    15:7   Promise—God
    15:8   Complaint—Abraham
    15:9-17 Ritual of Assurance
        Instructions—God, 15:9
        Beginning of Ritual, 15:10-11
        Speech of Promise—God, 15:12-16
        Completion of Ritual, 15:17
    15:18-21 Concluding Speech of Promise—God

EXPLANATORY NOTES

Dialogue About the Promise 15:1-21

15:1-6 Dialogue Concerning the Promise of Descendants

God speaks first, addressing Abraham in language similar to that with which a prophet would address a king before the king went out to battle (Van Seters, 1975: 254). The word of assurance, *fear not,* we find frequently on the lips of a priest or a prophet who brings good news to one threatened, ill, or suffering (Exod. 14:13; Isa. 41:13; Luke 2:10). The word of promise, accompanying this word of assurance, speaks in general terms of a *reward.* Like God's self-introduction as *shield,* the *reward* reflects the military flavor present in the speech.

The context of God's speech in 15:1 is not a military battle as such. More generally, God comes to Abraham speaking the language of power. For his part, Abraham has not seen much of God's power to produce on the promise. "What can you give me since I remain child-less?" (NIV). Abraham's present situation provides no demonstration of

God's power. The last half verse of 15:2 defies translation. Parallelism between 15:2 and 3 has provided the generally agreed-upon translation we find in the RSV, NASB, and others.

15:2	15:3
I continue childless	You have given me no offspring
Heir of my house is Eliezer	A house servant will be my heir
of Damascus	

The meaning is reasonably clear even if the translation cannot be. Abraham complains that because he has no child, another person, perhaps the steward of his house, will inherit everything.

Looking closely at the language used in this exchange helps us experience the tension between God and Abraham in this dialogue. God speaks first, using military power language (v. 1). Abraham answers with language drawn from the legal customs concerning inheritance (v. 2). God then directs Abraham to creation: *Look toward heaven and number the stars* (v. 5). The language takes yet another turn with the reiteration of the promise: "One who comes forth from your own body, he shall be your heir" (v. 4, NASB). In that short dialogue the language has shifted four times: military, legal, creation, promise.

The dialogue concludes with two statements by the narrator: one concerning Abraham, the other, God. As for Abraham, the narrator says simply, "He trusts Yahweh" (v. 6a). "Trust" may better capture the active character of the Hebrew word (*'aman*) than the word *believe*. The word "believe" for us often connotes a passive affirmation. The text does not give us any reason why Abraham trusted Yahweh. That must remain a mystery and a miracle (Brueggemann, 1982: 145).

The statement concerning God is similarly brief; God "credited" it to him as righteousness (v. 6b, NIV). We must not forget von Rad's reminder: "*Righteousness* is not an ideal, absolute norm which is above men, but rather a term of relationship" (1973: 185). Trust, not proof or work, grounds the relationships between God and Abraham. God declares that good enough. In this declaration of acceptance we are reminded of the statement of acceptance by the Israelite priests in the worship service—a declaration based on right behavior: "*Who shall ascend the hill of the Lord? . . . The one who has clean hands and a pure heart* (Ps. 24:3-4). In Genesis 15:6 we find no priestly examination of behavior, only a simple statement by the narrator that God reckoned Abraham's trust sufficient.

Dialogue Concerning the Promise of Land 15:7-21

The second dialogue begins like the first with God's self-introduction: *I am Yahweh.* Similar liturgical language introduces the Decalogue: *I am Yahweh your God, who brought you out of the land of Egypt . . . "* (Exod. 20:2). In 15:7, the introduction is followed with a specific promise—the promise of land. In 15:8 Abraham responds to the announcement exactly as he did in verses 2 and 3 with a complaint: *Lord, Yahweh, how am I to know. . . ?*

God responds again with instructions, this time not for Abraham to look at the stars, but that he prepare for a ritual (15:6). The ritual described seems similar to the one alluded to in Jeremiah 34:18. Similar rituals in the ancient Near East indicate that oaths were secured between the two halves of animal, thus binding parties to the agreement. The split animal may have illustrated the consequences on the parties should they violate the oath. Abraham follows the instructions and prepares for the oath ritual. The *birds of prey* represent an even more mysterious element (v. 11). They may represent an evil omen, or perhaps just a foreboding element lurking in the divine commitment and promise (Vawter, 1977:210-211). *[Covenant, p. 315.]*

In 15:12 Abraham becomes completely passive (cf. 2:21). Only God speaks and acts for the rest of the unit. God's speech of promise in 15:13-16 deals directly with the delay of the land promise: the promise of the land will have a long history. The family of Abraham must learn to live with delay. But Abraham's life will not consist only of delay. He can expect to live a long and full life and to be buried peacefully in the company of the ancestors (Kaiser and Lohse: 50-51). In the course of this saga, Abraham does not again complain about the delay of the land promise.

In 15:17 fire symbolizes God's action. God alone carries out the ritual. God alone assumes the obligations of this oath. God chooses to be bound to the promise without requiring any comparable ritual action or oath from Abraham. The one-sided character of the commitment carries into the final speech of promise, this time given as covenant (vv. 18-21). While Abraham sleeps, God sets in covenant the promise that the family of Abraham and Sarah will one day have a home and secures that promise with a divine oath. Though its fulfillment will arrive long after his death, Abraham too will be gathered into that promise. *[Promise in the Family Stories, p. 325.]*

THE TEXT IN BIBLICAL CONTEXT

Genesis 15:6 provided reason for Luther to write a commentary on Genesis. His comments on this verse summarize the Reformation perspective that "faith alone justifies and saves" *(Luther's Commentary:* 264). This Pauline reading of our text (Rom. 4) was also important to the Anabaptist wing of the Reformation. However, Menno Simons was somewhat more concerned than Luther to link obedience inseparably with faith *(Complete Works:* 121ff.). We would misread Luther's understanding of this text, however, if we assumed that faith does not issue in obedience *(Luther's Commentary:* 268). He simply did not want us to get the direction mixed up. In the midst of an Anabaptist community emphasizing discipleship, Luther deserves a careful hearing on Genesis 15. Neither in 15:6 nor elsewhere does this text talk about Abraham's responsibilities. Instead the text speaks of a trust that does not know what God's future may require but embraces it nonetheless. God reckons that embracing as solid enough ground for the relationship.

Calvin also focused on Genesis 15:6, but he emphasized another aspect of the verse: the miracle that surrounds Abraham's acceptance by God *(Calvin's Commentaries:* 404ff.). For Calvin, this text illustrates God's graciousness. Calvin's concern was to lift up the grace of God expressed in accepting Abraham and in providing Abraham the faith needed to trust God's future. The unit as a whole grounds the future of the promise certainly not in Abraham's obedience, and not even in Abraham's faith. Rather, both Abraham's faith and his future rest in the grace of God. In the midst of barrenness, Abraham could come to rely on the Promise Maker. That too "must be accounted as a miracle from God" (Brueggemann, 1982: 144-145).

THE TEXT IN THE LIFE OF THE CHURCH

In Genesis 15 Abraham complains about the delay of the promise. Nevertheless, the narrator assures us that Abraham trusts and that God accepts him on that basis. Complaint and trust in the Old Testament cannot be set over against one another as mutually exclusive. To be sure, complaint and trust argue with one another, but they do not exclude one another, as the lament psalms show us (cf. Ps. 22).

We often equate complaint with rejection, assuming that a complaint directed against us necessarily means we are not trusted or accepted. This in turn prevents us from really understanding complaint against God in the Psalms, Job, and especially by Jesus (Mark 14:34-36; 15:34). But complaint means that one takes the one who has promised seriously enough to be angry when things do not work out as promised.

God too takes complaint seriously. While complaint does not mean rejection and unbelief, it does indicate that the relationship is in danger. For Abraham, delay in the promise precipitated a crisis. He took the Promise Maker seriously, but the results were disappointing. God responded to Abraham's complaint, not with instant gratification, sudden fulfillment of the promise, but with unilateral and unconditional bonding to the eventual accomplishment of the promise. Through ritual oath, through covenant, God reaffirmed a commitment to the promise of blessing. God's speech does not ignore the fact of delay, but declares Yahweh's intent to remain bound irrevocably through the delay to the fulfillment.

Delay in God's promise remains an irritation for some but a matter of life and death for others. For a few, the presence of wealth or friends are a cushion against the anguish of homelessness and barrenness. Others have no such cushion except the cry, *O Lord God, what wilt thou give me?* (15:2). God has continued to respond, *Lo, I am with you always, to the close of the age* (Matt. 28:20).

Genesis 16:1 – 21:34

A Story About an Heir

PREVIEW

In Genesis 16:1—21:34 the saga of Abraham contains a long story about an heir. In Genesis 15 the saga told of an encounter between God and Abraham concerning the promise of an heir and the promise of land. God remained unconditionally committed to the promise of the land, but in God's speech to a sleeping Abraham (15:13-16) the fulfillment of that promise looked far into the future. Although mentioned in the repetition of the ancestral promises (e.g., 17:8), the promise of land essentially disappears from the rest of this saga. The saga turns instead to the promise of an heir. What is the future of that promise?

This long story starts with the birth of Ishmael (Gen. 16) and concludes with Isaac (Gen. 21). Both boys are born into the midst of conflict between Sarah and her servant, Hagar. The story moves from 16:1, *Now Sarai, Abram's wife, bore him no children,* to 21:2, *And Sarah conceived, and bore Abraham a son....* But the conflict between the two women creates trouble which further threatens the family's future.

This is not only a story of two women in conflict. Their conflict results in part from the inexplicable delay in the fulfillment of God's promise. The delay of the promise is accented not only by the long circuitous route the narrative follows, but also by the periodic references to the age of the couple made both by a narrator (16:16; 17:1, 24; 21:5) and by Abraham and Sarah themselves (17:17; 18:12). The story of the birth of an heir takes place, not as an isolated event, but in the midst of family

116

conflict, parental anxiety and wider community problems (Gen. 19).

Genesis 17:1—18:15, located in the center of this story, provides the annunciation of Isaac, first to Abraham (17:15-19) and then indirectly at least to Sarah (18:10-14). This section contains other elements of course, related to the complicated threads of the story, but in terms of the main story line these chapters provide a twofold announcement of the birth of the promised son.

The narrative "aside" provided by the Sodom tale (18:16—19:38) further emphasizes the delay. No sooner is the birth announced than the mother of the promised heir drops out of the drama completely! Sarah reemerges in Genesis 20:1-18, along with the ever-present problem of fertility. This time, save for divine intervention, the promised son might have been born in the household of Abimelech, king of Gerar.

The story of an heir closes with the birth of Isaac (Gen. 21), a baby born into complicated circumstances, but nonetheless the promised heir (21:12). And yet the unit does not quite end. With the phrase *at that time* (21:22) an additional episode appears. This introductory phrase serves to *connect* this episode with Genesis 16—21, in contrast to the disjunctive sense in the phrase with which Genesis 22 begins, *after these things* (RSV, NASB). This concluding episode functions to put at least a little narrative "time" between the birth of Isaac (21:1-21) and the meeting on Moriah (Gen. 22).

The following brief outline of the whole unit will be supplemented at the beginning of each section by a more detailed outline.

OUTLINE

The Annunciation and Birth of Ishmael, 16:1-16
16:1	Introduction
16:2-6	Family Conflict Concerning an Heir
16:7-14	The Annunciation
16:15-16	The Birth of Ishmael

The Annunciation of Isaac, 17:1—18:15
17:1-27	To Abraham
18:1-15	To Sarah

The Tale of Sodom and Lot, 18:16—19:38

A Tale of Threat to the Ancestral Mother, 20:1-18

Birth of Isaac, 21:1-21

Concluding Episode, 21:22-34

EXPLANATORY NOTES

The Annunciation and Birth of Ishmael 16:1-16

The introduction of this "story about an heir," while very brief, establishes the tension immediately (v. 1). This introductory narration tells us three things about Sarah. The first two we already now. She has a husband and no children. The last item is new: Sarah has an Egyptian maid, Hagar. These three elements eventually will provide the promised heir but also permanently divide the Abrahamic family.

16:2-6 Family Conflict Concerning an Heir

Sarah takes the initiative to deal with the absence of children. In the speech she interprets her barrenness as God's action toward her personally (v. 2a). The mother of the promised heir does not experience her infertility in terms of God's promise—nor does Abraham in response to her suggestion. For Sarah barrenness has become a deeply personal problem. We can hear both anguish and bitterness in her instructions to Abraham.

As we shall find through this whole story about an heir, Abraham becomes passive when it comes to dealing with Sarah's barrenness. In response to Sarah's instruction, he simply complies. We are not told the reason for Abraham's passivity. He acts decisively at other moments in the story, dealing with other problems: the visit of three strangers (Gen. 18), the problem of Sodom (Gen. 19), the threat to his own safety (Gen. 20). But in the family conflict concerning the barrenness, Abraham takes no initiative to explain the problem or to solve it. Both of those he leaves to Sarah.

The plan of Sarah to deal with her infertility apparently follows the legal custom in the ancient Near East, as we learn from the second millennium B.C. Babylonian Code of Hammurabi as well as texts from other ancient libraries. Even Sarah's demand that Hagar be returned to the status of servant follows legal procedure.

Our narrative, however, emphasizes more Sarah's anger and anguish than legal custom. The two speeches of Sarah (vv. 2, 5) suggest a woman who has nearly run out of options. The barren woman acts toward fertility but reaps contempt. In her second speech (v. 5), Sarah brings accusation against Abraham as well as Hagar. Abraham's response does not directly address her complaint, but indirectly seems to concede Sarah's legal right to the control of Hagar.

The conflict comes to a head in 16:6. In response to Sarah's treatment of her, Hagar runs away. The narrator does not evaluate any of this, neither directly applauding nor condemning Sarah, Hagar, or Abraham. The narrative portrays all of the characters as victim and aggressor. Sarah, who is victimized by barrenness, by Hagar, and by Abraham, turns on both of them, becoming the victimizer. Hagar, the servant, too moves from oppressed to oppressor, then back again to oppressed. Abraham, with his passive complacence may have irritated the situation, but he too was a victim of barrenness. The drama closes with an angry wife, a runaway, pregnant servant woman, and a bewildered (?) husband.

16:7-14 The Annunciation

When we read the phrase "angel of the Lord," we often imagine winged, divine beings who look like people. Our picture of angels has developed as a composite from a number of biblical and extra-biblical traditions (Westermann, 1979). The biblical texts themselves speak simply of "messengers of God," often not distinguishable from ordinary people. Characteristically, the angels carry a message from the Lord. Therefore, as in this text, the appearance of an angel can be understood as an encounter with God (v. 13). The appearance of an angel constitutes only one way in which God comes to humankind, but in the biblical texts it appears as a frequent means of divine communication to announce to a woman or man a coming birth. Often such announcement comes to a barren woman or couple (Luke 1:11-20). In this case the messenger-angel comes to Hagar, a woman whose fertility, not sterility, has become a problem.

The opening dialogue at the spring establishes Hagar as a refugee from Sarah (16:8-12). Then follow three speeches by the messenger: instruction to return (v. 9), promise of descendants (v. 10), and announcement of birth, name, and destiny (vv. 11-12). The statement of Ishmael's destiny characterizes him as a restless man constantly in conflict with other family members. And indeed when this saga concludes (25:18), the two sons of Abraham live separated from one another (Neff, 1972: 51-60).

In the familiar language of the promise to the ancestors, the speech of the angel to Hagar affirms God's commitment to those other than Abraham and Sarah (Brueggemann, 1982: 153). Hagar and Ishmael may not be the carriers of *the* promise, but they also have a future in the horizon of God's concern. At the point in the narrative where we might expect a narrow focus on the "chosen" community, we find instead God's care for those whom the chosen have sometimes excluded and even oppressed.

16:15-16 The Birth of Ishmael

Genesis 16:15 notes Ishmael's birth in a very matter-of-fact way, a contrast from the tension earlier in the narrative. This chronicle style concludes the narrative as such, but leaves the conflict between Sarah and Hagar unresolved. The reader does not know for sure whether Abraham has an heir or not.

The Annunciation of Isaac
Genesis 17:1 – 18:15

PREVIEW

The annunciation of the birth, name, and destiny of Isaac occurs twice in the saga. The first time, the annunciation happens in the context of God's encounter with Abraham (17:1-27). This encounter is organized as if it were a dialogue, but in fact Abraham speaks only once. A second annunciation happens in the context of a visitation to Abraham and Sarah by three unknown visitors (18:1-15). Sarah hears and responds to this annunciation although the speech is not addressed directly to her.

OUTLINE

The Announcement to Abraham, 17:1-27
      17:1-2   Initial Divine Speech
      17:3a   Abraham's Reaction
      17:3b-16 Main Divine Speeches
          Concerning Covenant, 17:3b-8
          Concerning Circumcision, 17:9-14
          Concerning a Promise of a Son, 17:15-16
      17:17-18 Abraham's Response
      17:19-21 Concluding Divine Speech
      17:20-27 Conclusion

The Announcement to Abraham and Sarah, 18:1-15
      18:1-2a Appearance of Visitors
      18:2b-8 Act of Hospitality
      18:9-15 Annunciation

EXPLANATORY NOTES

The Announcement to Abraham 17:1-27

17:1-3a Initial Divine Speech and Abraham's Reaction

Obviously, to call Genesis 17:1—18:15 the annunciation of Isaac is to speak of its role in the flow of the Abraham saga at a point where the problem of an heir has become the central issue. Indeed in this initial speech and response (vv. 1-3a), the promise of multiplication of descendants opens the door to the announcement of a son which will come later in this encounter.

Other elements appear in this initial speech. We will meet them in more detail in subsequent divine speeches. The speech begins with a word of self-introduction, "I am El Shaddai." Most English versions follow the common practice which goes back to Greek translation and rabbinic usage and translate this ancient title for God, "God Almighty." Texts from some of the religious communities surrounding Israel suggest that this was a common divine title. Whatever the ancient meaning of the phrase El Shaddai, perhaps God of the mountain/plain, our text does not find that original meaning important. Now the phrase functions as a characteristic title for God used by one stream of tradition in the family sagas of Genesis.

After this self-introduction, God gives Abraham instructions: *Walk before me, and be blameless.* Most likely that phrase functions as an announcement of Abraham's place in relationship to God more than as an "action" demanded of Abraham. Some interpreters have taken the phrase to require certain behavior. These two imperatives do expect action, but the nature of that action cannot be defined in terms of specific ethical or moral precepts. The word *blameless (tamim)* in Hebrew refers to wholeness of relationship (von Rad, 1972: 198). In this unit (17:1-27), the human action which establishes that relational solidarity with God is circumcision, a sign of participation in the community of God. Hence a decision to belong to the people of God (and not be cut off, 17:14), is the most this unit expects Abraham to do in order to *walk before me, and be blameless.*

The introductory speech also announces the promise of covenant. Genesis 17:2 clearly declares this covenant as gift: "I will give (Hebrew, *natan)* my covenant between you and me." In spite of its awkwardness, this more literal translation portrays the "gift" quality of the covenant better than translations such as, "I will establish (or make) a covenant between you and me." [*Covenant, p. 315.*]

In reaction to God's presence and speech, Abraham *fell on his face*

(v. 3a). This common act of homage functions in the Old Testament to express awe and fear in the presence of God or a divine messenger (Josh. 5:13-15) or even before the king (1 Sam. 25:23).

17:3b-8 Divine Speech Concerning Covenant

As in chapter 15, here the promises of descendants and land are placed in the context of covenant. As in the "initial speech" (17:1-2), covenant comes as a gift, not an agreement. The covenant is not accompanied by a ceremony in which the two parties agree to the defined relationship, but God announces to Abraham the covenant which is to be not only for Abraham but for his descendants.

This gift of an unending covenant with the descendants of Abraham became a critical affirmation for Israel in the time of the exile in Babylon (586-538 B.C.) Most of the other points on which the people could ground themselves had been lost with the destruction of Jerusalem, the removal of the Davidic king, and their deportation from the land. At that moment the community reached back to God's "forever" covenant with the landless Abraham. Out of this tradition they could reach toward the future, trusting God would be there. Israel realized repeatedly the role the past plays in opening up new possibilities for the future. Of course, these ancestral stories could be reinterpreted in such a manner as to close down the future. But more often the saga of Abraham spoke to Israel of new possibilities.

In this speech concerning covenant (vv. 4-8) a different name, or better a longer spelling of his name, signaled the coming of the new to Abraham. In terms of the origins of the names, the change from Abram to Abraham likely reflects a different dialect rather than a totally different name. The same type of name change occurs with Sarah's name in 17:15. The narrative gives importance to the name change beyond the etymology of the names. With this slight variation in the spelling, together with an explanation for the name change, the speech expressly reinforces the promise of descendants. Notice that the promise of offspring brackets (vv. 4b and 5b) the announcement of the name change (v. 5a). Abraham, who has had God's promise confirmed by word and covenant, now carries the promise of descendants visibly in his name, "father of a multitude of nations."

This speech includes the promise of land also (15:8), but the focus rests on the promise of descendants and God's commitment to be with the family of Abraham forever. Paul, writing to the Christians at Rome, reminds them of this unending promise (Rom. 4:16-17) and the hope that this covenant provides for the future.

17:9-14 Divine Speech Concerning Circumcision

The second divine speech in this series takes the form of instructions. Abraham is instructed to attend to the circumcision of every male in the community. Circumcision as a ritual goes back earlier in human history than we can follow. It functions among various peoples as a puberty rite, marriage rite, occasionally as an infant initiation rite, and of course as a hygenic, medical practice. In the ancient Near East circumcision seems to have been common among various northwest Semitic people, including the inhabitants of Canaan, but not among all the peoples of Canaan, e.g., the Philistines.

In this speech, circumcision is understood as a sign of the covenant. The covenant community is formed through this act of inclusion. Circumcision does not make the individual a "godly" person, but incorporates one into the community with whom God has an unending covenant. Failure or refusal to circumcise cuts one off from participation and so breaks covenant (v. 14). Von Rad notes that "cut off from his people" does not refer to the death penalty but exclusion from the community of the covenant (1972: 201).

In its polemic against circumcision as a religious rite, the Christian community has closed its eyes to connections between this understanding of circumcision and Christian baptism. Infant baptism, to be sure, but also adult baptism in the believers church tradition functions as a ritual of inclusion. In the baptismal promises, one at the same time affirms Jesus as Lord and accepts participation in the body of Christ. Those two are not split off from one another. Most Christians realize that the same danger the early Christians found in circumcision can also happen with baptism. The ritual action can become an initiation rite into a community which no longer lives out God's covenant. Baptism (unlike circumcision) can also become a problem when the ritual is understood to be a symbol of a relationship between an individual and God without reference to the covenant community.

17:15-16 Divine Speech Concerning a Promise of a Son

The announcement of a son to be born to Abraham and Sarah comes in this last of the series of speeches of God. The speech begins with a name change for Sarah which corresponds to that of Abraham in 17:5. Again the change likely represents a shift in spelling associated with a different dialect. But in the speech the new spelling, "Sarah," provides a visible symbol of blessing. Sarah shall be a mother: *I will give you a son by her* (v. 16). Like Abraham (17:5), Sarah carries God's promise as close as her name, *mother of nations*.

This announcement picks up the main thread of this "story about an heir." But in terms of the whole story, the announcement to Abraham of a son *by Sarah* gives rise to a major complication, Ishmael.

17:17-18 Abraham's Response

Abraham reacts to the annunciation speech, not with joy and celebration, but with consternation: it is a complication in his life. The narrative first reports Abraham's "private" response (v. 17) and then his one and only speech to God in this encounter (v. 18). Abraham falls on his face, the expression of homage and reverence that we met in 17:3. But this time the "fall" serves to cover up a private reaction to the announcement of a son. Abraham laughs to himself about children at Sarah's and his age. But to God Abraham speaks of a more practical matter, Ishmael. This response of Abraham recalls all the times we have responded one way to ourselves and quite another in public.

17:19-21 Concluding Divine Speech

In this completion of the annunciation, all the traditional elements are present: the announcement of birth, name, and destiny of the coming son. But the presence of Ishmael has complicated this annunciation. The destiny of the already born and named son is given (v. 20). Ishmael is promised blessing, fertility, and success. However, covenant is granted not to Ishmael, but to Isaac and to his posterity forever (vv. 19, 21). The line of Abraham through Isaac will carry the covenant into the future. As Ishmael and Isaac move into the future, the difference between them will not show up in the blessings of God that come to people generally—those that God provides to all. But the story line of God's promise will be traced through Isaac—not by virtue of anything Abraham or Isaac did, but by God's decision. The temptation exists for the community chosen to carry God's promise to see that as a basis for pride. But whenever the tradition tells the story of why one group carries the promise rather than another, the reason for that choice remains a mystery of God's providence (Deut. 7:6-7). [*Covenant, p. 315.*]

All the stories concerning Isaac's birth connect the name with "laughing" (17:17; 18:12; 21:6). Perhaps the name *Isaac* at one time referred to the laughter of God or the celebrative laughter at a birth, but those references are mostly gone from this saga (Westermann, 1985: 269). Instead, the laughter belongs to Abraham and Sarah, laughter found at the boundary between dream and reality. Almost always someone laughs when close to that boundary—laughter at the possibility that the dream might become reality, laughter when the promise and the dream come to be. The boundary between the promise and birth of a son, Abraham and Sarah found uncomfortable, laughable.

17:22-27 Conclusion

The conclusion of the encounter between God and Abraham finds Abraham carrying out the instructions he had received. But Abraham's execution of the instructions has the effect of including Ishmael in the covenant. While historically the Semitic groups known in the biblical tradition as Ishmaelites may have practiced circumcision, the action of Abraham causes problems in the flow of this saga. God's speech (vv. 19-21) set two different destinies for the two sons. Abraham's action incorporating Ishamel into the covenant community, while consistent with the instruction to circumcise all males in the household (17:10-13), confuses the matter of destiny. This circumcision carries out Abraham's request for Ishmael's future more than God's determination of Ishmael's future. The text presents this incongruity without comment.

The Announcement to Abraham and Sarah 18:1-15

18:1-2a Appearance of Visitors

The scene shifts abruptly to a second appearance. However, unlike the encounter in chapter 17, this one does not consist of a series of speeches, but we find instead elements of a tale. The tale begins, not with the introduction of the main characters, but with the phrase, *the Lord appeared to him* (NASB, RSV). In the flow of the saga, the *to him* refers to Abraham, corresponding to the phrase *the Lord appeared to Abraham* in 17:1. Hence, 18:1 establishes this narrative alongside Genesis 17 as a second encounter between Abraham and God.

The tale itself begins with Abraham looking up and finding three men standing in front of him. The narrator has told us that this is an appearance of God, but Abraham sees only three strangers.

18:2b-8 Act of Hospitality

In this section we find a very elaborate description of hospitality, including Abraham's own action of servicing the guests' needs for washing and eating. We can see in the flow of the narrative that Abraham acts as a host without peer. The host offers a "piece of bread" (v. 5, NASB) and then directs the preparation of a major feast. The Hebrew verbs portray Abraham frantically running to and fro getting this meal together with the help of Sarah and a servant (vv. 6-7), and then standing by quietly while the sojourners eat (v. 8).

18:9-15 Annunciation

The announcement of the birth of a child in the context of such a visit occurs in other stories in the ancient world, as it does also in the story of Elisha's visit to the Shunammite woman in 2 Kings 4. But here the visitation motif plays a role in relationship not only to the annunciation of Isaac but also to the Sodom narrative that follows. In fact, whereas in many such visitation stories the visitors use the host's expression of hospitality to test whether the couple should be granted fertility, in the flow of the Abraham saga that is never a question. The announcement of a son has already been given once (17:15-19), and here the announcement is repeated a second time. The audience includes Sarah, who is eavesdropping behind the door.

In this second announcement of a child, the focus is less on the announcement itself than on Sarah's response to the annunciation. The narrator reminds the listener of the ages of the couple and states that Sarah was past menopause. Sarah, laughing to herself, echoes that reminder with a probable touch of sarcasm. She wonders whether this annunciation implied that she was to once again experience *pleasure* (v. 12). According to the word order of the Hebrew—reflected best in the NASB—Sarah emphasizes not her age, but the age of Abraham. Perhaps Sarah's understanding of the problem included not only her menopause, but Abraham's infertility or impotence. In any case, Sarah responds to the annunciation in the same way Abraham had, with laughter (17:17).

Suddenly the narrative ceases to be the visitation of three strangers, but the appearance of the Lord, as 18:1 has signaled. God responds to Sarah's laugh with two questions: *Why did Sarah laugh?* and *Is anything too hard for the Lord?* God's speech concludes with a repetition of the announcement of birth.

The question *Is anything too hard for the Lord?* (v. 14) constitutes the key question for this "story about an heir." The question is easy to answer abstractly for anyone in the "family of Abraham." Of course nothing is too hard for the Lord. But what is easy to answer in theory becomes a different matter in the concrete human experience of barrenness. And indeed neither Sarah nor Abraham answers the question. Abraham makes no response, even though the question was put directly to him. Sarah avoids the question by denying that she laughed. The narrative ends with the question unanswered by Abraham and Sarah and by the events of the saga so far.

God's speech, *No, but you did laugh*, concludes the announcement of the birth, name, and destiny of Isaac which began back in Genesis

17:1. God works with and through people who laugh the laugh of doubt. The tradition proclaims that nothing is too hard for the Lord (Jer. 32:17; Mark 10:27; Luke 1:37)—not that Yahweh will do all things, but that God's promises will not fail (Brueggemann, 1982: 161). Nevertheless, for those who wait for the promise, private doubt/laughter even with public denial of doubt/laughter seems more common. The ones who laugh and deny laughing are those who know the agony of a prolonged wait even while taking the promise seriously.

The Tale of Sodom and Lot

Genesis 18:16 – 19:38

PREVIEW

The tale of Sodom and Lot begins with a note that functions as transition between the annunciation of Isaac and this tale (18:15). The visitors set off toward Sodom accompanied by Abraham. Remember that back in Genesis 16, following the annunciation of Ishmael, we found the report of his birth. A report of conception and/or birth regularly follows immediately after the annunciation, as illustrated also in the narrative of the Shunammite woman (1 Kings 4) and Mary (Luke 1—2). But that does not happen in this saga. Instead, the scene shifts away from the announcement of a son, leaving Sarah and Abraham with yet a longer wait.

The story line picks up a previous narrative thread which was set aside after chapter 14. This tale concerning Sodom and Lot has three sections. The initial section consists of divine soliloquy and Abraham's intercession on behalf of Sodom, 18:16-33. The second section relates the story of the destruction of Sodom, 19:1-29. Then the unit concludes with an episode concerning Lot and his daughters, the final appearance of Lot in the saga. 19:30-38.

OUTLINE

Prologue to the Table, 18:16-33
      18:16   Journey Note
      18:17-21 Divine Soliloquies
      18:22   Journey Note
      18:23-32 Abraham's Intercession
      18:33   Concluding Note

EXPLANATORY NOTES

Prologue to the Tale 18:16-33

18:17-21 Divine Soliloquies

In these two speeches (vv. 17-19 and 20-21) God brings together Abraham and the outrageous situation in Sodom. The connection is made explicit at two points. Life in Sodom and the *way* Abraham is responsible to promote sit in direct opposition to one another. Life in Sodom has produced the cry of oppression, *ṣaʿaqah* (18:20-21; cf. the same word in Exod. 2:23). Abraham's responsibility (v. 19) was to promote the doing of *righteousness and justice (sedaqah* and *mišpat).*

Righteousness and justice programmatically describes the way of the Lord (v. 19). The cry of oppression manifestly witnesses to the absence of righteousness and justice. All these words involve the character of community interaction (cf. the poetic play on these same words in Isa. 5:7). *Righteousness* does not refer to a catalog of virtues, as Genesis 38:26 will also make clear. Nor is *justice* in this word pair reducible to a code of laws. Rather, righteousness/justice portrays a way of living in community that promotes life for all its members—a life promoting social order. The cry of the oppressed arises out of a death-producing social order.

Through Abraham's chosenness God acts to promote life, not only for Abraham's family but for all families. God's soliloquy speaks of Abraham's life-promoting role through the familiar promise language of this saga: "in him all the nations of the earth will be blessed" (NASB). But as noted, the divine speeches use other language to express the same thing, language associated with the prophetic tradition, "righteousness and justice" (Amos 5:24; Isa. 5:7) and words familiar to the psalmists, "the way of Yahweh" (Ps. 25:8-10; 86:11). According to these soliloquies, God decides not to hide the problem of the outcry of death from the one whose task remains to promote life.

18:22 Journey Note

Most of these transitional sentences in narrative can go with little comment, but this one hides an interesting problem. Most of our translations use the "corrected" version of the Hebrew text and thus read "Abraham remained standing before Yahweh" (NIV). The scribes have noted that they changed the text from the original reading: "Yahweh remained standing before Abraham." The original reading might imply that Abraham was the one "in charge." It seems that the earlier reading did not sufficiently "protect" God's sovereignty.

God is capable of caring for the matter of sovereignty and does not need our protection. The original text knows something else about God. In the biblical tradition Yahweh is radically relational. Whether the text speaks of that relationship in terms of covenant, parent and child, or even bride and groom, relationship between God and the people remains primary. The boundary between people and God, i.e., divine sovereignty, does become an issue in such stories as the Garden of Eden and Tower of Babel (Gen. 3 and 11). In the polite form of address he uses, Abraham acknowledges God's sovereignty. Nevertheless, in the original reading of this text Yahweh remains standing before Abraham in genuine dialogue without endangering God's sovereignty: *And the Word became flesh and dwelt among us* (John 1:14).

18:23-32 Abraham's Intercession

In order to understand this dialogue better, we need to remember something about different ways in which the ancient world worked with the question of justice. We normally assume individual responsibility for justice: I pay the consequences for my acts and mine alone. However, that structure works only in certain areas of personal behavior. In many more areas the individual one-to-one ratio of act and consequence will not work. Most actions involve many more than just one person, and the consequences fall on others even though not all are equally at fault. We will all pay the consequences for environmental destruction or nuclear disaster, even though some work hard to care for the environment and to prevent nuclear war. In ancient Israel this corporate understanding of act and consequence was crucial as a way of looking at justice. Hence it should follow that if Sodom were inhabited by a sinful few, they endangered the future of the whole city (cf. the story of Achan, Josh. 7).

It is possible to imagine that the righteous few might escape in this conventional approach to social justice (which in fact happens in Genesis 19; Brueggemann, 1982: 171). But the outcome here remains uncertain because usually the sin of one affects the whole community.

Abraham opens the discussion over the fate of Sodom by reminding God of the divine responsibility to be fair (v. 23). A system lacks fairness when the righteous are destroyed with the wicked. This would lead us to expect Abraham to argue for a two-way approach, one fate for the wicked, one for the righteous. But he does not. Acting as one chosen to promote life, Abraham suggests instead that the conventional system be turned upside down. He maintains the one-destiny system and boldly proposes to the one standing before him—in question form—that the future of everyone be determined not by the wicked ones in the midst of the community, but by the righteous ones. Rather than the rotten many threatening the future of all, could the healthy few preserve the future for everyone? And God agrees!

The rest of the negotiations concern how many healthy people there must be to preserve the whole community, but most important to the dialogue is the operating principle. We might insist that only a two-way approach is fair. But Abraham's intercession seeks to promote life for all, which, according to God, he was specially chosen to do (Gen. 18:18).

Tale of Destruction 19:1-29

19:1-2 Arrival of Visitors

The central narrative begins with Lot sitting at the city gate when he saw two strangers. Immediately he greeted them in the same way Abraham had earlier (18:2). In his opening speech Lot offers the two visitors hospitality, as Abraham had done. But instead of accepting, as in the previous story (18:1-5), these visitors refuse Lot's offer. They propose instead to spend the night in the city square! That refusal by the guests comes as a surprise. Hospitality stories do not normally go this way. The problem occasionally arises that no one will offer hospitality (Judg. 19:15), but not that sojourners refuse it and sleep in the square.

This first exchange signals to the listener that Lot will have problems. And indeed, through the whole tale, Lot fails to get done what needs to happen. Lot tries to protect his guests but ends up being protected by them (19:10). Lot tries to convince his family to leave, but they think he is joking (19:14). After all his efforts to save his guests, Lot insists that he, himself, cannot make it to the mountains in time and so asks for permission to flee to a little town closer at hand (19:19-20). Later Lot fears to stay in that town himself and ends up in the mountains after all

(19:30). In all this, Lot appears as a bungler and buffoon (Coats, 1983: 144).

However, the portrait of Lot in the narrative is sympathetic. He tries to be a proper host. His guests are the ones who refuse and accept his hospitality only when Lot will not take "no" for an answer (19:3). He wants the mob at the door to be different, addressing them in very polite language as *my brothers* (19:7). Lot offers his own family to protect his guests (19:8), yet he also wants to save his family (19:14). The flow of the narrative draws the listener toward Lot. He acts appropriately most of the time, but his work brings no harvest. Thought he tries, Lot cannot "be a blessing" to others as Abraham can (12:3).

19:3-11 Act of Hospitality

Lot overcomes his visitors' reluctance and prepares a meal for them. But before bedtime the men of the city surround Lot's house. The narrator makes certain that no one misunderstands: *all* the men come. The men of Sodom demand that the visitors be turned over to them. Lot's speech notes the evil of homosexual rape (19:7-8). Yet the foremost concern of this narrative is the Sodomites' violation of the custom of hospitality, a "law" which has an almost sacral character in this ancient world (Vawter, 1977: 235). The sojourners who take refuge inside the gates of a town or the door of a house, whether those persons be friends, strangers, or even enemies, become special persons during the visit. By having *all* the men of the city intent on homosexual rape, the narrative reinforces beyond any doubt God's announcement that Sodom deserves destruction.

Tradition knows Sodom as a proverbially wicked city. At the heart of the problem lies abuse against those who are hungry and thirsty and have no place to lay their head.

> Behold this was the guilt of your sister Sodom: she and her daughters had pride, surfeit of food and prosperous ease, but did not aid the poor and needy. (Ezek. 16:49)

The broad range of biblical texts using Sodom as a negative example suggests that the primary problem in Sodom was inhospitable social practice not only homosexuality or even homosexual rape.

Lot offers his daughters to the mob in place of the visitors. Some have wondered whether this offer indicated the relative low value of women. It might be that Lot did not care much about his daughters. However, the flow of the narrative as it follows from Lot's offer of hospitality to the visitors encourages us rather to think the opposite. He had offered the best hospitality (v. 3). Lot's offer to substitute his two virgin daughters can be seen as an extension of that caring enough to offer the very best. Lot offers all the resources of his family to minister to and protect these strangers.

19:12-22 Rescue

God had determined to *go down* to verify the accusation against Sodom (Gen. 18:21). The collective violation of the law of hospitality proved conclusive. The visitors to Lot announce the verdict together with the sentence: *for we are about to destroy this place, because the great outcry against its people has become great before the Lord* (v. 13).

The rescue itself is narrated in a way that expresses exasperation. Lot cannot get his family to take the matter seriously (v. 14). And the messengers/angels end up having a terrible time getting Lot to agree to be rescued. Lot responds to the urging of the angels by lingering. So the narrator says the men seized Lot by the hand, brought him out, and set him down outside the gates, explaining, "Flee, do not look back, do not stop, flee!" (vv. 16-17). Lot worries that he cannot make it. In a long speech which wastes precious time in the narrative Lot asks for a change in plans (vv. 18-20). One (of the men?) agrees, but asks him to get on with it. The rescue ends with Lot's arrival in Zoar, leaving the listener breathing a sigh of relief.

19:23-26 Destruction of Sodom

The narrative uses traditional cataclysmic language to describe the destruction, thus emphasizing its totality. Lot's wife shared the future of the city because she "looked behind" (v. 26). Clearly the narrative wants us to understand that she disobeyed the instruction in the rescuers' speech not to "look behind" (19:17). But the Hebrew text does not make clear where she looked, suggesting that she looked "behind him" (Lot?). This ambiguity results in some variation in translations.

19:27-29 Conclusion

Brueggemann notes that Genesis 18:16—19:38 preserves several different perspectives on the question of sin and the future of humanity (1982: 166-176). The tale of the destruction of Sodom understands destiny to follow as a direct consequence of actions. The acts of the men of Sodom resulted in their destruction. The act of Lot toward his visitors, however inept, resulted in Lot's deliverance. However, the dialogue between God and Abraham in 18:23-32 suggested that the relationship between sin and the future might not be so direct. Perhaps the few righteous in the midst of a sinful situation can affect a good future for even the wicked.

This concluding paragraph to the tale (19:27-29) reflects perhaps yet another perspective on the issue. The narrator observes that Lot's future depended on Abraham (v. 29). Perhaps neither Lot's hospitality (9:3) nor God's compassion for Lot (19:16) accounted for Lot's escape. Rather, it was God's "remembering" Abraham that enabled Lot to escape this disaster. God remembered Noah and those with him, and that changed the future for Noah (8:1). But this is different. God remembers Abraham and rescues Lot! The narrator's comments do not evaluate Lot as either wicked or righteous, so that is not at stake. Rather, God's commitment to one person result in God's deliverance of another.

The biblical tradition does not give a simplistic answer to the question of transgression and punishment. Acts have consequences. Justice may be the simple working out of that process, but not always. Righteousness counts for something also, aiding even those who are unrighteous. Also, God's covenant with one can become the occasion of blessing for all (Rom. 5:15).

A Concluding Episode 19:30-38

Lot may have escaped, but in the narrative he does not escape with much. He and his daughters live up in the hills in a cave. If the present appears bleak, the future promises even less. In that moment the daughters take charge. These two women remain unnamed, known only by their relationship to Lot, *daughters,* to each other, *first-born* and *younger,* and to their offspring, "mothers" of Moab and Ammon. Still they take charge of Lot's future.

The daughters act to become pregnant by their father. As listeners we might well condemn the daughters for arranging incest and belittle Lot for his drunken participation. To be sure, the tradition legislates against incest (Lev. 20), but if that judgment is to be applied to this situation, the narrative gives us no hint. More likely we are to see this as the action of very marginal people toward the future (see also Gen. 38). Narratively, the two daughters have no future, but they act and bring forth two sons, the ancestors of two peoples.

Just a word about the relationship between this episode in the hills and the ongoing story about an heir for Sarah and Abraham. After the annunciation to Abraham and Sarah, another ends up with the child. That has happened twice now. Fertility finds Hagar and the two daughters of Lot, but Sarah remains barren. Abraham, who has been an agent of blessing to others, the carrier of promise, still lacks a future.

A Tale of Threat to the Ancestral Mother

Genesis 20:1-18

PREVIEW

The abrupt introduction in Genesis 20 can leave the reader confused. Have we not been here before with Abraham passing off Sarah as his sister (12:10—13:1)? This introductory of transitional sentence (20:1) takes Abraham far south into the desert—Kadesh and Shur—and then brings him back up again west of Beersheba and Hebron, where most of the Abraham stories are set. According to the chronology of the saga, Sarah is ninety plus, and yet she is taken into Abimelech's house to be a "wife." We see that the saga does not concentrate on some matters that often concern us, such as geographical precision and chronological logic. [Dating of the Philistines, p. 317]. Sagas of faith can seldom be reduced to geographical and chronological categories. This story concerns the coming of an heir as fulfillment of God's promise. To try to force all the other elements to fit perfectly is to miss the major story line.

Certainly in the saga we are back where we found ourselves just after Abraham received the promise. For Sarah and Abraham the delay in the promise continues, regardless of how often it has been renewed by words, oath, and covenant. From God's standpoint, Abraham continues to act in ways sometimes faithful but other times endangering the promise.

OUTLINE

Introduction, 20:1

Complication, 20:2
    20:2a Speech of Abraham
    20:2b Result

Resolution, 20:3-18
    20:3-8   Lawsuit: God versus Abimelech
    20:8-13   Controversy: Abimelech Against Abraham
    20:14-18 Conclusion

EXPLANATORY NOTES
Complication 20:2

As is common with Hebrew narrative, this tale centers in speeches, i.e., dialogue between the main characters. However, unexpectedly the story opens with a speech by Abraham, but without a stated addressee. The lack of description invites the reader to imagine the situation. Immediately Sarah finds herself in danger of becoming a member of Abimelech's household (v. 2). Again the importance of that circumstance is not given in this tale itself. In fact this verse does not give us a hint that Abraham's speech and the subsequent result create any problem. However, set within the context the complication is enormous. The violation of Sarah's marriage comes immediately to the front in God's lawsuit (Gen. 20:3-18). But still more is at stake. The annunciation of Isaac (Gen. 17:18) has tied the future directly to Sarah in a way that was not even the case in the first tale about danger for the ancestral mother (Gen. 12:10—13:1). God is bonded not only with Abraham through promise, oath and covenant, but with Sarah through annunciation. Abraham has put the whole of God's future in danger, not just Sarah's.

Resolution 20:3-18

20:3-7 Lawsuit: God Versus Abimelech

A trial takes place—a trial in the night during Abimelech's dream. God speaks as prosecutor: *You are a dead man* (v. 3). The accusation comes from Abimelech's potential violation of Sarah's marriage. Prior to Abimelech's response, the narrator makes sure the listeners understand the violation as potential and not actual. Abimelech's speech in his own defense begins with a counter accusation concerning a potential violation by God: "Will you kill a righteous people?" (v. 4). After observing that both Abraham and Sarah had stated their relationship to be brother and sister, Abimelech claims integrity of heart and innocence of hands. As the context and the parallelism of the two phrases indicate, these two terms talk not about moral rectitude but relational integrity. Although the narrator says he had a right to do so, Abimelech does not argue that he has not touched Sarah, but that he has acted with relational integrity toward Sarah and Abraham.

The trial concludes with God affirming Abimelech's innocence (v. 6) and instructing him to restore *the man's wife.* The unexpected part of God's speech is the statement that Abraham is a prophet and will intercede on behalf of Abimelech. Indeed the prophetic literature shows the prophet in that role (Amos 7; 1 Kings 17:20; Jer. 15:1), although both priest and king can also function as intercessor (Lev. 16; 2 Sam. 12:16). The Bible illustrates that petition was not the domain of one office or official. Hence we need not be surprised that Abraham could be portrayed as intercessor here (so also Gen. 18). That Abraham would be called prophet *(nabi)* is unusual and could indicate that this story was passed on in circles close to the prophetic traditions.

20:8-13 Controversy: Abimelech Against Abraham

Armed with an acquittal in his trial with God, Abimelech turns on Abraham with accusatory questions followed by a statement (v. 9). Not finished yet, Abimelech speaks again with another accusatory question (v. 10). This gives us a good example of one way in which Hebrew narrative deals with feelings. We are not told directly that Abimelech was angry, but the character of his speeches provoke feelings of rage in the listener. *[Characteristics of Hebrew Narrative, p. 313.]*

Abraham seeks to defend himself against these accusations (vv. 11-13). The narrator does not evaluate Abraham's defense. That again falls to the reader. But one can easily conclude that the sympathies of the narrative lie with Abimelech, not Abraham. To be sure, Abraham entered the area as a stranger, subject to the danger of being an alien, but Abimelech obviously does "fear God." He acts out that reverence far more than Abraham does. Even if Sarah is Abraham's half sister—the narrative leaves the readers to evaluate Abraham's claim in that regard—still the information Abraham withholds is the critical datum. At best Abraham, in his own self interest, misled Abimelech, jeopardizing Sarah and a lot of innocent residents of Gerar.

20:14-18 Conclusion

The unit concludes with Abimelech carrying out the instruction of God to return Sarah. The description of his actions demonstrates that Abimelech goes far beyond the minimum in his restoration of Sarah to Abraham. The threat of deportation (cf. 12:19-20) has been replaced by the offer to allow Abraham to settle wherever he chooses. Animals, servants, and money are lavished on Abraham and Sarah. Abimlech does everything he can to heal the damage caused by the situation, even though he is in no way guilty (Westermann, 1966: 401).

Abraham does intercede in Abimelech's behalf, and fertility returns to the women of Gerar. They once again begin to bear children. Notice the irony of the last sentence. When Sarah became one of them, all the women of Gerar became barren. Now their wombs are "reopened." But Sarah remains barren.

The Birth of Isaac

Genesis 21:1-21

PREVIEW

The saga arrives at last at the end of the wait for the promised child. This section began with a report of Sarah's barrenness (16:1) and the attempt to solve the problem by adoption. That failed through a combination of human conflict and divine decree. After the announcement that Sarah herself would be the mother (Gen. 17 and 18), the wait continued while everyone else seemed to be having babies. But now God *visits* Sarah as promised (21:1).

In spite of the anticipation, the birth report itself might go by unnoticed. It lies buried between episodes of Abraham's conflict with the people who control the land in which he lives, Abimelech and the residents of Gerar. The birth report itself is overshadowed by the far more dramatic narrative concerning the destiny of Ishmael (21:8-21). Nevertheless, in the midst of neighborhood conflict and domestic unhappiness, the child, Isaac, is born.

OUTLINE

The Report of the Birth   21:1-7
    21:1   Fulfillment of Promise
    21:2-5 Birth Events
    21:6-7 Response of Sarah

The Problem of the Other Child   21:8-21
    21:8-11   Crisis
    21:12-21 Resolution
        Speech of God, 21:12-13
        Action of Abraham, 21:14
        Near death of Ishamel, 21:15-21
            Crisis,   21:15-16
            Divine intervention, 21:17-19a
            Conclusion, 21:19b-21

EXPLANATORY NOTES

The Report of Isaac's Birth 21:1-7

The birth report begins with a statement that this is the promised birth (21:1). The narrative states this fact once: *The Lord visited Sarah as he*

had said (v. 1a). The parallel phrase restates the same thing: *The Lord
did to Sarah as he had promised* (v. 1b). However brief the description
of the birth, the narrative leaves no doubt that this is the one for which
the story has been waiting.

Apparently the birth of the promised one never happens at the
"right" time and convenient place. Like most other births, Isaac's seems
of minor importance compared to much more "important" events, both
foreign and domestic. Even though Isaac was not born at the right time
for Abraham and Sarah, the narrator tells us that the birth happened in
God's "appointed time" (v. 2, NASB).

The importance of the birth is not lost on Sarah. Abraham carries
out the expected post-birth activities, naming and circumcision (vv. 3-4).
Sarah alone speaks. She speaks of the fact that now she can laugh again
and others too will laugh. Laughter has always been associated with
Isaac's birth, as his name implies. Before it was the laughter of Abraham
and Sarah who knew themselves too old to become parents (17:17;
18:12). Now Sarah's laughter celebrates the birth, and others laugh also.
The Hebrew text leaves it open for us to decide whether the others are
laughing along with Sarah (NASB, NIV) about the situation (RSV?) or
perhaps even at Sarah, the old-age mother (v. 6).

The Problem of the Other Child 21:8-21

The joy of the birth did not last long, according to the saga. Isaac was
born into a family that already had an heir, Ishmael. In the various
translations we see the difficulty in translating the Hebrew in 21:9. The
RSV reads with the ancient Greek and Latin texts translating: *Sarah saw
the son of Hagar . . . playing with her son.* The NASB and NIV go with
another possible translation: "Sarah saw the son of Hagar . . . mocking."
The word translated "mocking" in the NIV and "playing" in the RSV is
the word to "laugh" which we have seen as a play on Isaac's name (Gen.
17:17; 18:12; 21:7).

The "story of the heir" (Gen. 16) has seen the conflict as between
Sarah and Hagar, not between Sarah and Ishmael or between the two
sons. In this particular episode, Ishmael is pictured as young enough to
be carried on Hagar's back (21:14-15, RSV, a fact ambiguous in the Hebrew and hidden by the NASB and NIV translations). We should
probably not think of Ishmael as creating tension by his behavior; his
presence is complication enough. Genesis 21 portrays Hagar and Ishmael in a very sympathetic light. We would do well to use a translation
like "playing" or "laughing" for 21:9 even if we choose not to include the

phrase attested to in the ancient Greek and Latin translators, "with her son Isaac." Sarah's speech to Abraham refers to the major complication in the family, two heirs for one inheritance (v. 10).

Given Hebrew narrative's reticence to describe the feelings of the characters in a story, preferring instead to let the readers imagine the feelings through speeches and narration of action, 21:11 stands out. The conflict produces immense anxiety in Abraham. The Hebrew word *ra'a* means something that causes suffering. Our word "distress" or "displeasing" seems too controlled. The division of his family split Abraham as well. *On account of his son,* the text reads—Abraham has two sons!

To this crisis God speaks (vv. 12-13). God instructs Abraham to do as Sarah demands. God will do what Abraham cannot—care for the sons of Abraham. So Abraham, arising early, prepares Hagar and her son for departure. We are not told what anyone feels at this moment in the narrative. Instead, the preparation reads with the same deliberateness we shall find in Genesis 22 when Abraham and Isaac depart for Moriah. No words are reported as Abraham sends a son and his mother off into the desert (v. 14).

As the reader might expect, the water runs out, so Hagar sets or almost throws (according to the Hebrew) the child under a shrub (v. 15). She goes some distance away pleading to no one in particular, "Do not let me see the boy die" (v. 16, NASB). The mother or the child—the Hebrew text is unclear—perhaps we should imagine both, cry.

The biblical tradition regularly recites that God hears the cries of the distressed (Exod. 2:23; 1 Sam. 7:8-9; Ps. 107:19). Hence also to this dire situation God speaks a word of deliverance (vv. 17-18). According to that word, the boy will not only have a present, but a future as well. The narrative ends with the deliverance of Hagar and her son and the boy's future beginning to work itself out (vv. 19-21).

We have labeled this section "the problem of the other child." We know from the saga that the boy's name is Ishmael, and yet the text never uses the child's name. The child is known in the narrative only as *the son of Hagar the Egyptian* (v. 9); Abraham's *son* (v. 11), "the son of this maid" (v. 13, NASB), or simply *the child.* The boy has no identity in himself in this narrative. The future happens to him because of the anger, the jealousy, and the care of those around him. He lives his life as the victim and sometimes the benefactor of promises made and kept by others.

Abraham and Abimelech: A Concluding Episode

Genesis 21:22-34

PREVIEW

The concluding episode in this story about an heir returns to the interaction between Abraham and Abimelech. [Dating of the Philistines, p. 317.] Although somewhat choppy in the present text, the narrative centers around an oath and a covenant between these two men.

OUTLINE

Oath, 21:22-24

Covenant, 21:25-32a
    21:25-26   Disputation
    21:27-32a   Ritual
Concluding Comments 21:32b-34

EXPLANATORY NOTES

Oath 21:22-24

The birth of Isaac happened, not as an isolated event in God's special history, but in the context of events that took no notice of his arrival. The narrative expresses that by placing the birth in the midst of an ongoing story about Abraham and Abimelech. Apparently the world did not stop to give attention to this birth. Even Abraham's attention was elsewhere.

Nevertheless, Abimelech's speech to Abraham contains an ironic twist when placed next to the birth narrative and the consequent difficulties concerning Hagar and Ishmael: *God is with you in all that you do* (v. 22). The reader might well like to hear Abraham's response to that comment, but the story does not stop for that. Instead, Abimelech requests an oath from Abraham. He asks Abraham not to *deal falsely (šaqar)* with him or his descendants. Abimelech requests the opposite of treachery, namely *hesed* ("loyalty," "kindness," "steadfast love").

One can hardly explain the word *hesed* briefly. We have no adequate English equivalent for *hesed*. Basically, *hesed* involves a voluntary response by one person to the essential needs of another. The nature of the response obviously depends on the situation. In the Old Testament, *hesed* seldom refers to customary acts of kindness or favors, but to a needed response to a dangerous situation or individual problem. A "*hesed*" response has a voluntary element even if supported by an oath (Sakenfeld, 1978). *Hesed* happens when one sees another in danger or need and gives assistance. Such assistance may or may not be requested. Abimelech senses himself in danger from the one possessing divine blessing (v. 22) and grounds his request for *hesed* in the way he has acted toward Abraham in the past.

Covenant 21:25-32a

The next scene opens with a dispute over water. Survival depended on access to water, a most precious commodity in that dry land. Abraham accuses Abimelech of seizing wells that belong to his family (v. 25). Abimelech denies knowledge of any such theft. With that, the two make a covenant.

The covenant-making ritual is bracketed by two general statements; "The two of them/they cut a covenant" (vv. 27b, 32a). The ritual itself involves seven ewe lambs as a gift from Abraham to Abimelech. The gift of seven fits the name of the place, Beersheba, which can mean "the well of seven." Beersheba can also mean the "well of the oath." Subsequently, that play on the place name, Beersheba, is also used: *there both of them swore an oath* (v. 31). This seems to be one occasion in which the whole narrative is closely tied to a play on the name of the place, including the regular formula for such etiologies: "thus the name of that place was called...."

Concluding Comments 21:32b-34

This concluding episode further emphasizes Abraham's connection with the sanctuary at Beersheba. Besides taking the oath and making a covenant with Abimelech, Abraham planted a sacred tree there (v. 33a). Abraham worships there (v. 33b). Whatever else one hears in this section, Abraham's connection with this sanctuary dare not be missed.

Certainly a close tie with Abraham to the "well" sanctuary enhanced the importance of Beersheba in later Israel. [*Dating of the Philistines, p. 317.*] But this etiology will not allow that connection to be used simply as a matter of self-indulgent pride. Notice, the narrative celebrates Beersheba as the place of covenant between Abraham and the residents of what later was to become Philistia: a covenant with the uncircumcised with whom disputes arise over important matters like water! Abraham agrees to an oath, promising to do *hesed* for those who are not a part of God's people. Remembering that Abraham worshiped "here" might be advantageous for the residents of Beersheba, but the narrative challenges a self-centered use of that memory.

THE TEXT IN BIBLICAL CONTEXT

Having explored the long "story about an heir," (16:1—21:34) we now turn to the role this story has played in the life of the tradition. The story of God's making a way for the promise to continue from the first genera- tion to the second and on to the subsequent generations reminded the community that they too were carriers of the promise, a promise that through them God would effect blessing to all other families. The liturgy reinforced that understanding by the regular identification of Yahweh as the God of Abraham, Isaac and Jacob—each new generation.

This story of an heir did not allow the continuation of the promise to be reduced to a genetic connection. Ishmael was legitimately the firstborn, but by God's choice Isaac carried the promise. Neither by Isaac's righteousness nor by Ishmael's failure did the promise belong to Isaac, but only by God's choice. Paul reaffirmed that the future of the promise was not reducible to genetic connection or any other human basis for presuming on the promise. Even yet the future of the promise depends on God's choice (Rom. 9:6-8). This proclamation comes as hope to those who by human ways of reckoning have no chance to be promise carriers. It warns all who assume that by right of birth, sex, de- nominational affiliation, or any other criterion of qualification, they can presume to carry the promise. The future remains a matter of God's freedom of choice not preset by identifiable human credentials.

In Galatians 4 Paul uses the conflict between Sarah and Hagar to talk about "two ways." He uses an allegorical method of interpretation to make his point. An allegorical interpretation uses various details in the story and equates them with items quite different from their original referent. Hence in Galatians 4 Hagar stands for a covenant of law (Mt. Sinai). Sarah represents the new covenant according to the Spirit. Paul likely means to use the text to differentiate Judaism and Christianity, proclaiming Christianity as the rightful heir of the promise, a direction quite different from the story as a part of the Abrahamic saga. Indeed, in his zeal for the matter at hand, Paul takes some details of the story in ways we would not choose. Nevertheless, lines do run back and forth between the Genesis story and Paul's interpretation. For both, the deci- sion about the future of the promise does not lie in human hands. In the Genesis saga Ishmael will not be the carrier of the promise, no matter how legal the process of his birth, how much Abraham loves him, or even how much his being cast out is the socially conventional, but per- sonally unjust result of a domestic power struggle. For Paul the new Jerusalem is free of human control (Gal. 4:26). The future of the promise will depend on God making the barren fruitful, not on a world which presumes, plans, and seeks to produce the future (Brueggemann, 1982: 184).

THE TEXT IN THE LIFE OF THE CHURCH

Many elements mentioned as we walked through this story might be lifted up for a special note in the concluding paragraphs. The freedom of God in respect to the future of the promise received attention in the preceding section. But we cannot fail to notice the regard the narrative has for those "not chosen." To be sure, the not chosen are not idealized as the innocent victims of an arbitrary God. Lot seems sincere but incompetent. That incompetence plays a role in the disasters that befall him. He acts recklessly when the situation calls for discretion and timidly when boldness is required. Hagar apparently wants to be the power in the family as much as Sarah. Her fertility gives Hagar an advantage which she does not hesitate to exploit. Nevertheless, the stories do not portray the not chosen as more "sinful" than the chosen. When dealing with Abimelech, Abraham chooses to protect himself when the situation calls for trust. And Sarah exploits her position to oppress Hagar when she has opportunity. In this narrative both the chosen and not chosen are real people, they are not stereotyped as good and evil.

Luther suggests that Abraham's love of Ishmael almost took his attention away from the promise *(Luther's Commentary:* 390). Perhaps we might suggest a different way to understand what Luther observed. God does not let any of the "not chosen" wander beyond the range of divine care, whether they are related to the "family" or are just neighbors in the land. The residents of Sodom, portrayed as the collective personification of evil, force God to deal with them out of justice. They have no future. But all others, ranging from Sarah to Hagar, from Abraham to Abimelech, are gifted in some way with a future by God.

In the center of the story sit Sarah and Abraham waiting for the future. While others around them receive a future, Sarah remains barren. While friends and loved ones laugh *with* the gift of life, Sarah and Abraham laugh *at* the promise of life. They make do with the laughter which covers the tears of disappointment and the cynical laughter that has given up hope—the laughter of the barren. But finally as promised, God transforms the laughter. With Isaac, Sarah and Abraham move by God's grace from barren laughter to the laughter of life.

Genesis 22:1-19

The Story of a Test

PREVIEW

Perhaps the most intense of all the narratives in the Abraham saga, Genesis 22:1-19 identifies itself as a narrative about a "test" (v. 1). Functioning as the counterpart to the promise of a son (Gen. 15), this narrative is marked off as a single unit by the phrase, *after these things* (vv. 1, 20) and the journey which the divine speech directs (vv. 2-19).

Other literary characteristics bind this narrative together as a unit. Most visible is the tension created by the divine command to offer Isaac as a burnt offering and the resolution of that threat to Isaac's life with the speech of the angel (vv. 11ff.). One other element bears noticing. In many biblical Hebrew narratives, key words and phrases *(Leitwörter)* hold the story together, often providing important windows into the meaning of the text. This narrative provides us a good example of such a *Leitwort. [Characteristics of Hebrew Narrative, p. 315.]*

In the previous "story about an heir" (16:1—21:34) the word "son" (Hebrew, *ben)* was repeated about 25 times when referring to an heir for Abraham and Sarah. Now in Genesis 22:1-19 the word *son* appears ten times on the lips of all the main characters and the narrator of the drama. Everyone, save Isaac himself, reminds the readers that this story is about a *son*. The speeches of God and the angel speak to Abraham about his *son*, his *only son*, the son he *loves* (vv. 2, 12, 16). Abraham speaks directly to Isaac only two lines, both of them are punctuated at the end with *my son* (vv. 7-8).

Thus *son* is the key word in this narrative. It connects this narrative with Genesis 15, where Abraham first goes to God about the problem of a *son*. It connects with Genesis 16—21 where the *son* provides the theme that carries through the whole story. But *son* in Genesis 22 is more than a connecting device. The key word *son* initiates, intensifies, and at last relaxes the drama. Abraham, who gave permission to send one son out into the desert to die, now walks silently to Moriah to meet God and offer back in a fiery sacrifice his "promised" son.

The way the interpreter understands this text affects how it is displayed in outline form. Certainly direct address is critical in Hebrew narrative, and hence Brueggemann organizes the unit around the points of dialogue and direct address (1982: 186). The opening phrase indicates that this narrative reports a "test" of Abraham's obedience and that too could be the clue for organizing the unit (Coats, 1983: 157-158). The focal point of the action falls in 22:9-14, so that the unit could be organized with the rest of the unit moving toward and away from that action center. All of these help display important features of the text. The outline here goes yet another direction. In the opening dialogue God instructs Abraham to make a journey. That journey carries the narrative from verse 3 through the end in verse 19. Hence this drama is here set within the context of a journey.

OUTLINE

Introduction, 22:1a

Opening Dialogue, 22:1b-2
    Call—God
    Response—Abraham
    Instructions—God

Execution of Instructions—Journey, 22:3-19
        22:3   Preparations and Departure
        22:4-8 Arrival
            Instructions to Servants, 22:4-5
            Walk to the Place, 22:6-8
        22:9-14 Sacrifice
            Son, 22:9-10
            Dialogue with Angel, 22:11-12
            Lamb, 22:13
            Concluding Etiology, 22:14
        22:15-18 Speech of the Angel
        22:19   Departure and Return

EXPLANATORY NOTES

Introduction 22:1a

As noted above, this opening phrase or sentence introduces this narrative as a test. Although the divine promise in 12:1-3, the famine in 12:10, and the arrival of visitors in chapter 18 all may have had hidden elements of a test, only here does the narrator inform the reader that we have a test. Thereby, we, as the readers, can direct some of our attention away from the danger to Isaac, to the precarious situation of Abraham in his relationship to God. But Abraham does not have the luxury of that information. Abraham must go through the drama not knowing until the angel's final speech (and that by inference), that he has passed the test (22:16-17). In fact, most of us enter into the story in such a way that we too do not know/remember that this is a test. We experience it only as an intense drama of love and danger.

Execution of Instructions—Journey 22:3-19

22:1b-2 Opening Dialogue

The instructions of God seem incomprehensible to us. The narrative does not tell us how Abraham received them. Indeed the narrative all the way through does not tell us anything directly about Abraham's thoughts and feelings. So upon receiving the instruction to take his son, the only one, the one he loves, and offer him as a burnt offering on a hilltop, Abraham gives no audible reply. The listeners are left with their own feelings upon hearing the instructions that came to Abraham. Perhaps silent action is all that can be narrated.

Abraham's thoughts are not the only element that remain a mystery in this dialogue. Where shall we locate the place where this sacrifice is to happen? Most of our translations follow the Masoretic Hebrew text and identify the place as *Moriah,* the location upon which, according to 2 Chronicles 3:1, Solomon built the temple. Several things make us wonder if Moriah is the earliest reading and/or if the two Moriahs are the same. No other ancient text has the location as Moriah. The other texts do not agree among themselves, but none of them have Moriah. Second Chronicles 3:1 has "Mount Moriah," which makes more sense than the *land of Moriah,* as found here. Finally, nowhere else in Genesis 22 does the text refer to the location by name. It seems best to let it go at that and not try to specify the location.

One other unusual note about God's speech. The divine speech begins with a word of entreaty, the Hebrew *na'.* This small "particle" appears in a divine command only here and Isaiah 7:3 (Crenshaw, 1975:

254). Why this entreaty by God, a particle that turns an imperative toward petition? Perhaps not only Abraham, but also God has a great deal at stake in this meeting on the mountain.

22:3 Preparations and Departure

The narrator talks in a quite matter-of-fact manner about the preparations for the journey. In the context of the whole saga, Sarah appears conspicuous here by her absence. We are not told anything about thoughts or words spoken to Sarah, Isaac, or anyone else. Abraham simply takes two of his young men along, wood for an offering, and Isaac, *his son*. Silently Abraham begins to execute God's instructions.

22:4-7 Arrival at the Place

Sighting *the place*, Abraham stops, leaving behind the two young men and the animals. Abraham's instruction to the two lads have the same ambiguity found in his later words to Isaac. He tells them that *the lad* and I go there and "we" will worship and "we" will return (v. 5, NIV). That may be correct, but it hides the danger and drama to come and involves information which Abraham cannot know at this point in the story. One further unusual element: while God, Abraham, and the narrator conspicuously refer to Isaac as *son*, here Abraham uses the term *lad* or "young man," seemingly emphasizing relational distance. Perhaps Abraham needs words which detach him from the situation when speaking publicly. There will be no spectators from here on, just Abraham and Isaac, *his son*.

The two of them walk on together in "poignant and eloquent silence" (Speiser, 1964: 165). Footsteps seem to be the only sound. Nothing in the narrative detracts attention from the two walking together. We know nothing about how they looked or what they saw—just the two of them, one old, one young, a father and son.

The silence breaks with Isaac's speech: "Dad." "Yes, my son." "I see the fire and the wood, but where is the lamb for the sacrifice?" "God will provide a lamb for the sacrifice, my son." Tacking *my son* awkwardly onto the end of the statement chills the soul as it reinforces the drama: "the lamb of sacrifice, my son" (Crenshaw, 1975: 247-248). The speaking ends. Again the reader hears only footsteps. All else remains unexpressed: dark, hidden, unknown (Auerbach: 9-12).

22:9-14 Sacrifice

At the critical point, when we would expect the narrative to slow down to prepare for the sacrifice on the mountains (von Rad, 1972:

241), surprisingly the binding and laying of Isaac on the altar appears as a quick series of verbs: *built,* "arranged," *bound, laid.* The narrative has not slowed enough! The son lies there on the altar before the listener is ready, given the long silence of the walk to the place. Now the narrative words do come more slowly. Abraham reached out his hand and took hold of the knife. He had one purpose: *to slay his son* (v. 10)—all this in narrative silence.

Then the silence is broken (v. 11)—broken by a messenger/angel of God with new instructions: *Do not.* The angel does not speak directly about Abraham's intention to kill his son, saying instead, "Do not *reach out* your hand *to* the lad, and do nothing to him" (v. 12). Perhaps the angel too needed distance from the near disaster. The angel proclaims, *Now I know you fear God.* "Fear of God" has fundamentally to do not with a disposition or feeling either for or in awe of God, but rather an obedience which does not protect even what is most precious but trusts God with the future (Brueggemann and Wolff, 1975: 72).

Abraham lifts his eyes for a second time. The first time he saw *the place* (22:4). This time he sees a ram and he completes the sacrifice. Abraham names the place: *Yahweh yireh,* a name as ambiguous as this event has been. The word *yireh* can be a play on the Hebrew word "to see," which in 22:8 we normally translate "provide." But it can also play off the word "fear"/"obey." So this may be the place where "Yahweh is seen" or "Yahweh is obeyed" or "Yahweh provides"—probably all of those. In the context of this event, it remains a place beyond naming.

22:15-18 Speech of the Angel

This has been a very private event: no one except Abraham and Isaac have been present on that mountain. But this very private moment has very public consequences. It has everything to do with the flow of the saga. Hence the promises set out in Genesis 12:1-3 and subsequently confirmed by oath and covenant are repeated here. In this repetition the promises are proclaimed in the heightened form of a song of celebration. Using a common method of intensifying a word by adding an infinitive form to the verb, the promise reads: "I will doubly bless you and doubly multiply your descendants" (v. 17). The promise is supported still further by an oath grounded in God's own being (v. 16). Even God's celebration and joy in the speech cannot be contained.

22:19 Departure and Return

In the flow of the saga Abraham's journey began at Beersheba (21:33). And now he returns there. A curious element appears in this departure and return. Isaac is missing—left on the mountain? (Crenshaw 1975: 246). Abraham goes back to the two young men: *and they . . . went together* (v. 19)—the same words used of Abraham and Isaac on the way to the mountain (22:6, 8). Perhaps we should assume Isaac was there also, though not mentioned. But then again, perhaps Isaac moves from the mountain into the future, while Abraham's responsibility to the promise has been completed and with that he returns to Beersheba. Isaac remains a bit of a mystery. The next figure whom the tradition follows in detail is not Isaac but Jacob. Not all carriers of the promise occupy the center stage.

THE TEXT IN BIBLICAL CONTEXT

The drama of the near sacrifice of Isaac has inspired classical works of art and theology. Soren Kierkegaard experienced Abraham on Moriah as the second father of the race, the father of faith—one who acted on faith in face of the unethical and irrational, the emotionally absurd (1983: 9-123). Rembrandt captured the terror of the moment in a 1635 painting *(The Bible in Art: The Old Testament:* 48). Countless other poets, artists, teachers, and preachers, some remembered, most not, have wondered about and marveled at this story in the Abraham saga.

Testing by God is a familiar motif in the Bible. The Deuteronomic tradition sees God's testing as an important way to interpret many of the difficulties Israel encounters, beginning with the experience in the wilderness:

> And you shall remember all the way the Lord your God has led you these forty years in the wilderness, that he might humble you, testing you to know what was in your heart. . . . (Deut. 8:2—cf. Deut. 13:3; Judg. 2:22).

The New Testament narrates the experience of Jesus as one who is tested in the wilderness to know what is in the heart (Matt. 4:1-11 and parallels).

The passion narrative does not explicitly call the Garden of Gethsemane a test of Jesus, but the drama and danger of that moment closely parallel the experience of Abraham on the mountain. God demands that the carrier of the promise give up any control or claim on the promise. At that moment there is no future for the promise carrier. The future of the blessing of all the nations of the earth rests in God's hands alone. As the promise carrier surrenders any claim to that role, God reaffirms the promise through a ram caught in a thicket and a stone rolled away from a tomb. The testing and providing on the mountain called

Moriah becomes the crucifixion and resurrection in the faith of the New Testament (Brueggemann, 1982: 194).

The connections some interpreters have drawn between the danger and drama of the near sacrifice of Isaac and the crucifixion-resurrection of Jesus has led at times to a blending of these two stories into one. This merging began early in the church's interpretation of Genesis 22. Irenaeus and Tertullian related the wood which Isaac carried to the cross Jesus bore *(Ante-Nicene Fathers,* Vol. I, III, IV.) Apparently the merging of the near sacrifice of Isaac with the Passion narrative of Jesus was reflected rather generally in the worship of the early church *(Ante-Nicene Fathers,* Vol. II: 530).

In a somewhat similar interpretative direction, the Jewish tradition emphasized Isaac's role as exemplary martyr, later suggesting also that Isaac's willingness to be sacrificed acted as atonement for the sins of Israel and the Gentiles (Davies and Chilton, 1978: 514-546). Although the identification of the two stories has continued, the Reformers were rather more restrained than earlier interpreters, preferring to stress Abraham's faith and obedience rather than Isaac as a "type" of Christ *(Luther's Commentary II:* 7-24; Menno Simons, 1956: 351-352). That Reformation direction continues to commend itself to us.

THE TEXT IN THE LIFE OF THE CHURCH

God's celebration of Abraham's passing the test (22:15-18) suggests that like Abraham, God had a lot at stake on this mountain called Moriah. God had promised Abraham without qualification to use him to be the agent of blessing to all the nations of the earth. Despite God's regularly repeating the promise and confirming that promise with oath and covenant, Abraham's career gave no clear indication that he could carry the promise. On the one hand, Abraham acted decisively to bring blessing to Lot (chapters 14 and 18), but the same person lied to protect himself, thus endangering other people (12:10-20; 20:1-13). The same persons who acted out of trust in the promisemaker (15:6; 17:22-27) tried to force the fulfillment of the promise (chapter 16) and laughed at the idea that the promise could ever be realized (17:17; 18:12). The saga often portrays the chosen Abraham and Sarah in a way that makes the listener wonder if someone has made a mistake. Could that wondering have brought God to Moriah to meet Abraham?

Even in their trust (15:6), Abraham and Sarah seemed unclear that they could count on God. Famine greeted their arrival in the land of promise (chapter 12) followed by strife in the family (chapter 13) and war in the countryside (chapter 14). Then there came the wait—the long interminable wait for a son. They lived with barrenness while fertility surrounded them: Ishmael, Moab, Amon, the household of Abimelech. Finally near the end of their life, Sarah gave birth to Isaac. The experience of Sarah and Abraham with God's promise seemed to include more waiting and wondering than enjoying and celebrating.

God and Abraham with Isaac met on the mountain. God took the risk that Abraham would respond. Abraham took the risk that God would provide. The man took a knife in his hand. A ram was caught in the thicket. Abraham had his promise and his son. God had an agent of blessing for all the families of the earth.

God met a person on another mount—Mount Calvary. Jesus risked his life. God risked a Son. God found one who could bear the cross. Jesus found that God would provide. And all the families of the earth receive blessing.

Genesis 22:20 – 25:18

Abraham's Testamentary Activities and Death

PREVIEW

The Abraham saga concludes with a unit on his testamentary activities, the things he does in his last years. We find the same sort of conclusion to the Jacob saga and the story of Joseph. In each of the accounts the major figure engages in the final activities which conclude the story and prepare for the next generation (see also Gen. 35; 48—50).

This unit begins and ends with a genealogy and a death report (Gen. 22:20—25:18). These elements bracket an extended narrative about Abraham's effort to obtain a bride for Isaac. Actually the structure of the unit does not fit together quite as neatly as that sounds. The unit begins with a genealogy which points to the birth of Rebekah, who is to be the second mother of Israel (22:20-24), followed by the death and burial of the first mother, Sarah (23:1-20). Following the narrative in which Abraham obtains a suitable wife for Isaac (24:1-67) comes a concluding genealogy and the report of Abraham's death (25:1-11). After that we find a "postscript" to the narrative which begins with the formula "these are the generations" (25:12). This postscript lists the genealogy of Ishmael (25:12-16) and reports his death (25:17-18).

OUTLINE

EXPLANATORY NOTES

Genealogy of Nahor 22:20-24

This genealogy presents itself to us as a speech to Abraham by an un-known speaker: *It was told to Abraham . . .* (v. 20). The primary purpose is to communicate to Abraham the genealogy of Rebekah.

The genealogy lists eight children born to Abraham's brother Nahor by Milcah. The names of Nahor and Milcah take us all the way back to the genealogy with which the Abraham saga began (11:29). The key name in this list is the last of the eight children, Bethuel, the father of Rebekah. We are told twice in this short genealogy that Nahor is Abraham's brother (vv. 22, 23). This genealogy functions in the unit not just to provide news about Abraham's family living elsewhere, but as introduction to the old man's unfinished task—securing the second-generation family of the promise. Isaac must be securely married—within the family. This genealogy prepares for the eventuality that Rebekah will be Israel's second mother. [*Reading Genealogies, p. 326.*]

Report of Sarah's Death 23:1-20

23:1-2 Sarah's Death

In a way characteristic of the genealogical framework of the saga, the death of Sarah is reported as it would be in an obituary notice. But the text does not leave us with only that straightforward notice, it adds, *Abraham went in to mourn for Sarah and to weep for her* (v. 2). Israel's first mother is dead: a woman victimized by barrenness (11:30; 16:1) and by Abraham's urge toward self-protection (12:11-13; 20:2), a woman who tried to make the promise happen and ended up hating the results of her plan (16:1-6; 21:8-10). But most of her life Sarah waited, sometimes in the foreground, but more often behind the scenes—waited for the promised son. In the flow of the saga, soon after the son is born and safe, the mother is dead.

23:3-20 Sarah's Burial

Abraham as a resident alien or sojourner had no property of his own. Apparently such people could acquire property, but only with the permission of the dominant community (Westermann, 1966: 457). Toward that end Abraham approaches *the Hittites* for permission to obtain land on which to bury Sarah. In the past, scholars have related Abraham's negotiations to elements from ancient Hittite law, the Hittites being a non-Semitic group living in Anatolia (modern Turkey). More recent study suggests that the Hittites mentioned in the Genesis family stories are one of a number of non-Abrahamic family groups living in Canaan, not necessarily equatable with the former inhabitants of Anatolia (de Vaux, 1978: 255-256).

The negotiations between Abraham and the townsfolk appear both overly polite and very intense. Abraham introduces himself as a resident alien and asks them to *give* him land to bury his *dead* (v. 4). The word *give (natan)* functions as the key word throughout the negotiations (vv. 4, 9, 11, 13). This will be a matter of buying and selling, not giving. Intense bargaining will be hidden beneath the polite and deferential language of public discourse.

The residents answer Abraham's humility (v. 4), calling Abraham the mightiest prince, or, if we want to translate *'elohim* differently, divine prince (v. 6). Abraham has put himself at the bottom of the social ladder and they put him at the top. Their answer also invites a specific proposal which Abraham then makes. Speaking very politely, Abraham offers full price if Ephron will *give* the cave at *Machpelah* (vv. 8-9). Ephron, as one of the elders addressing Abraham as *my Lord,* offers to *give* the field and *give* the cave also. Three times Ephron repeats the word *give* (23:11

Abraham, bowing for the second time, offers to *give* the price of the field (v. 13). Ephron, claiming that money is nothing between friends, sets what appears to be a very high price (compared for example to the fifty shekels David paid for the temple site in Jerusalem, 2 Sam. 24:24) (Vawter, 1977: 265). The *prince, Lord* Abraham, agreed to the gift at full price (23:16). The intense bargaining concealed beneath the overly differential language of public discourse makes the scene almost comic.

The transaction at the city gate is completed and Sarah is buried (vv. 19-20). We might expect some connection between this purchase and the promise of land. At last the family possesses some land. But in the text we find no mention of that. Abraham does indeed own land, a cemetery cave. One suspects that as fulfillment of the land promise, a cemetery is hardly what Abraham had expected. Nevertheless, Sarah is buried in a cave which will hold several of the ancestors (25:9; 49:29-31), thus completing the first of Abraham's final or testamentary activities.

Story of Isaac's Marriage 24:1-67

24:1-9 Introduction

Abraham continues the task of putting his house in order by arranging for the marriage of his son Isaac. The arrangements for that marriage are told in the form of a short story, more formally called a *novella*. In this last narrative of the Abraham saga the narrator can at last call Abraham *blessed* (v. 1). The whole saga began with a promise of blessing (Gen. 12:1-3) and now it reaches its conclusion with that pronouncement. One matter remains yet, and for that Abraham enlists the aid of his most senior servant, the manager of all he has (v. 2). The story line of this novella follows the work of a good and faithful servant, declaring that in God's providence the patient work of such a servant will bear fruit. The servant remains unnamed throughout the story. But this good servant acts as the quiet hero of the story, even though not directly the benefactor of its successful conclusion.

The story begins with Abraham calling the servant to the task of obtaining a wife for Isaac from Abraham's kindred, the family Abraham had been directed to leave at the beginning of the saga (12:3). Abraham seeks to secure the servant's loyalty with an oath, including a ritual in which the person being placed under oath touches the source of fertility—the *life* of the one asking for the oath (vv. 2, 9; also 47:29). Abraham declares the inhabitants of Canaan disqualified as a source for a woman to become Isaac's wife. This will be an endogamous marriage, a marriage kept within the family.

The servant raises the possibility that a suitable woman will not come in response to the servant's request: perhaps Isaac himself should return to the land from which Abraham came (v. 5). That option Abraham absolutely rejects (v. 6). At the end of his speech (v. 8) Abraham states once more that Isaac must not be taken back to the family territory in Mesopotamia. The future of the Abraham family rests in *this land.*

Although the narrative shows us a resolute Abraham, the old man does not simply presume the mission for a wife will succeed. He stipulates that if a suitable woman will not follow the servant back to Isaac, the servant is no longer obligated by the oath (v. 8). The course of the family's pilgrimage in this saga warns even Abraham against presuming on God's providence. Abraham acts toward the promise but without any guarantee that any particular action will be successful.

24:10 Journey: Departure

The servant gathers gifts together and departs. Central to this narrative is an understanding of a good servant or steward (Roth 177-187). Proverbs 13:17 describes the role of the servant-messenger:

> A bad messenger causes trouble,
> A loyal envoy brings healing.

This journey pictures the work of a loyal envoy.

The narrative moves along on a web of key words describing the instructions and work of this faithful servant-messenger. The movement of the narrative is carried by the messenger's "going" (halak, e.g., 24:4, 10, 42, 56). The tension of the narrative rests on whether Rebekah will go (halak and yaṣa, e.g., 24:5, 8, 55, 58). Whereas the movement of the people is carried by the words go/go out, God's quiet presence is conveyed through the words bless (barak, 24:1, 31, 35, 60) and lead (nahah, 24:27, 48). Still another key word grounds negotiations between the servant and the family—ḥesed, steadfast love/loyalty (24:12, 14, 27, 49). The servant acts as the vehicle through which all these words function in the story: the going and coming, the blessing and leading, the steadfast love and loyalty.

24:11-27 Arrival and Encounter at the Well

The scene at the well is bracketed by the servant's two prayers (vv. 12, 17). Repetition in the opening prayer emphasizes the servant's petitions that God act out of steadfast love and loyalty (ḥesed) toward Abraham (vv. 12, 14). In his prayer, the servant stipulates the conditions by which he will identify the wife for Isaac. To meet the conditions, the woman must not only respond to his need for water but to the thirst of the camels as well. Such action would be a model of hospitality and indeed even of God's *hesed*—voluntary action in response to the serious need of a person (Sakenfeld, 1978).

A woman appears even before the servant finishes his prayer (v. 15). The narrator in lengthy comments tells us that she is a member of Abraham's family, beautiful, and unmarried (vv. 15-16). Rebekah responds quickly to the need of the servant for drink and to the camels' thirst (v. 20). Everything happens so fast that the narrator's comment in 24:21 produces at least a smile: "Silently the man watched her to know whether or not Yahweh had brought success to his journey." The amusing scene of this beautiful woman running back and forth watering the camels while the man stands silently evaluating the situation theologically will likely produce quite different responses in readers.

The servant then lavishes gifts on the woman and inquires concerning her father's name and whether the family could give him hospitality (vv. 22-23). She repeats some of her genealogy and affirms her family's willingness and ability to provide hospitality. The scene then closes as it opened, with a prayer by the servant, this time a prayer of thanks (v. 27).

The search for both bride and hospitality gives the whole drama a comic tinge. It is as if both of them know the real but unspoken agenda, thus causing the matter of hospitality to take on an exaggerated importance. The servant gives jewelry, which in the agenda of hospitality appears to be payment for water and service, but in fact is part of the gift of the groom's family to the bride's family. Having been asked for her father's name, Rebekah responds with enough genealogy for all to know he belongs to Abraham's family. Hebrew humor, often expressed through incongruity, irony, and understatement, has room to play in this scene.

24:28-54a Negotiations for a Bride

Humor follows the narrative to Rebekah's house. She runs to *her mother's* home with a report of the visit (v. 28). The narrator introduces us to her brother Laban, who as the family spokesperson, runs to the watering place. The narrator then backs up and tells us *why* Laban ran to the well in the first place—he saw the jewelry and heard his sister's words (v. 30). We cannot be sure what words Laban heard—perhaps it was the rattle of jewelry. Laban then pronounces the servant "blessed of Yahweh" and brings him into the house (v. 31).

Just as he is about to eat the food laid before him, the servant stops to tell why he came (v. 33). We then find a long, long speech by the servant in which he gives an account of everything, including his own fear that when he finds the right woman she will not come (vv. 34-49). A comparison between what Abraham said and what the servant reports shows only minor changes, but we have learned in Hebrew narrative to pay attention to such minor variations (Alter, 1981: 77-78). The servant begins by stating that Abraham has become very rich and that Isaac has inherited all the wealth (vv. 35-36). The servant then emphasizes that he is to get a wife from Abraham's *father's house* (v. 38), but completely leaves out Abraham's warning—repeated twice—not to return Isaac to the father's homeland! The servant states that by permitting Rebekah to marry Isaac the family can show its steadfast love and loyalty (*ḥesed*) to Abraham. This statement exerts further pressure on the situation (v. 49). Laban and Bethuel accede to the request quickly—too quickly, the reader senses (vv. 50-51).

Bethuel is mentioned only here as having a part in the negotiations, which elsewhere involve only Laban (v. 50). Perhaps the father's name slipped in accidentally (Francisco, 1973: 196). The presence of the name in the received text provides the comic element of the father popping into the narrative to agree to the marriage and then disappearing again. Abraham's servant then completes giving the gifts to the bride's family (v. 53). Christians from the African churches suggest that Western Christians may misunderstand those gifts by regarding these as the "bridal price," as though a man were buying a wife. Such gifts are given to the bride's family to ingratiate the groom's family with the bride's family so that the bride's family will give permission for the marriage. African Christians, where a similiar marriage system often still exists, stress that such a marriage system is not a process of buying and selling. Although women did not have the same kind of choice about marriage that current Western women have, neither did the men.

24:54b-61 Departure

The dialogue the next morning demonstrates that all is not yet finished. The servant asks permission to take Rebekah and leave (v. 54b). But Rebekah's mother (who has not appeared in the negotiations thus far) and Laban ask that the trip be delayed. Difficulty in translating the Hebrew text leaves the reader unclear about how long a delay they suggested—ten days(?). In any case they request a substantial delay. The servant objects, implying possible divine approval for the quick departure. The brother and mother agree to let the daughter decide. The tension is broken when Rebekah agrees to go and they send her away with a royal blessing (Coats, 1983: 169).

24:62-67 Conclusion

The short story concludes with the marriage. The saga of Jacob (Gen. 25:19—36:43) remembers the marriage between Rebekah and Isaac as a sometimes troubled union. But Rebekah has agreed to the marriage. Moreover, Isaac loves her (v. 67). With this marriage the family of Abraham now has in place its second generation, Rebekah and Isaac. The marriage can be called providential in that the marriage fit into God's purpose. However, the narrative stresses not only God's control of events, but also the wise and faithful action of people. Through moments, sometimes funny, sometimes tense, people negotiate their way within God's providence. We find no division between good people and evil people, but just ordinary people—worried about their family, impressed by wealth, awkward in some moments, shrewd in others. Many of the actions we find here recur regularly in betrothal and marriage stories—the journey to another land, the meeting at the well, and the negotiations over the marriage concluded by a meal (Alter, 1981: 52). We find twists and turns that make this story distinctive, but no dramatic divine interventions. The characters in this story find God in the ordinary, conventional events.

Genealogy of Abraham 25:1-6

Abraham took another wife, Keturah. This marriage issues in six sons, two of whom the text follows into the third and fourth generation— Midian and Jokshan. The names we can identify appear to be Semitic groups engaged in trades and commerce throughout the area.

With 25:5-6 the text shifts away from a strict genealogy to talk about Abraham's relationship to his *children*. Abraham gave them gifts and sent them out. They were not Isaac. To Isaac, Abraham gave *all*. The genealogy protects the "promisedness" of Isaac while affirming that others belong in the family. *[Reading Genealogies, p. 326.]*

Report of Abraham's Death and Burial 25:7-11

The report of Abraham's death emphasizes that he died in peace: long life, gray hair, satisfied, *gathered to his people* (v. 8). The text does not recall the turmoil of his life pilgrimage, but only the satisfaction at the end of life. Isaac and Ishmael appear together at the death of their father. The tradition has no need to protect the primacy of Isaac in the burial of Abraham, but immediately thereafter separation reasserts itself.

God blesses Isaac. *[Promise in the Family Stories, p. 325.]* Ishmael disappears from the narratives.

Postscript: Ishmael 25:12-18

Although the narratives do not follow Ishmael's story, his branch of the family does have a history, as this postscript reminds us. Even if Ishmael's story is lost to the biblical tradition, this genealogy knows that his is not an insignificant people, but princes and tribes living in farm villages and encampments protected by stone walls. The final phrase (v. 18b) is a tribal saying found also in Genesis 16:12. This saying captures the conflictual character of the pilgrimage of the Ishmael branch of the Abraham family. The Ishmael tradition, by which the Islamic Arab community traces its parentage to Abraham, brings that conflict to our very day.

THE TEXT IN BIBLICAL CONTEXT

We will meet again, at the end of the Joseph novella, the final or testamentary activities of an ancestor of our faith (Gen. 48—50). This moment in the life pilgrimage of a biblical character often proves to be the central moment for the faith community. At the conclusion of life the central task is to pass on the tradition. The heritage can be passed on by words, by the institution of ritual, or by actions which ensure continuity between the past and the future.

In the testamentary activities of Joseph we will find words and ritual of blessing (so also Isaac, Gen. 27). The remembered final activities of Moses are given to us in the form of a sermon delivered to the community ready to enter into the Promised Land (Deut.). Samuel also delivers a speech portrayed as a testamentary sermon (1 Sam. 12). In the flow of the present Samuel narrative that sermon proves not to be his final testament; but in it, Samuel connects the past with the future in his anointing of David (1 Sam. 16). David too gives his choice of a successor as his last act (1 Kings 1). Samuel and David have to choose who, among those competing to carry the tradition, will be chosen. Abraham, similarly acts to ensure that Isaac will carry the tradition into the future. In no case does the testamentary action of the parent guarantee that the future will be untroubled. But Abraham, Joseph, Moses, Samuel, and David at the end of their lives act to make the future possible. They cannot control what is done with that heritage.

The New Testament too knows about testamentary activities. Zechariah, like his Hebrew ancestor Joseph, pronounces blessing on his son in his final days. But the center of the New Testament lies in the testamentary activities of Jesus preserved in what we know as the "Passion narrative." By words and ritual at a final meal, Jesus prepares his disciples for the future, connecting the church inseparably with his life and death. By words from the cross preserved in the narrative, Jesus opens life to a thief who had no future and to a mother about to lose her son.

But the gospel narratives do not end Jesus' testamentary activities on the cross. He continues to make way for the future after the cross by meeting a woman in the garden, two men on the road to Emmaus, the disciples on the shore of the sea, in a house in a small village, and on a Galilean hilltop.

THE TEXT IN THE LIFE OF THE CHURCH

The theme of the good and faithful servant is deeply a part of the believers church heritage. Almost more than the well-known names of our heritage, we prize the contribution of the servant who quietly works in the community. We cherish the stories of those gentle people, our mothers and fathers, who gave whatever they could in service to heal the broken, to feed the hungry, to make life possible for others. Most of these persons, like the servant of Abraham, remain anonymous. But insofar as we can identify a behavioral center within the Christian faith, that center is service.

Undoubtedly this emphasis on service as the mark of a true Christian is both our strength and our weakness. Out of that emphasis on service have emerged innumerable service agencies in North America and around the world engaged in activities ranging from disaster relief work to international student exchange. On the other hand, we take so much pride in the phrase "good and faithful servant" that we look askance at those people whose Christianity does not issue in such service.

As ones who know the servant from the inside, we can tell also about the "servant's" doubts—the moments when we wish that the story would give us a name, providing a future for us. But the life of the unnamed servant does not end in name recognition. It ends, as we find it in this narrative, with the servant faithfully discharging the assignment and disappearing from the story.

Part 3

The Saga of Jacob

Genesis 25:19 – 36:43

The Saga of Jacob

PREVIEW

The saga of Abraham began with God's word directing Abraham to move from Mesopotamia to a new land (Gen. 12). The story ended with the death first of Sarah, then Abraham. The second major ancestral narrative begins differently, with the birth of Jacob and Esau, and ends with the death first of Jacob's wife Rachel and then of Isaac. Because it concludes with the death of Isaac in parallel with the Abraham saga, one would be justified in designating this the saga of Isaac (von Rad, 1973: 263; Coats, 1983: 177). But in the narrative itself Jacob, not Isaac, functions as the central character. In the next saga (Gen. 37—50) Joseph, not Jacob, occupies that place.

A careful reading of the saga reveals its complexity. Various threads are introduced, dropped, and then picked up again. One motif present from beginning to end is conflict. Conflict in the Isaac family affects almost all possible relationships. The family conflict reaches beyond the immediate family to touch distant relatives and next-door neighbors. Conflict marks even Jacob's relationship with God. Nor does the conclusion of the saga bring a resolution of all the family conflict. Instead continued estrangement, accommodation and partial reconciliation characterize the denouement of the Jacob saga (Coats, 1979: 82-106).

Although most prominent, conflict is not the only motif threading its way through the narrative. The promises which energized the Abraham saga also emerge periodically in this saga (26:3-4; 28:3-4, 13-16; 32:12;

35:11-12). Even more than "promise," the presence or absence of blessing is critical to the Jacob material (Westermann, 1980: 93). Obviously,
the Jacob/Esau story centers in the struggle over blessing. But also the
Laban/Jacob and the Leah/Rachel narratives hinge on the presence or
absence of blessing (30:2, 23, 27). Blessing, the power for a fruitful, prosperous life, complicates all the stories, pitting the less blessed Esau
against the more blessed Jacob, the less fertile Rachel against the more
fertile Leah. Being the more blessed does not ensure one's happiness,
however, as both Jacob and Leah experience. But neither is there any
great pleasure in being the less blessed, as the pilgrimages of Rachel and
Esau demonstrate.

In spite of the complexity of this saga, the narrative displays an
overarching symmetry (called chiamus). *[Charactertistics of Hebrew Narrative, p. 313.]* The saga opens and closes with texts concerning birth,
death, and genealogy (25:19-26; 35:16—36:43). Inside those brackets
we find two narratives which interrupt the basic story line—Isaac in
Gerar (26) and the violation of Dinah (34). The conflict between Jacob
and Esau appears in the next section, moving in from both the beginning
and end of the saga (27 and 33). Chapters 28 and 32 narrate two critical
encounters between Jacob and God. From chapter 29 to 31 stretches
the story of Jacob and Laban. But in the center of that story (29:31—
30:24) lies the conflict between Rachel and Leah. Put in chart form the
overarching symmetry looks like this (cf. also Westermann, 1966: 500;
Brueggemann, 1982: 211-213).

A. Birth and genealogy	25:19-34
B. Digression from the main plot	26
C. Jacob and Esau	27
D. God and Jacob	28
E. Jacob and Laban	29:1-30
F. Rachel and Leah	29:31—30:24
e. Jacob and Laban	30:25—31:55
d. God and Jacob	32
c. Jacob and Esau	33
b. Digression from the main plot	34
a. Birth, death, and genealogy	35

It might be possible to press the details of this symmetry much
farther (Fishbane 40-62). But the narrative will not be tightly pushed into
any schema. Other directions are also at work in the narrative, suggesting different outlines to the material. For example, one could organize
an outline of the saga by following the notes about journeys of the family
(Westermann, 1980: 76, 85-86, 93). These notations appear mostly in

the seams between the conflict stories. Most discussions treat these notations of journeys made by the family or part of the family as incidental.
Certainly the tense stories of conflict generate the energy in the saga.
But these brief remarks noting that "Isaac went" here or "Jacob left"
there provide a framework for the powerful stories, a framework
rendered invisible if we ignore the journey notations.

If the saga is viewed through these seemingly incidental journey
notes, the reader can observe even more energy in the narrative. The
story has almost no times of rest and quiet. The family is either in conflict
or on the move, and often the two dynamics overlap. The sagas of Abraham and Joseph have moments when the narrative relaxes, but in the
saga of Jacob we find little of that. Even sleep is disturbed, and a night at
a riverbank holds the terror of attack.

Using the journey notes as a way to organize the material, an outline
of the saga would look like this.

OUTLINE

Introduction, 25:19-34

Report of the Family Pilgrimage, 26:1—35:29
    26:1—28:9 Isaac
        Journey to Gerar and Beersheba, 26:1-33
        Conflict in the Family, 26:34—28:9
    28:10—35:29   Jacob
        Journey to Haran and back, 28:10—33:20
          Encounter on the way, 28:10-22
          Sojourn in Haran, 29:1—31:55
          On the Way Back, 32:1—33:20
        Conflict with Shechem, 34:1-31
        Concluding Journeys, 35:1-29

Conclusion, 36:1-43

By looking at these two different outlines, one using literary chiasm
and the second following the transitional journey notes, we can see the
complexity of this literary masterpiece. No single reading can do it justice, no single interpretation will prove exhaustive. It is hoped the commentary that follows will provide an avenue by which each reader can
enter the saga of Jacob and personally experience the pilgrimage of this .
family in conflict. A more detailed outline of each unit will appear as the
unit is discussed below.

Introduction to the Jacob Saga

PREVIEW

The saga of Jacob begins with the "generation" formula *('eleh toledot)* (v. 19a) that we have found marking the transition between other significant units in Genesis (e.g., 5:1; 10:1; 11:27). The formula is not always translated the same depending on whether narrative or genealogical list follows immediately thereafter. In this case only a brief genealogical note (25:19b-20) follows the generations formula, then the text moves into narrative introducing the saga. This narrative introduction consists of two episodes: a narrative about the birth of Esau and Jacob (vv. 21-26) and an anecdote concerning the inheritance right of the firstborn, Esau (25:27-34). *[Characteristics of Hebrew Narrative, p. 313.]*

OUTLINE

Superscription, 25:19a

Genealogical Note, 25:19b-20

Birth Narrative, 25:21-26
  25:21   Conception
  25:22-23 Pregnancy
  25:24-26a Birth
  25:26b   Genealogical Note

Anecdote of Conflict, 25:27-34
  25:27-28 Exposition
  25:29-34 Incident

EXPLANATORY NOTES
Jacob's Birth and Youth 25:21-34
25:21-26 Birth Narrative

This is the story of a generation born in conflict. Nevertheless, this "third generation" exists because of God's response to Isaac's intercession. For like Sarah, Rebekah, the "right" woman, finds herself barren (Gen. 24). But this saga is unlike the Sarah and Abraham saga in that Rebekah's barrenness does not become a dominant motif. Instead, the narrator tells us quite simply that Isaac petitioned God concerning Rebekah's infertility: God answered and Rebekah conceived (v. 21). Barrenness in this text becomes the occasion not for anxiety, but for the affirmation of God's presence in the genesis of the next generation.

Anxiety arises in this generation, not from barrenness, but from conflict. The conflict goes back as far as the mother's womb. In this introductory narrative, Rebekah carries not only the next generation but the anxiety that accompanies it. She cries out in words which in the Hebrew text are nearly incoherent, as illustrated by the wide variation in the different translations (v. 22a). Rebekah's lament contains at least the question, "Why me?" (cf. NIV) and perhaps even a wish to die (cf. RSV).

Out of this anguish Rebekah "goes to seek" a response from God (v. 22b). This language normally invokes a picture of a journey to a sanctuary and a standard ritual through which an answer is obtained from God. The narrative tells us nothing about the ritual, but only reports the answer in the poetic form of a divine oracle.

The oracle itself is ambiguous (v. 23). The first two poetic lines speak of division, separation moving beyond the family to larger political entities. The oracle expects a power struggle in which the younger shall be the stronger and the elder end up as servant. The horizon of the oracle extends beyond this particular saga, relating perhaps to the time when Edom was a vassal to David's Israel (2 Sam. 8:14). Several times the text blurs the distinction between the family rivalry, Jacob/Esau, and the national conflict, Israel/Edom. This blessing reminds us that no level of social organization is immune from conflict and division, domination and subordination. Conflict at one level in a society affects all other levels.

But how is God related to the "destiny" as announced by the oracle? The oracle does not offer an explanation which would allow the construction of a doctrine concerning destiny. The first thing to note is that the oracle is stated in the passive—such and such will happen, not in the active—God will do. Second, we find an oracle which does not in its detail check with the events of the immediate Jacob and Esau story.

At most the text affirms that the matter of destiny is not resolved automatically by social custom or law, as for example by primogeniture (i.e., order of birth). God's world offers more surprises than custom usually allows. In addition, this oracle affirms God's presence as the future happens even when that future includes division and domination. The exact role of God cannot be decided beforehand.

The birth report itself (vv. 24-26) establishes the two boys as twins, then promptly seeks to distinguish between the two. Esau is not here equated with Edom, but the red, 'adomoni, anticipates that equation later on (25:30). The word red/ruddy when used to describe a male in the Bible refers to one who is quite handsome, e.g., David (1 Sam. 16:12; 17:42, cf. Song of Sol. 5:10). The hair, se'ar, relates to the name Esau, 'esaw, although that equation is not very close. The closer equation with hairy is to Seir, one name for the Edomite region (Gen. 32:3).

The narrative describes Jacob not in terms of physical feature, but action. He was born with his hand hanging on to his brother's heel, so the narrative relates his name to the Hebrew word for heel, 'ageb. Although this wordplay functions within the narrative, it does not likely represent the philological origin of the name. Later Esau relates Jacob's name to the verb form of the word ('aqab), which means to cheat or defraud. The descriptions seem to poke fun at both boys: one as a hairy monster and the other one hanging on to his brother's heel. It seems wise not to press the details of the description much further than the humorous description of two newborn babies.

25:27-34 Anecdote of Conflict

The introduction carries the struggle between the two brothers further with an anecdote. The narration which introduces the incident observes that the conflict extends beyond the two boys to the whole family. The twins are described quite differently: Esau became a hunter, a man of the field; Jacob preferred life in the tents (v. 27). Jacob is called tam, which may mean mild-mannered, perhaps reticent, or even naive (cf. similar use of the noun in 2 Sam. 15:11). Isaac loved Esau, who liked the taste of wild game. Rebekah loved Jacob for reasons not stated (v. 28). The division darkly forecast in the birth oracle (v. 23) has begun to affect even unexpected parts of the community: brothers going two different directions, father aligned with one, mother with the other.

The incident itself finds Esau desperate for food and water, as the Hebrew word ('ayep) indicates. He asks Jacob for some of the red stuff, "red, red," the Hebrew words say (v. 30). The narrative emphasizes the critical nature of Esau's situation by having him repeat what the narrator has told us: Esau was desperate for something to drink. Jacob responds by asking for Esau's birthright, his special place as the firstborn son (v. 31). Esau immediately agrees, declaring that he would lose it anyway if he died for lack of water. Jacob still will not give him anything to eat or drink. He wants an oath from Esau and gets it (v. 33). The narrative then closes quickly with a staccato of verbs: *Esau . . . ate . . . drank . . . rose . . . went* (v. 34).

The narrator concludes with a statement seemingly critical of Esau: *Thus Esau despised his birthright* (v. 34). Perhaps Esau took too lightly his place in the family. That statement may balance a narrative which in all ways shows Jacob to be a problem. It would be an understatement to call Jacob an "opportunist." He saw his brother in need, critical need, and took advantage of the situation. Esau himself calls that "fraud" (27:36). The offer of hospitality extended by Abraham to three strangers (Gen. 18) and even by Lot (Gen. 19), Jacob refuses to his own brother! Instead, Jacob uses his brother's need for hospitality as an opportunity to extort from him first place in the family.

THE TEXT IN BIBLICAL CONTEXT

Much of the biblical drama serves to illustrate the proverb repeated in the New Testament: *Many that are first will be last, and the last first* (Matt. 19:30). This proverb often functions as an affirmation of eventual justice, as in Matthew. It brings hope to those who are presently oppressed. In God's realm there will be no such oppression. God's order will invert what now is and those who have never been invited to a feast will have the first places at the messianic banquet.

But the familiar proverb about inversion does not always describe future justice. In the election theology of Deuteronomy, Israel has been elected first even though she was the least, not primarily in the interest of justice, but because of God's love and faithfulness to the promises (Deut. 7:6-8). Sometimes the inversion can be explained in other ways, such as to keep the wise or the righteous from boasting of their own achievements: *Let the one who boasts, boast of the Lord* (1 Cor. 1:31).

Luther suggests that the inversion of the customary in this anecdote comes according to the plan of God. Esau was at fault for selling his birthright, according to Luther. Jacob did no wrong because he cannot be faulted for buying something that already belonged to him by divine right *(Luther's Commentary,* II: 67; so also Calvin, *Commentary,* II: 54-55). The narrator in Genesis neither absolves Esau of all responsibility, nor claims that Esau deserved to lose his birthright. Nor does the text claim that the birthright belonged to Jacob by divine right. The Genesis text only says that God announced the inversion (25:23).

Neither fairness, divine promise, nor pedagogical purpose adequately explains this inversion of the place of the firstborn—only the surprising openness that characterizes God's world. Cain, Esau, and Job felt themselves victimized by the surprise factor in God's world. But without that openness there could be only justice, obedience, and instruction, no grace through God's most unexpected surprise—the man from Nazareth.

THE TEXT IN THE LIFE OF THE CHURCH

The narrative signals immediately that the characters in this saga cannot be separated into good people and evil people. Both Jacob and Esau acted in ways that were sometimes worthy of praise and other times blame. Esau's entitlement as firstborn in the family was taken from him not because of his own sin, but by his opportunistic brother and the surprising inversion of custom which happens occasionally in God's world. And yet Esau was not only an innocent victim. He did not take sufficient care of his birthright.

Jacob did not offer hospitality to his brother, but used his brother's need to extort the family inheritance from Esau. And yet the saga will later tell us that with all his faults, Jacob was chosen by God to carry the ancestral promise into the third generation.

We find in Isaac and Rebekah the same mixture of behavior. They were specially chosen by God for each other and as bearers of the promise (Gen. 17—18; 21; 24). And yet as parents Rebekah and Isaac formed alliances with different children, coalitions that would prove destructive to the family.

We wish at times for a simple world in which the good people are chosen to carry God's blessing and the evil people are destroyed, either by God or human agents of God's wrath. But the nonviolent witness in the faith community is predicated in part on a very realistic understanding of human nature. There are no good people and evil people. If we look for the opportunist Jacob and the careless Esau, we find they are us. The only separation between people that we can see clearly is between those who know themselves in need of God's forgiveness and those who do not. For those who know their own sin the gospel offers forgiveness. For those who do not, the gospel presents both a challenge and the intercessory words of Jesus: *Father, forgive them; for they know not what they do* (Luke 23:34).

Genesis 26:1-33

Isaac's Journey to Gerar and Beersheba

PREVIEW

No way of organizing the Jacob saga enables every piece to fit easily. To make a new unit with each itinerary note would split apart material which according to other signals in the text ought to be treated as a whole. This unit contains several notes about a journey of Isaac which takes him and at least Rebekah first to Gerar and then by steps to Beersheba. To separate this unit into individual movements, treating each separately, would disregard elements that hold the entire unit together. Isaac and Abimelech function as the main characters in the whole narrative, moving through conflict to a covenant of accommodation. The unit is bracketed by two appearances of God to Isaac, each with words of promise grounded in God's relationship with Abraham (vv. 2-5, 24). [Promise in the Family Stories, p. 325.] God's blessing of Isaac announced in those divine oracles provides one of the sources of tension between the two main characters, Isaac and Abimelech.

The tale of Isaac in Gerar relates for the third time a story in which the ancestral mother—this time Rebekah—nearly becomes a part of a foreign household. As in Genesis 12:10-20 and 20:1-18, the ancestral family here lives in a foreign land. In order to protect himself from presumed danger, the father (Abraham or Isaac) tries to pass his wife off as his sister. The foreign ruler thereupon has the option of taking the beautiful foreigner as his wife. However, the ruler is stopped from making that a permanent arrangement either by divine intervention or by circumstances.

Having now arrived at the third of these danger stories, we should note in a little more detail their similarities and differences (see Koch: 11-131; and Polzin: 81-98). Two of the stories concern Abraham and Sarah (Gen. 12; 20) and one Isaac and Rebekah (Gen. 26). In one the foreign ruler is the Pharaoh in Egypt (Gen. 12) and in two the king of the "Philistines" (Gen. 20; 26). In two stories the family's move to a foreign land comes in response to famine (Gen. 12; 26). In the other the journey happens without reason stated (Gen. 20). In two stories, divine intervention stops the marriage between Sarah/Rebekah and the foreign ruler (Gen. 12; 20) and in one (Gen. 26) the ruler chooses to protect Rebekah when he learns by chance that she is married. The tale in Genesis 12 could presumably allow the relationship between Sarah and Pharaoh to be consummated before the divine intervention strikes. In Genesis 20 the intervention of God comes in a dream before the relationship between the king and Sarah is completed. In Genesis 26 Rebekah does not even get to the king's house before Abimelech happens on the information that stops his decision to marry Rebekah.

How then are we to understand the relationship between the three? We cannot be completely sure. Some suggest they represent a historical report of three different incidents (Kidner, 1967). That conjecture emphasizes the differences between the three at the expense of the similarities. Others suggest there may have been one story, the other two representing literary variations of that one story (Van Seters, 1983). That concentrates on the similarities of the three stories and assumes a literary process of rewriting. It seems reasonable at least to assume that the tale evolved as it was passed on in oral and perhaps even written form. Rather than concentrating on the origin, the present faith community might more fruitfully explore why the Hebrew community chose to pass on to us this tale about the ancestral fathers and mothers. What are we to hear in this oft-repeated tale of danger to the ancestral mother? At least we can say that this story serves to illustrate that the divine promise was carried in earthen vessels.

OUTLINE

Introduction, 26:1a

Report of Isaac's Journey, 26:1b-33
    26:1b-16 To Gerar
        Itinerary Note, 26:1b

Theophany and Result, 26:2-6
Confrontation with Abimelech, 26:7-11
Conclusion, 26:12-16

26:17-22 To the "Valley" of Gerar
Itinerary Note, 26:17
Well Etiologies, 26:18-22
Wells of Abraham, 26:18
Esek, 26:19-21
Rehoboth, 26:22

26:23-33 To Beersheba
Itinerary Note, 26:23
Theophany and Result, 26:24-25
Concluding Confrontation, 26:26-33

EXPLANATORY NOTES

Report of Isaac's Journey to Gerar 26:1-16

The introduction to this tale (v. 1) explicitly relates it to the first tale of danger to the ancestral mother in the Abraham saga (Gen. 12). In the semiarid land of Palestine, famine is an ever-present danger. Famine plays a role in each of the ancestral sagas; it is a key element in the whole Joseph saga which follows.

26:2-6 Theophany

We will find it characteristic of this saga, more than the sagas of Abraham and Joseph, that God appears to a person "on the way," moving from one place to another (28:10-17; 32:1-2, 22-32). Here God appears to Isaac, giving first instructions (26:2-3a) and then a promise (vv. 3b-5). The instructions, stated negatively, then positively, direct Isaac not to go to Egypt, but to stay/sojourn in *this land*. In terms of the flow of the story this instruction has the effect of keeping Isaac in a very dry land, perhaps quite as dry as the one the famine had forced him to leave (von Rad, 1973: 270). Be that as it may, the oracle stops Isaac from going to Egypt, the traditional land of food in times of Palestinian drought (Gen. 12; 42). This speech also passes on to the Isaac generation the promises which had energized the Abraham saga. In fact this speech includes nearly the whole range of promises which appear in the ancestral stories: promise of presence, blessing and land, promise of multiplication of descendants, and blessing on all nations through this family. The only promise missing is the specific promise of a son so central to the Abraham and Sarah story. The covenant oath with Abraham (v. 3) and Abraham's obedient response (v. 5) become the ground for the extension of the promises into the second generation.

The promises of God do not play as prominent a role in this narrative (Gen. 25—36) as they did in the Abraham saga. In addition, our familiarity with the story may cause us to overlook the importance of the next generation inheriting the promises that gave meaning to their "parents' " life. Nothing in the promises assumes that they are transferrable. But by God's word, supported by Abraham's obedience, these promises are transferred. It remains to be seen what the heirs of the promise will do with their heritage.

26:7-11 Confrontation with Abimelech

In this narrative, famine has forced Isaac into a foreign territory. Fear, engendered by the unknown, strikes Isaac. He does not know how he will be received, and he fears the worst. This tale is unlike the other two tales about danger to the ancestral mother (Gen. 12; 20) in that Isaac does not ask Rebekah to claim to be his sister. He says it himself, straightaway, when asked about "his wife." The narrative does not tell us much of what Isaac imagined might happen, only that Rebekah was beautiful and that Isaac presumed the men of the place would *kill* him *on account* of his wife. The reticence of the narrator to say more allows the reader to imagine along with Isaac (v. 7).

Abimelech, by chance observation, sees Isaac "playing" with Rebekah in a way that tells him the two are not brother and sister (v. 8). The word "playing" (a form of *sahaq)* is the same one used in the Abraham saga as a play on Isaac's name (21:6). Here the word has a sexual connotation, which it does also in Genesis 39:14, 19 (cf. Exod. 32:6 and perhaps Judg. 16:25). In angry words, Abimelech demands an explanation (v. 9). Isaac does not say much except that he thought he might die *on account of* Rebekah. Abimelech does not respond directly to Isaac's defense but tells Isaac that his action has placed the people of Gerar in serious danger. Warning his people in the strongest terms to leave Isaac and Rebekah alone, Abimelech drops the matter (v. 11).

26:12-16 Conclusion in Gerar

The narrative in Gerar concludes by describing the result of God's blessing on Isaac (vv. 12-14). Here the blessing of God brings Isaac wealth and prosperity. But blessing also brings the envy of those around him. The man who came as a refugee from famine has prospered so much as to generate the envy of his neighbors (vv. 14-15). This part of the tale ends with a complete reversal. Isaac, the refugee who feared the men of that place, has become Isaac, the blessed, whose strength now occasions his expulsion (v. 16). Abimelech, who in a previous speech sought to protect Isaac and Rebekah from being harmed by his people, now directs Isaac to leave so as to protect the people of Gerar!

Isaac's Journey to the Valley of Gerar 26:17-22

Following Abimelech's speech deporting him, Isaac moves to what is usually translated the *valley of Gerar*. In the arid Negev, we should not think of a green valley. The Hebrew uses the word *naḥal*, a dry streambed called a "wadi." With Isaac "dwelling" in that wadi (v. 17), the narrative turns to the problem of water. Maintaining its cross-reference to the Abraham saga (so also 26:1, 15), the text remarks almost parenthetically that Isaac reopened and named the wells Abraham had dug. The story then turns to the discovery of a new well (v. 19), a well of "living water" *(mayim ḥayyim)*. This presumably refers to flowing water, perhaps an artesian well, as differentiated from the stagnant pond that might exist in a dry streambed.

Not surprisingly, this new well creates a water crisis in the arid land (v. 20). So Isaac's family digs a new well, which also becomes the object of dispute with the herdsmen and/or farmers of the region (v. 21). Moving further on, they dig a third well, which they are allowed to maintain for themselves. These short notations of conflict remind us that contention over scarce natural resources is an age-old problem.

Most of us would want Isaac to fight for his rights to the water. However, the narrative pictures Isaac as not fighting for his wells, but moving on and digging others. We have seen the contrasts which jar this story—Isaac, the bearer of God's promises/Isaac, the fearful one/Isaac, the famine refugee/Isaac, the wealthy sojourner. Now we find Isaac, deported because he was "too powerful" to live among the people of Gerar, quietly moving on when confronted by the same people. The weak one becomes strong but Isaac chooses not to use that strength to fight.

Isaac's Journey to Beersheba 26:23-33

The final stop in Isaac's journey brings him to Beersheba (v. 23). As the journey began with an appearance of God (theophany) (26:2-5), so it concludes in the same way. The oracle in 26:24 contains many of the elements of the previous oracle (26:2-5) but in an abbreviated form: promise of presence, blessing, multiplication of offspring, grounded in God's relationship with Abraham. *[Promise in the Family Stories, p. 325, and Blessing in Genesis, p. 312.]* The function of the speeches in the unit may be more important than the details of the content, all of which is traditional promise material. By serving as "bookends" at the beginning and end of Isaac's journey, the speeches keep the unit expressly theological. These bookends affirm God's presence in Isaac's pilgrimage, even with no dramatic divine intervention along the way.

The confrontation between Abimelech and Isaac in 26:26-31 begins, as did the first one, with an accusing question (26:9). This time Isaac asks the question: *Why have you come to me?* (v. 27). Isaac's visitors state what the narrator has told us: Isaac is blessed by God. They want a covenant that ensures their safety from the now powerful Isaac. The reversal from Isaac as the famine refugee to Isaac as the powerful blessed one has affected the whole of his world.

What the well disputes implied about Isaac's use of his wealth and power now comes to the surface in Abimelech's request for a covenant (vv. 28-29). Isaac does not respond to the request with direct speech. Instead, he acts, extending them hospitality, exchanging oaths with them and sending them away in peace *(šalom)* (26:30-31).

At that moment another well is discovered, a new water supply. Beersheba, they name that well. The Hebrew *be'er* means "well." The Hebrew consonants *šb'* can form several Hebrew words. The story of the naming of Beersheba in the Abraham saga (21:30) plays off the Hebrew word "seven" *(šeba')* and "swearing an oath" *(šaba')*. The number seven does not play a role in this story, but "oath" does. The word *šaba'*, "satisfied/plenty," is also built on the same three Hebrew consonants. That word also has an important role in this tale. It balances the word with which the story began, *ra'ab*, famine.

The unit has moved from famine (26:1) to a well of plenty (26:33); from fear that the men of Gerar would kill Isaac (26:7) to making a feast for all (26:30); from conflict and confrontation to peace. One cannot say that the conclusion of the story is idyllic. The covenant with Abimelech is a nonaggression pact, not a reconciliation (Coats, 1983: 194). We will not find idyllic endings in the Jacob saga. Nevertheless, an ending characterized by hospitality and peace, an oath of mutual nonaggression and a well of plenty constitutes a moment of relaxation in a narrative which otherwise knows mostly anger and anguish, confrontation and conflict.

THE TEXT IN BIBLICAL CONTEXT

Luther remarks about Isaac's lying about his wife: "I certainly cannot excuse the patriarchs, as some do, nor do I want to excuse them" *(Genesis, II: 80)*. Instead, he takes comfort from the missteps of his ancestors in the faith: "There are in Christ's kingdom those who at times are strong and then again weak." Certainly all in the Jacob saga show themselves at times strong and then again weak. The remainder of Israel's story finds the faith carried by people who do not provide untarnished models of faithfulness. The New Testament knows that the followers of Jesus exhibit the same ebb and flow of faithfulness. Luther's observations rightly remind us that such missteps then and now should provide the community an occasion to celebrate God's forgiving faithfulness rather than be overcome with self-guilt or destroyed by condemning anger.

The weak moment of Isaac in the narrative makes itself quite visible to the reader. The strong moment of Isaac may be so quiet as to be overlooked or even mistaken for weakness. Even though strong, Isaac chose to move on rather than fight for the right to control water. Even though wronged, Isaac chose to sign a nonaggression agreement with the one who had deported him. In a similar use of power, the one from Nazareth, even though it was to mean his death, *set his face to go to Jerusalem* (Luke 9:51).

THE TEXT IN THE LIFE OF THE CHURCH

We have noted that this tale delights in contrasts: famine to plenty, weak to strong, conflict to accommodation. In his final confrontation with Isaac, Abimelech states twice that the blessing of Yahweh accounts for the contrasts in the story (26:28-29). Certainly in this narrative the quiet working of God's blessing on Isaac is the hidden factor which cannot be controlled by Abimelech nor destroyed by Isaac's problematic behavior. To Isaac, God's blessing brings wealth and power, water and prosperity, all very material fruits of blessing. Here material wealth and divine blessing are not at odds (Brueggemann, 1982: 222-224).

Many of us come from a tradition that is very well aware of the problems attendant on a simple equation of divine blessing and material wealth. The biblical tradition also knows that wealth is dangerous and cannot be used as an easy measure of divine favor (Mark 10:25; Jer. 5:26-29; 9:23; 17:11; Ezek. 22:12-13; Prov. 11:1-8, 28 among others). On the other hand, this tale about the blessing of Isaac reminds us that we can fall prey to the equally simplistic equation of wealth and sin. We often wonder if it is possible for those who have riches to enter the kingdom of God (Mark 10:23-27). The tradition, by preserving texts in which divine blessing brings wealth and others in which wealth becomes a stumbling block (Mark 10:17-22), at the very least prevents any oversimplifications about divine blessing and material prosperity. Those of us who are reasonably prosperous and are aware of the spiritual danger of material wealth must not forget that from the very beginning, Genesis witnesses to God's blessing on *all* humanity, a blessing that envisions a satisifed, prosperous, and peaceful world (Gen. 1).

Genesis 26:34 – 28:9

Conflict in the Family

PREVIEW

This story tells about conflict in the family which divides parents from children and children from one another, and which even aligns the husband and wife against each other. Given the destiny of this family as heirs of God's promise, the crisis in the family is not only sociological but theological. The reader must wonder, not only whether the family can survive, but what will happen to God's promises. Those promises in the Abraham and Sarah saga survived the prolonged sterility of the ancestral mother and a threat from God's own command, but now the future of the promises may be squandered by a family wrecked by jealousy, deception, and power struggle.

This tale cannot be reduced to one disruptive incident with a single offending person. Families are more complicated than that, and this one is no exception. We find here two different stories of strife in the family merged into one narrative. The familiar one pits Rebekah and Jacob against Esau and Isaac in a struggle to control the family inheritance (27:1-45). The other conflict, less familiar, involves the question of suitable wives for Esau and Jacob and puts especially Rebekah at odds with Esau and his wives (26:34-35; 27:46—28:9). Whatever the history of the tale, in the received text these two stories have been woven to-

181

gether, creating very complicated dynamics resolved only by family separation.

Perhaps no tale better illustrates the central role of dialogue in Hebrew narrative than this tale of strife in Isaac's family (Alter, 1981: 63-87). *[Characteristics of Hebrew Narrative, p. 313.]* The central part of the story, the report of blessing (27:1-40), consists of four scenes, each of which involves dialogue between members of the family. Following those tension-filled conversations, Jacob is dispatched to the family's Mesopotamian homeland (27:41—28:5). Again dialogue between the principal characters carries the narrative action. The narration about Esau's marriages brackets the tale of family strife and serves to complicate the story still further (26:34-35; 28:6-9).

OUTLINE

Prologue: Esau's Marriage, 26:34-35

Report of Blessing, 27:1-40
     27:1-4   Scene 1: Isaac and Esau
     27:5-17   Scene 2: Rebekah and Jacob
     27:18-29 Scene 3: Jacob and Isaac
     27:30-40 Scene 4: Esau and Isaac

Denouement, 27:41—28:5

Epilogue: Esau's Marriage, 28:6-9

EXPLANATORY NOTES

Conflict in the Family 26:34—28:9

26:34-35 Prologue: Esau's Marriage

The tale of strife begins with a brief remark concerning Esau's marriage to native women, but women who were outside the family. These marriages caused a bitter spirit *(morat ruaḥ)* to prevail for Isaac and Rebekah (v. 35). The narrative does not tell us why this was so: either because of the action of the wives or perhaps simply because Esau married "out of the family" (Gen. 24). This prologue to the major conflict of the tale aligns Isaac and Rebekah against Esau, a different alignment than the later conflict will provide. Nevertheless, the process has begun whereby Esau becomes a marginal member of the family, a status sealed by the epilogue (28:6-7).

Report of Blessing 27:1-40

27:1-4 Scene 1: Isaac and Esau

The first scene in the report of the blessing centers in a dialogue between Isaac and Esau. Both an introductory sentence (v. 1a) and Isaac's speech (v. 2) set this scene at the deathbed of Isaac, even though the saga does not report his death until Genesis 35:29.

The scene contains several of the literary elements that will bond the whole tale together. The five senses constitute one motif running throughout. The sense of sight and taste first play a role in the drama. Later the senses of touch (27:12, 22), sound (27:22), and smell (27:27) move to the foreground.

The key word in the narrative is *blessing (brk)*. [*Blessing in Genesis, p. 312.*] The Hebrew consonants of *blessing (brk)*, connect this key word with the Hebrew word *birthright (bkrh)*, the key word in the anecdote about conflict between Jacob and Esau (25:27-34) (Fokkelman: 107). Such literary devices, which remain almost invisible in translation, serve to bond various individual parts together for the reader, whether or not the literary elements were designed for that purpose. The question of intent, whether the storytellers and writers who passed this saga along intentionally used those literary devices, is one we cannot answer. It may have happened as a natural part of the art or accidentally as the saga was passed on. Be that as it may, we have inherited beautiful Hebrew narrative. [*Characteristics of Hebrew Narrative, p. 313.*]

This opening scene assumes the blessing of the elder son by the father as a common part of the final activities of the elderly head of the family. The blessing, along with the right of birth of the elder son, makes that son the primary carrier of the family heritage. Of course this involves material wealth, but more is involved than just property. The elder son becomes the head of the family, the one who carries the family tradition: defining the family's understanding of itself, speaking for the family, and carrying out the family's life direction. Theologically, for this family it also meant being the bearer of God's promises into the next generation. Isaac, then, prepares to pass on life to his son in quite a normal fashion. But that normal process stands in tension with the divine oracle which accompanied Rebekah's pregnancy (25:23) and the incident in which Jacob extorted the birthright from Esau (25:29-34).

27:5-17 Scene 2: Rebekah and Jacob

Scene 2 introduces a direct complication to the normal process of Isaac's blessing his older son. Rebekah conspires to have that blessing go to Jacob. In the dialogue between Rebekah and Jacob (v. 6-13), the mother lays out her plan to deceive Isaac. Jacob objects, not, as the reader might expect, to the fact of deception, but to the plan—he fears that the deception might not work: he might end up cursed instead of blessed (vv. 11-12). Rebekah dismisses his worry, agreeing to accept on herself any negative consequence. Now we have a different alignment in the family than we found in the prologue to this unit (26:34-35). There Isaac and Rebekah were together against Esau. Here we find the acting out of coalitions which the narrator gave us in the saga's introduction: Isaac and Esau; Rebekah and Jacob (25:28).

Rebekah takes the initiative to direct events away from their natural course. This redirection will take the family toward the end anticipated by the divine oracle which attended Rebekah's pregnancy (25:23). This leaves the readers caught between the divine oracle, which expected the younger to be the dominant son, and the devious maneuvering of the mother and younger son to accomplish that fact. Nowhere does the faith tradition excuse deception of the blind and deaf (Lev. 19:14; Deut. 27:18; von Rad, 1973: 277). Nevertheless, the narrative proceeds without evaluating the actions of the family. The story tells itself, creating its own drama and ambiguity.

27:18-29 Scene 3: Jacob and Isaac

This scene focuses on the dialogue between Isaac and his son; but which son? It is a complicated dialogue in which Isaac twice blesses the son standing before him (vv. 23, 27). Perhaps some of its complicated character can be traced to changes that came about as this story was passed on in different locales and through many generations. But, however it happened, the final dialogue creates an intense encounter in which Isaac cannot figure out and also cannot quite trust what he is told. Jacob, in turn, faces the danger that his father will discover the truth. The peril of that danger ebbs and flows throughout the encounter. It looks as if the danger has passed with the statement in verse 23 that Isaac had blessed the son before him, only to erupt again with the father's next speech: *Are you really my son Esau?* (v. 24).

In his speeches in the dialogue, Isaac constantly seeks to unravel the mystery standing before him. Precluded by age from using sight, he tries to take in the data provided by sound and touch, smell and taste. The results are confusing. The food tastes like the foods he enjoys with Esau. Touch pictures for him the hair-covered body of his older son. The odor of the garments reflects the life of his hunting and herding son. Only sound gave cause to wonder. The words declared the son to be Esau, but the sound was that of Jacob. How can he be sure? Isaac's inquiry prompts Jacob to reiterate in all ways the deception he and Rebekah have arranged. Occasionally the dialogue requires Jacob to invent explanations quickly. The most intriguing of these comes in response to Isaac's wondering how the food could have been prepared so quickly after his request. Jacob replies, "Yahweh, your God, brought about my success" (v. 20). With that, Jacob has pulled God into the deception, dramatically using the divine name. Yet the divine oracle at Rebekah's pregnancy (25:23) expects the primacy of Jacob which this scheme intends to produce. Perhaps hidden amidst the deception and exploitation, God has worked in ways beyond the provision of a quick and tasty meal for a dying father.

It is a kiss that finally convinces the blind man and completes the betrayal (v. 27). The blessing pronounced by Isaac announces, first, fertility for the fields, and second, political prominence (vv. 28-29). The third element in the blessing makes the success of others dependent on their relationship to Jacob. With that blessing, the scene abruptly closes. [Blessing in Genesis, p. 312.]

27:30-40 Scene 4: Esau and Isaac

Immediately, according to the narrative, Esau arrives at Isaac's side. The narrator makes the reader anticipate that a slightly earlier arrival would have changed the end of the tale (v. 30). The dialogue between father and older son reaches deep into the rage, despair, and grief that comes when a future has been irretrievably lost to the scheming deception of others. Esau begins offering his father the requested food (note that with Jacob much the same dialogue occurs but in different order, 27:18-19). Isaac asks the question debated in Scene 3: Who are you? (v. 32). Hearing his son's response, Isaac shakes uncontrollably and asks a question which needs no answer: Whom did I bless before you? (v. 33).

Esau needs no further explanation either, but dissolves into a plea for blessing (v. 34). Denied that blessing, Esau in subsequent speeches, expresses the whole range of emotion: anger at Jacob, despair for his own future, a tearful but tenacious appeal for some kind of blessing (vv. 34, 36, 38). The range and intensity of the emotions gripping the two men can best be appreciated by rereading the dialogue closely.

Finally Esau is blessed or is sent away with a "nonblessing." The Hebrew words are ambiguous. The poetry can be read to grant Esau fertility of the fields, much the same blessing that Jacob received (see the footnote to v. 39 in RSV and NASB). But more often Esau's blessing is interpreted as a nonblessing: he shall live away from the fertile fields. The ambiguity of Esau's future continues as the *blessing* defines his political destiny: his future shall be one of conflict. He shall be subordinate to his brother—but not always (v. 40). This *blessing* can appropriately be heard in connection with the historical relationship between Israel and its Transjordanian neighbor, Edom, a relationship of conflict and shifting dominance. But in the context of this narrative, Esau's *blessing* serves notice to readers that some elements of this family's future remain unclear in spite of the success of the Rebekah-Jacob coalition. *[Blessing in Genesis, p. 312.]*

27:41 – 28:5 Denouement

The immediate consequence of Rebekah and Jacob's victory is Esau's hatred. Esau determines to kill his brother after his father's death, a death which is expected soon (v. 41). At this point in the tale Rebekah reenters the drama in much the same role she had before. She has access to information from unknown sources about Esau's intention to kill Jacob. Rebekah's speech again "instructs" Jacob, this time to flee from the household to live with his uncle in Mesopotamia (v. 45).

Rebekah does not stop with instructing Jacob. She goes also to Isaac. Here the story picks up a thread which has been absent since the prologue: the disappointment of both parents that Esau married native women rather than family members (26:35). In connection with that parental dispute with Esau, Rebekah's speech follows naturally (v. 46). She states her problem with bringing outsiders into the family in such a way as to prompt Isaac to send Jacob to Mesopotamia to find a wife from among the family (38:1-5). Many interpreters feel that a separate tale circulated that blamed Esau's intermarriage for the strife and division in the family. Now, however, that has been woven in as a subplot of the conflict over the paternal blessing. Whatever the material's history may be, in the present narrative Rebekah's prompting of Isaac takes on conspiratorial overtones. She uses the issue of Esau's marriages to effect the rescue of Jacob from danger. By having Isaac *send* Jacob away, Rebekah gives her favorite son's departure a cover of legitimacy.

Isaac does send out Jacob and in the sending speech pronounces over him the "family blessing" from the Abraham saga (28:3-4). The speech contains a blessing, including family and land. The language of this promise speech differs from most of the others, but the effect is to confer on Jacob the right and responsibility to carry the promise tradition which the whole ancestral story proclaims as this family's mission and destiny (von Rad, 1973: 282). Jacob has now moved to the prominent position in the family by his own exploitation, his mother's conspiracy and his father's pronouncement. He, not his older brother, will be the heir of the family, the one who carries on the faith heritage.

28:6-9 Epilogue: Esau's Marriage

In the prologue (26:33-34) Esau's marriages with local women, those outside the "family," set him at odds with his parents. The loss of his place as the blessed older son further pushed Esau to the edge of the family. Thus the epilogue begins with Esau sitting on the very edge of the family, perhaps not physically, but relationally. The narrator gives us Esau's rehearsal of the concluding events: Isaac's blessing of Jacob, sending Jacob to find a wife, Isaac's valuing marriage "in the family." In response to his parents' values, Esau marries again, this time "in the family," not his mother's family, but his father's. Esau marries a daughter of Ishmael, Abraham's "other" son, Esau's uncle.

Esau's marriage relates most directly to the public conflict over a suitable wife (26:33-34; 27:46—28:5) rather than the stolen blessing. Nevertheless, in the context of the whole story, the epilogue portrays Esau as a marginalized family member who deeply wanted to belong. He had been the son his father loved best. Now he had almost no place in the family. Seeing that his marriages had displeased Isaac, Esau acted. Perhaps he could marry back into the family. However, Esau married the daughter of Ishmael, who was as marginal as he. The narrative ends on that note, leaving Esau's relationship to the family unresolved.

THE TEXT IN BIBLICAL CONTEXT

The prophet Jeremiah, when describing the collapse of the community, uses language and pictures related to Jacob's stealing of the blessing:

> Beware of your friends;
>   do not trust your brothers.
> For every brother is a deceiver,
>   and every friend a slanderer. (Jer. 9:4, NIV)

That translation hides the word "Jacob" which the Hebrew text of Jeremiah contains in the next to the last line of the poetry. The line could also be translated: "For every brother is (like) Jacob."

As the faith community has worked with this story in the Jacob saga, it has struggled to understand the relationship between the deception by Rebekah and Jacob and God's choice of Jacob as the promise bearer. Some have suggested that perhaps Esau's surrender of the right of firstborn made Jacob the firstborn and his actions acceptable (Hershon:

163). Luther supposed that Rebekah's tenacious clinging to God's plan for the primacy of Jacob at least partly excused her actions (Commentary on Genesis, II: 108). But most have to concede, as Calvin did, that "seeking the blessing by fraud . . . was contrary to faith" (Commentary on the Books of Genesis, II: 88-89). We must answer for ourselves how God's way and Rebekah and Jacob's fraud fit together.

Our desire to make the way of God fit our understanding of divine intention may cause us to lay this story aside or try, as some of our predecessors did, to force it to "make sense." But the way of God simply will not be explained (Brueggemann, 1982: 235). God can choose a nondescript Near Eastern people to be the agent of blessing to all humanity. God's way can create a messianic line out of a king (David) convicted of adultery and murder. The way can follow an obscure Galilean to his death on a Roman cross.

THE TEXT IN THE LIFE OF THE CHURCH

No narrative in the Hebrew Bible makes itself more available as a study in family dynamics than does this tale. The more we watch closely what happens in family life, the more this narrative comes alive. The role of each person in this story merits discussion, but let us look briefly at Esau and Rebekah, the two characters less prominent than Jacob and Isaac in the whole sweep of the ancestral sagas.

Esau marries local women—Hittite, the text calls them. Abraham had taken steps to avoid such a marriage for Isaac, but the story gives us no reason to suspect that Esau acted out of rebellion or disobedience. He acted and found out later that his action contradicted the values held by his parents. Later he tried to correct and restore the family relationships by marrying a suitable woman. Throughout, this narrative portrays Esau sympathetically, even if he is pictured as an unusual-looking character. His actions, his reactions, his behavior, his feelings suit the situation: obedient when asked, hurt when wronged, angered when violated. Still he could do nothing to better his situation. Esau was the family member always "beside the point" (Brueggemann, 1982: 234) and yet oddly important to the family. Because of him some family values were clarified. All the family defined themselves as not Esau. He played the part of the one not chosen to carry the family heritage, seemingly bypassed even by God. The story does not assume he deserved this destiny. Must someone be "beside the point" in God's family or in ours?

Rebekah directs the action in this drama. Her speeches always prompt action, action congruent with what she wants. She never asks for information. She has the data—data others do not have and do not realize she possesses. The narrative is reticent in showing us Rebekah, and yet when she acts the family changes dramatically. She never speaks to Esau and he loses at every step. She always acts for Jacob. The reader senses a drivenness in her speeches to Jacob, an impatience in her instruction. With her husband, Isaac, she displays a private and public split. She is covertly aligned against him and Esau. However, when she addresses Isaac directly she appeals to their shared values and works to split him away from Esau. The portrayal of Rebekah is perhaps the least sympathetic of all. And yet where is God's way in the drama? Does God's way triumph because of the action of this powerful woman? Is the congruence between God's way and Rebekah's way merely coincidental? Finally, one would have to say that Rebekah, like Esau, paid a heavy price for her role in the family. In the course of the Jacob saga, she was never to see her beloved son again.

Genesis 28:10-22

Jacob's Encounter on the Journey Toward Haran

PREVIEW

The saga turns now to follow Jacob to the family's homeland in Mesopotamia and back. Jacob's Mesopotamian journey is bracketed by two encounters with God. On the way to Mesopotamia, God confronts Jacob at Bethel, on the journey back, at the river Jabbok (32:22-32). These two texts then form a literary transition between Jacob's conflict with Esau (Gen. 27 and 33) and his stay with Laban (Gen. 29—31). But beyond the literary function, these two "appearances" weave a theological thread into the narrative of Jacob's journey (28:10—35:22). Jacob must now reckon with the divine presence, however absent that God appears to be.

This encounter at Bethel is related not only to Genesis 32, but chapter 35, where God also appears to Jacob at Bethel. These two Bethel theophanies continue the thread of God's promise throughout the narrative. Historically they seem to point to Bethel as a prominent sanctuary from Israel's earliest times. This encounter between Jacob and God is cast in the form of a dream.

OUTLINE
Introduction, 28:10-11

Report of a Dream, 28:12-15
    28:12   Vision
    28:13-15 Audition
        Self-Introduction, 28:13a
        Promise, 28:13b-15
            Land, 28:13b
            Descendants, 28:14a
            Blessing to All, 28:14b
            Presence, 28:15

Report of Jacob's Response, 28:16-22
    28:16-17 Sayings
    28:18-19 Naming of Bethel
    28:20-22 Vow

EXPLANATORY NOTES

Jacob's Encounter on the Journey to Haran 28:10-22

Some key words which we will want to watch throughout this narrative appear straightaway in the introduction (vv. 10-11). Jacob arrived at "the place," or *a certain place (hammaqom)*. He took *one of the stones (*'eben)* to use a pillow. We start with a nameless place and an ordinary rock. Nevertheless, the way those two elements are introduced to the reader signals that *the place* and *the stones* may not be or remain as ordinary as they look at first. The narrative creates a feeling of anticipation in the introduction of these ordinary things.

Report of a Dream 28:12-15

Jacob dreamed, and suddenly, a stairway was set up on the earth, and the top of it reached to heaven. The reader senses more surprise and excitement in the Hebrew text than translations often convey. A dream generates the unexpected and unusual. This dream is no exception. "Suddenly God's messengers (angels) are going up and down" the stairs (v. 12). The Hebrew word "pathway" or "stairway" *(sullam)* suggests a stairway or path which connects the divine and human realms.

Then just as suddenly, God appears and speaks. As we expect of dreams, the action does not move in a smooth sequence, but irregularly jumps about. The jump to God's sudden self-introduction immediately ties this dream to Jacob's heritage (28:13). Indeed the speech gives to Jacob the heritage of promise which his ancestors had carried. These promises had enabled an infertile woman (Sarah) to bear a child (Gen. 21), a homeless refugee (Isaac) to grow strong and wealthy (Gen. 26), and one connected with the promise bearing ancestor (Lot) to be rescued from disaster (Gen. 19). The emphasis in this divine oracle of promise falls on the promise of presence (v. 15). The promise of presence or aid was also included in the oracle to the traveling Isaac (26:3, 24). However, here this very ancient blessing on the traveler appears in expanded form (Westermann, 1980: 140-143). While incorporating Jacob into the line of promise bearers, the most prominent promise in this narrative touches the fear and desire of a sojourner—divine presence, protection, and homecoming (Brueggemann, 1982: 245-246). *[Promises in the Family Stories, p. 325.]*

Jacob's Response 28:16-22

Immediately, Jacob awakens. The surprised dreamer's words are reported as traditional sayings, phrases that have become prominent in the worship language of the church (vv. 16-17). Perhaps the story's sayings were part of the liturgy of Israel's worship. But in the context of this narrative the words become expressions of Jacob's surprise when he experiences the presence of God in a place that appeared quite ordinary. These sayings pick up a key word which we noted in the introduction—*place. A certain place* is now experienced as God's *place,* "the house of God" *(beth-el).* The unexpected dream has transformed the common unnamed place into the sacred place named Bethel.

Jacob's words pick up the key word *place* and his actions pick up the second key word *stone* (v. 18). The same transformation which *the place* underwent has also changed one of the *stones.* The common stone has become a sacred pillar *(maṣṣebah).* Such sacred stones marked local sanctuaries throughout the ancient Near East, those of the Canaanites as well as the Hebrews. The *pillars* association with Canaanite religion made them an anathema especially in Deuteronomy (Deut. 12:3).

With the erection of the stone, Jacob's resting spot has been transformed from an ordinary place with stones for pillows to a "house of God" with a sacred pillar. The naming of the place as "house of God" (Bethel) seems almost parenthetical, even redundant. It likely represents expansion of the story as it was passed on, growth which can be observed elsewhere in the narrative (Vawter, 1977: 314-316).

Jacob concludes with a vow. In the vow he asks for what God had promised—provision for the traveler's needs: presence, protection, and homecoming (vv. 20-21). The vow reorients Jacob's journey. The journey had originated as flight to avoid assassination and a trip to find a wife suitable to his parents. Now, however, Jacob's journey becomes a pilgrimage with theological content. He goes to the same place for much the same purpose, but now he travels as a carrier of God's promises and with divine assurance of aid. In turn, accompanied by God's "traveling mercies," Jacob has committed himself to living with Yahweh as his God (vv. 21). To be sure, the character of God's promise and of Jacob's vow finds the Lord's commitment to Jacob unconditional, while Jacob says, *If* (v. 20). But the promise and the vow transform Jacob's journey as surely as an encounter with God changes a stony place into a sanctuary.

THE TEXT IN BIBLICAL CONTEXT

The Bible tells other stories about wayfarers who unexpectedly happen onto a sacred place and/or an encounter with God. The narrative of the liberation of Israel from Egypt begins with such a surprise encounter (Exod. 3). Moses, while "keeping" the flocks of his father-in-law, unexpectedly walked near an unusual shrub. That "bush" turned out to be a sanctuary. That encounter at the "mountain of God" changed the context of Moses' flight from Egypt, as Jacob's encounter at the "house of God" reshaped his flight from home.

The story of Elijah describes his flight from home to avoid persecution (1 Kings 19). He sat down under a tree, desiring to die. Unexpectedly an angel approached and directed him on a journey that would bring him to the mountain of God, where he too would encounter God (1 Kings 19:4-8). As with Jacob and Moses, this unexpected encounter transformed the way Elijah understood his world.

We should note the connection between these unexpected encounters with God and sanctuaries or sacred space. The meeting of God did not happen just anywhere, but at the mountain of God or the house of God. The biblical tradition, especially the Hebrew Bible, has a deep appreciation for sacred space. To a large degree, the surprise for Jacob and Moses was that the place they had come upon was sacred space. Elijah was directed to the mountain of God. That is not to say that in ancient Israel God could only meet a person at a shrine, but sacred *place* was crucial. A sanctuary carried the trembling expectation that God would appear there, as had happened to the ancestors. Therefore, after his dream Jacob could say, God *is in this place; and I did not know it. . . . This is none other than the house of God.* (28:16-17).

The New Testament certainly appears less conscious of sacred space than the Old Testament. But we need to be careful about saying that the New Testament declares the faith to be anti-sacred space. The central role of the temple in the Gospels, as for example, in the narrative of the "cleansing of temple" (Mark 11:15-18 and parallels) and the importance of Jerusalem even in pictures of the end (Rev. 21) warn us not to push the two Testaments too far apart on the importance of sacred space to the faith. God can appear at any place, but some space brings with it a history and an anticipation because, recognized or not, it *is none other than the house of God.*

THE TEXT IN THE LIFE OF THE CHURCH

At Bethel, Jacob's journey was transformed from a flight to avoid Esau's wrath and an errand to find a suitable wife, to the pilgrimage of one who bore God's promise. The reason for the journey remained unchanged, but through this dream the trip itself was dramatically "converted."

In much of the Christian community we think of conversion as a change in the character of the individual. While that remains an important way for us to talk about conversion, it is not clear that the ancient world had a notion of "character" similar to ours, as an inner core of a person that can be changed. Frequently "conversion" in the biblical tradition involved an encounter with God in which the group and/or individual received a different way to look at life. The person was changed in receiving a new context for life, but the change could not be described in terms of psychological transformation or behavioral change.

Neither the dream at Bethel nor the wrestling with God (Gen. 32) is the story of Jacob's character change. Jacob remains a "fighter," prone to conflict and adept at making the situation work for his benefit. But he now lives as one who carries God's promise. His life now opens up as a part of God's drama involving not only Jacob, not just his family, but all the families of the earth (28:14).

Many have interpreted Paul's conversion as a change in his character. But we need to look again at the narrative. Paul is a new person because he receives a new religious context for his life: *he is a chosen instrument of mine to carry my name before the Gentiles. . . .* (Acts 9:15). Paul's life has become a part of God's drama, which extends beyond his "family" to the Gentiles as well as the sons of Israel (Snyder, 1976: 738-739). Paul, like Jacob, may not behave differently. Paul remains opinionated and obstinate, as Jacob continues to manipulate situations, but their lives are not the same. They are a new creation.

Genesis 29:1 – 31:55

Jacob's Sojourn in Haran

PREVIEW

This short story concerning Jacob's sojourn in Haran narrates a second major conflict in the family. The characters in this drama include Jacob, Laban, Rachel, and Leah. Like the previous story (26:34—28:9), the narrative describes a developing siutation, one that aligns various persons at different times with and against one another.

The major conflict pits Jacob against Laban. Normally Rachel aligns herself with Jacob, but the two of them also bump up against each other. The other significant conflict finds Rachel against Leah. But the two sisters also stand together with Jacob against Laban.

This narrative has the characteristics of a short story or novella. Although set in the midst of a longer saga, this novella can be read on its own. We find no reference to the reason for Jacob's arrival in Haran, neither the strife with Esau nor the errand to find a suitable bride. The story opens with Jacob's arrival at a community well (29:2) and closes with the separation of Jacob and Laban (31:55).

The outline of this short story displays some of the symmetry or chiasmus that we have noted in the saga as a whole (Brueggemann, 1982: 249). [Characteristics of Hebrew Narrative, p. 313.] Like the story of Jacob's sojourn in Haran, the narrative begins with his arrival

(29:2-14). While conflict is the dominant motif of the short story, it is not present when Jacob arrives. Laban and Jacob then negotiate wages for the sojourner's work while there (29:15-20). That appears amiable, but a major eruption occurs in the fulfillment of their agreement (29:21-30). The novella leaves the relationship between Jacob and Laban to list the birth of Jacob's children by Leah and Rachel (29:31—30:24). What we find there is not just a listing, however. Woven in with the list is narrative concerning the conflict between Rachel and Leah. At the end of this center section, that dispute is dropped and the Laban/Jacob conflict is picked up again. Again we find the two of them negotiating Jacob's wages with another complication as the agreement is worked out (30:25-43). Finally, Jacob determines to leave (31:1-55). While the first meeting between the two was peaceful and joy-filled, the last meeting becomes confrontational and angry.

The unit can be outlined with Jacob's arrival and departure bracketing two agreements concerning wages between Jacob and Laban and a central section listing the birth of the offspring.

OUTLINE

Jacob's Arrival in Haran, 29:1-14
    29:1-3   Exposition
    29:4-14 Greetings
        Shepherds, 29:4-8
        Rachel, 29:9-12
        Laban, 29:13-14

An Agreement Concerning Wages, 29:15-30
    29:15-19 Negotiations
    29:20-30 Transaction—Conflict

The Birth of Offspring, 29:31—30:24
    29:31-35 To Leah
    30:1-8   To Bilhah-Rachel
    30:9-13   To Zilpah-Leah
    30:14-21 To Leah
    30:22-24 To Rachel

An Agreement Concerning Wages, 30:25-43
    30:25-34 Negotiations
    30:35-43 Transaction—Conflict

EXPLANATORY NOTES

Jacob's Arrival in Haran 29:1-14

This scene does not explicitly present itself as a betrothal scene. Nevertheless, readers familiar with such scenes in Hebrew narrative (e.g., Gen. 24) will know that more happens here than simply the arrival of a sojourner who is related to one of the shepherds of the area. On the surface the narrative reads simply as the arrival of a traveler. Jacob first speaks with the shepherds gathered at the well, learning that he has arrived at his mother's home community (vv. 4-6). In a subsequent exchange, Jacob undertakes to instruct the shepherds about how they are to go about their business (v. 7). They object, either implying that they need the strength of all the shepherds to lift the stone or that the custom of that place requires waiting until all shepherds are gathered before uncovering the well (v. 8).

At that moment another shepherd arrives, Rachel. Jacob walks up to the stone, rolls it away by himself, and draws water for her flocks (v. 10). The drawing of water by Jacob may involve heroic strength (Coats, 1983: 213) and hence function as a normal part of a betrothal scene. The stranger who greets the woman at the well and draws water for her flock initiates a bond between them (Williams, 1980: 109). In Genesis 24:16-23 and John 4:7-15 the pattern is reversed with the woman drawing the water for the stranger. Thereafter, Jacob goes to Rachel, greets her with a kiss and tears. Here Jacob introduces himself to what the reader might expect is a startled and perplexed Rachel (v. 12). Her response, however, follows the script of a betrothal scene. She runs and tells her father. All this is narrated for us in descriptive fashion.

In the third and final greeting upon Jacob's arrival, Laban takes the initiative away from the visitor. Laban extends Jacob hospitality and exuberantly declares solidarity with his guest: "You are my own flesh and bones!" (cf. Gen. 2:23 and 2 Sam. 5:1). This first scene ends on this note of complete harmony.

An Agreement Concerning Wages 29:15-30

Given the betrothal elements in the opening scene, one should expect negotiations concerning Jacob's marriage to Rachel. But the scene does not begin like that. Instead, Laban talks about how much he will pay Jacob to work for him. Jacob, as anticipated, is more interested in getting permission to marry Rachel than accumulating money. He proposes to work for seven years for no wage other than the privilege of marrying Rachel (v. 18). Jacob's offer was extremely generous from the monetary standpoint, but analogy from present-day practice among African tribal groups warns us against quickly describing this as paying money for Rachel. Within those groups, such practice is understood as ingratiating oneself with the family to win their permission for the marriage. From the outside, it may look like a pure business transaction. Rachel and Leah will use business language to describe how they understood it (31:15). But we need to be aware that filtering ancient Near East contract language through our own sense of how marriages should happen may not provide the best interpretation of marriage in the ancient Near East. While Laban agrees that this marriage is preferable to any other and invites Jacob to stay (v. 19), we must notice that Laban did not explicitly agree to give Rachel to Jacob after seven years.

The narrator tells the reader that Jacob's love of Rachel blinds him to time, work, and, as we shall see, the custom of his uncle's country (v. 26). After the agreed-upon time, Jacob asks permission to marry Rachel and the household prepares for a wedding. Laban invites all the men of the community to a premarriage feast. The feast is called a *misteh* from the Hebrew word *satah*, "to drink." We are probably to understand that following the feast Jacob was not in complete control of his faculties (Coats, 1983: 214).

Whatever the reason, Jacob did not recognize that Leah, not his beloved Rachel, shared his marriage bed. The Hebrew text uses language of surprise similar to that found in Jacob's dream: *In the morning, behold, it was Leah* (v. 25). Jacob had married the wrong woman! Jacob's three accusatory questions express his outrage at Laban. Laban defends himself by appeal to custom: a family does not give a younger daughter in marriage before her older sisters. Laban offers Rachel in marriage also, in return for more work after the second marriage. The scene ends quickly with Jacob trapped between his love for Rachel and his anger at his uncle/father-in-law; he agrees to the terms, marries Rachel, and then works for Laban (v. 30).

The harmony and solidarity between Jacob and Laban with which the narrative began has been irretrievably shattered by Laban's action, even if that action conformed to custom. The same fracture occurred between Jacob and Esau with the deception of Isaac by Rebekah and Jacob (27:1-45). Indeed the location of this tale of deception next to the earlier one generates some other possible parallels (Fishbane: 55). Not only does the deceiver become the deceived, but at issue in both is the right of the firstborn. Again Jacob tried to upset the birth order. This time it did not work. In both stories the deception creates victims. In the deception of Isaac everyone ended up victimized in one way or another, but none more than Esau. In this narrative it will be the same. All suffer the consequences, but Leah must hurt most—Jacob . . . *loved Rachel more than Leah* (v. 30).

The Birth of Offspring 29:31 – 30:24

The section functions as the center of the short story. While it lists the sons of Jacob, it does so in the context of a narrative of struggle, conflict, and suffering. For the first time in this Jacob and Laban novella, the narrator mentions God's direct intervention, and it concerns the matter of fertility. Seeing that Leah was "hated," God made her fertile, but Rachel remained barren. This section opens with a tense situation in which God is said to be a direct participant.

Two elements more than any other define a fulfilled life in this story: love and fertility. One finds here the beautiful Rachel, beloved, but barren, and the "ordinary" Leah, unloved but fertile. One has a situation in which each woman has part of life, but neither is fulfilled. Both long for the part of life they have been denied.

Leah expresses her longing in the meanings ascribed to the names she gives her sons. Reuben—"Perhaps now my husband will love me"; Simeon—"Yahweh heard that I am hated"; Levi—"Maybe now my husband will be joined to me"; Judah—*This time I will praise the Lord* (29:32-34). Each name can have several meanings, but Leah gives them an interpretation which traces her pilgrimage of pain, the pain of being the unloved, even hated. In the names the reader can feel the agony. Finally, with the last son, Leah turns away from her husband. She will not receive that for which she yearns most—love.

The second list of sons expresses Rachel's agony (30:1-8). She has the love her sister seeks but no child. In anguish Rachel demands from Jacob that which her life lacks (v. 1). Jacob strikes back, putting husband and wife at odds for the only time in the novella. In desperation, Rachel settles on the same process of adoption that Sarah had used when she was barren (Gen. 16). Rachel gives her personal attendant, Bilhah, to

Jacob as a surrogate wife. The children born from that union belong to Rachel. The names Rachel gives the sons again function to express her feelings. The names tell a story of anger and conflict, of hardness and determination: Dan—*God has judged me . . . and given me a son;* Naphtili—*I have wrestled . . . and prevailed.* The Hebrew text leaves unclear whether she wrestled "mightily" with her sister or with God and her sister (v. 8).

Leah's next move shows that she has not capitulated (30:9-13). She gives her maid to Jacob as a surrogate wife. The interpretation she gives to the sons born of this union express joy: Gad—"good fortune"; Asher—*Happy am I.* But the context of these names provides an element of pathos. She has six sons but still not the love of her husband.

Leah's next response shows love as still her deepest desire (vv. 14-16). Reuben brings to her "mandrakes," perhaps a fruit of the mandragoda, supposed to have a magical power to bring fertility (Westermann, 1985: 475). Immediately Rachel wants those—the key to what she lacks. Leah agrees to sell them to Rachel in return for what she wants—time with Jacob. Rachel agrees. Leah then meets Jacob coming from the field with words which match the anguish of Rachel's *Give me children, or I shall die* (30:1): "Come to me, for I have bought your services" (v. 16). The speeches of Rachel and Leah to Jacob in this unit express the human toll taken by the situation—loved and barren; unloved and fertile.

Leah named the son of this purchase Issacher—"God has given me my hire" (v. 18). Another son Leah named Zebulun—*now my husband will honor me, because I have borne him six sons* (v. 20, RSV, NIV). The word Leah uses—*zbl*—in unclear. It might mean "honor," "respect," or perhaps "accept." Whatever exactly she wants from Jacob, that does not come. Perhaps there exists a note of giving up in the report of the birth of a daughter, Dinah. The birth is reported in very formal listing style, without interpretation or comment (v. 21).

At the very end the narrator again reports God's intervention: *God remembered Rachel* (v. 22). God's remembering brings relief from the storm (Gen. 8:1), rescue from danger (Gen. 19:29), deliverance from oppression (Exod. 2:24), and here restoration of fertility. God, not the magical herb, changes Rachel's situation. Rachel has a son, but is it enough? She names the son Joseph—*May the Lord add to me another son!* (v. 24). On that note the unit ends with the sisters still at odds and their lives still not complete. Together they make a complete life (Cohen: 339-342), but they are not one. The narrative drops their conflict without reconciliation or resolution.

An Agreement Concerning Wages 30:25-43

The novella hurries back to Jacob and Laban and the question of Jacob's wages. But everything has changed from the first agreement (29:15-19). A long dialogue ensues between Laban and Jacob (vv. 25-34). Jacob wants to leave. Laban wants Jacob to stay (vv. 27-28). Whatever else has happened during his nephew's sojourn with him, Laban has become wealthy and acknowledges Jacob as the agent of that blessing. So Laban invites Jacob to set his own wages.

Jacob agrees that he has been the cause of his uncle's good fortune (vv. 29-30)! His speech sets Laban up for a hefty settlement (v. 31a). Then Jacob makes an odd request. He asks for the animals that are not normal. The usual is white sheep and dark/black goats, although animals with odd coloring happen often. Difficulties with the Hebrew text makes it impossible to sort out the exact terms of the agreement, as the variations in the translations indicate. Clearly Jacob asked for all the animals with abnormal coloring. Jacob declares that the color of the animals will prove his loyalty (ṣedeqah, RSV: honesty). Laban quickly agrees (v. 34).

But the relationship between Jacob and Laban has not been characterized by loyalty. It has become a story of conflict, and manipulation. Immediately the two men begin to adapt the agreement toward their own best interests (vv. 35-43). Trouble with the Hebrew text again prevents us from knowing exactly what happened. In spite of most translations the text does not seem to support the interpretation that Laban separated the various colored animals with the intention of stealing the ones that the wage agreement assigned to his nephew. The future multicolored animals were to be Jacob's wages, not the existing ones. Hence, Laban himself made the separation of the animals. He then put great distance between the two flocks (vv. 35-36), so that Jacob could not increase his wages from some of the already existing multicolored animals or by easily breeding new varicolored sheep and goats (Fokkelman: 149).

Jacob, however, will use magic to best his uncle. The narrative, unbroken by any speeches, describes Jacob's action with very determined Hebrew prose. Through his program of breeding, Jacob emerges with many strong multicolored animals, leaving Laban with a few weak solid-colored animals. The previous agreement left Jacob with two wives: one beautiful one and one with "weak eyes." He did not want the weak-eyed one. This agreement makes Jacob rich with large and beautiful flocks (v. 43), providing Laban with a few weak goats.

Deception follows this family: Jacob, who deceived his father and was deceived by his uncle, now deceives the one who deceived him. How long will this continue?

Jacob's Departure from Haran 31:1-55

31:1-3 Reasons for Departure

Jacob determines to leave. This unit begins by stating the reasons: (1) Laban's sons are complaining about Jacob's accumulation of wealth at their father's expense. (2) Laban has changed his attitude toward Jacob. The alienation is now as complete as the solidarity had been at Jacob's arrival (29:4). (3) God's word instructs Jacob to return home, promising divine aid. [Promises in the Family Stories, p. 325.]

31:4-16 Preparations

Genesis 31:4-13 reports a long speech in which Jacob seeks to persuade Rachel and Leah to go with him on the journey to his home. Jacob presents to his wives an interpretation of the conflict over the last wage and salary agreement that varies considerably from the narrator's report of 30:37-43.

Jacob begins his account with points not in dispute: (1) Laban's attitude has grown antagonistic to Jacob; (2) God has been with Jacob; (3) Jacob has worked hard serving Laban (vv. 5-6). Then Jacob turns to his interpretation of the events: Your father . . . cheated me and changed my wages ten times, but God did not permit him to harm me (v. 7). The narrator has told us nothing about a change in wages following the last agreement, but Jacob explains events as he understands them: Laban has tried to gain the advantage by changing the agreement concerning the newborn animals (vv. 8-9). Jacob asserts that it was not magic that had created the markings on the animals, as the narrator described, but God (vv. 10-12).

Perhaps the variance between the description of the events in the narration (30:37-43) and Jacob's interpretation of those events can be explained by the expansion of the story in its history (Vawter, 1977: 334-335). However, the text as it comes to us presents an interesting picture of the situation. The reader does not need to assume that Jacob was deliberately lying or that all must be harmonized, e.g., Jacob explaining things the narrator left out (Fokkelman: 157-162). By presenting the reader with two versions of the events, the novella invites the listener to become involved in the drama. Most of us have had experience with widely differing interpretations of events which arise in the midst of tension and conflict. Always the parties to the dispute genuinely believe that theirs is the only accurate report, as any mediator to a dispute well knows.

The two women, Rachel and Leah, side with Jacob, but the reason they give is not grounded in the justice of Jacob's case. They have their own grievance against their father (31:14-15). Rachel and Leah declare Laban has treated them as *foreigners (nokriyoth)*. Laban has *sold* them and used up the proceeds. They apparently interpret the marriage arrangement by Laban as "selling," an interpretation consistent with the words used in some ancient Near East marriage agreements. Again, to describe the agreement by which Rachel and Leah were married as "selling," involving a "bridal price," is only one way to interpret those events (Vawter, 1977: 335). Again we find the family embroiled in unending conflict. This time Rachel and Leah unite against their father.

31:17-32 Jacob's Flight

The narrative moves directly to describe Jacob's departure (vv. 17-21). Again Jacob's departure constitutes flight. In a parenthetical comment the narrator reports that Rachel *stole* Laban's "teraphim" (v. 19). We do not know exactly the nature of these objects. They can be understood in different ways. But one can say here they seem to be religious heirlooms (Vawter, 1977: 339). In addition, Jacob "stole the heart" of Laban by running away in secret (v. 20). The translations "deceived" and *outwitted* (NASB, NIV, RSV) lose the parallelism between Rachel's and Jacob's theft. To "steal the heart" can mean "to deceive," but elsewhere it involves taking away a person's ability to discern and act appropriately (2 Sam. 15:6; 1 Kings 12:27; H. W. Wolff, 1974: 48, 53). The narrative describes Jacob's secret departure as a further irritation in the ongoing feud; certainly it does not contribute to the resolution of the feud.

31:22-24 Pursuit by Laban

The departure enrages Laban, and the narrative builds toward another confrontation. The mounting tension is interrupted by the report of Laban's dream (v. 24). The divine speech contains an element of ambiguity in English: "Be careful lest you speak with (or "do to") Jacob good or evil." This seems to be an idiomatic expression warning Laban not to use force against Jacob (von Rad, 1973: 308).

31:25-54 Confrontation

As has become common in their relationship, the wronged party opens the dispute with a series of accusatory questions (vv. 26-28, cf. 29:25; 31:36). Laban's basic accusation charges Jacob with "stealing his heart" ("cheat," RSV; "deceive," NASB, NIV). This charge repeats the narrative statement at Jacob's departure (31:20). Laban details the charge: Laban did not have a chance to say farewell to his daughters (vv. 26-28). Jacob's stealth violated the process of parting, a process essential to the family. Only at the end of the accusatory speech does Laban mention the stolen goods (v. 30).

Jacob does not deny the charge but defends himself by explaining his motive: fear (v. 31). But Jacob's response heats up over the issue of the stolen religious heirlooms. The main focus of Laban's accusation is lost when Jacob takes up the matter of the stolen heirlooms. He seizes the offensive, declaring himself and all his household innocent. Jacob even takes an oath vowing death to the one caught with the stolen goods.

Laban follows Jacob's redirection of the dispute and sets about in search of his belongings. Again narrative tension mounts as Laban enters Rachel's tent (v. 33). The narrator tells the reader that Rachel is sitting on the stolen heirlooms. When he approaches, Rachel tells her father that menstruation requires her to stay where she is. Laban leaves without finding his religious heirlooms (v. 35).

Now Jacob feels justified in using the form of the accusatory question (v. 36). Clearly alienation and antagonism are the primary problem. What they argue about—stolen hearts, religious heirlooms, false accusations—is secondary to the battle itself. Jacob has won this time. He celebrates his victory by a long speech describing himself as innocent and wronged—preserved only by divine protection. Again Jacob includes matters not mentioned earlier in the novella. Jacob declares that he absorbed any losses to Laban's flocks and that he constantly suffered from insomnia and inclement weather (vv. 39-40).

Laban has little room to maneuver: he cannot find his stolen goods and God's intervention has warned him against using force. In short, clipped sentences Laban declares that even though everything belongs to him, he cannot do anything about it (v. 43). So Laban proposes a covenant between the two of them (v. 44). Without comment Jacob begins arranging stones. The story began with stones—the stone at Bethel (28:10-22) and the stone covering the well (29:2-10) and it will end with stones.

The covenant between Jacob and Laban is not a covenant of reconciliation but a treaty of nonaggression (vv. 48-53). [Covenant, p. 315.] They agree not to cross over the stone boundary line to harm each other (v. 52). Jacob agrees not to mistreat Laban's daughters or to take other wives so as to diminish the importance of Leah and Rachel. The Hebrew text concerning the naming of the spot is difficult (vv. 47-49), perhaps owing to different names used for this boundary marker in the tradition. The treaty described here likely had a place in the ongoing relationship between Israel and its Aramean neighbors. This covenant has continued to have a place in the liturgical language of the faith community as the Mizpah benediction:

> May the Lord watch between you and me,
> While we are absent, one from another.
> (31:49, translation mine)

However, the worship use of this benediction seldom remembers the unreconciled antagonism between Jacob and Laban which characterizes its biblical context.

THE TEXT IN BIBLICAL CONTEXT

Much of the action in this story follows a natural flow from act to consequence. Deceit brings anger and retribution. These in turn produce more deceit and anger. The novella becomes a real-life illustration of an unending cycle of violation. Even God is drawn into the cycle, granting fertility to Leah because "Leah was hated" (29:31). No one acts to interrupt the cycle on his or her own. Always the characters act on the basis of real or perceived wrongs done to them. It is a tragic story of escalating anger with no one to change the course of events, save God's intervention telling Jacob to leave (31:3) and Laban not to use force (31:24). Whatever the precise meaning of the enigmatic speech by God to Laban (31:24), it has the effect of redirecting the course of events. The speech prevents Laban from acting out the atmosphere of hostility which had developed in the narrative. So Laban proposes to resolve the crisis by covenant. This covenant would allow the two of them to walk toward a future in which they would act differently toward each other even if they continued to feel hostile and wary.

The covenant broke down the dividing wall of hostility (Eph. 2:14) at the level of behavior, if not at the level of feeling. In this story it is Laban who finally acts differently, if only out of divine demand. In response to divine instruction, Laban ends up giving Jacob "the last word." Laban starts to defend himself, but turns instead to covenant (31:43-44). [Covenant, p. 315.]

However we are to understand the Gospels' report of Jesus' largely silent demeanor at his trial, Jesus voluntarily gives his accusers the last word, and in the crucifixion it appears that theirs is the last action. But to respond in kind would only continue the cycle of hostility, as the Jacob and Laban story shows. A different future becomes possible in the crucifixion words: *Father, forgive them; for they know not what they do* (Luke 23:34) (cf. Lehmann, 1975: 64-70).

THE TEXT IN THE LIFE OF THE CHURCH

The other persistent conflict in the narrative rages between Leah and Rachel. But with them the cause does not reside in acts of deceit or violation one against the other. Their conflict erupts out of situations over which they have no control. Rachel is loved but barren; Leah, fertile but unloved. They struggle, pleading with God and manipulating their circumstances, to gain the love and fertility needed to fulfill their life. It does not happen. The narrative never tells us that Jacob's attitude toward Leah changed. Although God's remembering grants Rachel one son, when the story closes she remains unsatisfied. According to a subsequent account, Rachel's next birth would take her life. She named her second child *son of my sorrow* (Gen. 35:17-18).

It would be easy to moralize on the story, and to assert that Leah and Rachel should have been satisfied with what they had and not long for what they lacked. But the biblical text does not do that, not for Leah and Rachel, not for Hannah (1 Sam. 1), not for the Hebrew slaves in Egypt (Exod. 2), not for anyone caught in an intolerable life situation. The psalms of Israel's worship are utterly realistic about the suffering of one blocked by circumstances from life, abundant life. Such persons live with reproach, even if only the unintended reproach of one who takes for granted the very blessings of life that the oppressed can only pray for.

To those caught in half a life, the Bible offers not reproach or platitudes but God's remembering. To those longing for love or stagnated by a sterile world, the faith offers not blame or jargon but one who has come that we might have a full life (John 10:10). We might define a full life differently than this narrative, maybe even objecting to its definition of life for a woman: to be loved by a man and have children, especially sons. But, however a full life is defined, the problem remains the same. Some folks, maybe all, will find themselves living in a situation which blocks them from reaching the fullness of life. They know the anguish of Leah and the hostility of Rachel. Ministry, like the Bible, takes that agony utterly seriously even while offering a word of hope.

Genesis 32:1 – 33:20

Jacob on the Way Back

PREVIEW

The narrative has resolved the relationship between Jacob and Laban, not with reconciliation, but with separation and a covenant of nonaggression (31:44-50). Now the saga turns back to the relationship dropped in 27:41-45 with Jacob's flight to his mother's homeland, the conflict between Jacob and Esau. Almost immediately the narrative directs our attention to Jacob standing at the border of "his brother's" territory. Jacob sends a message to *my lord Esau*, asking for acceptance—*favor in your sight* (32:4-5). We cannot forget Esau's last words about Jacob: *I will kill my brother Jacob* (27:41). The narrative has reintroduced tension almost before we can relax from the last problem.

Jacob's return to his own home has two distinct elements blended into a single narrative. Jacob's preparations for meeting with Esau is bracketed by two encounters with the divine. Twice Jacob is met quite unexpectedly by God or God's messengers, 32:1-2 and 32:22-32. Both these encounters interrupt the reunion between Jacob and Esau (32:3-21; 33:1-17). Even though the two encounters with God disrupt the narrative flow and may well have been passed on in the community separate from the saga, their inclusion in the text as we have received it creates a different narrative climate for the reunion between the two brothers.

In Genesis 32 most English translations number the verses differently than the Hebrew Bible. We will follow the English translations in the verse numbers.

207

OUTLINE

Encounter at Mahanaim, 32:1-2

Preparations to Meet Esau, 32:3-21
    32:3-6 Sending Messengers
        Commissioning Speech, 32:3-5
        Messenger's Report, 32:6
    32:7-21 Jacob's Response
        Statement of Fear, 32:7a
        Result, 32:7b-21
            Arranging Family, 32:7b-8
            Petitioning God, 32:9-12
            Selecting a Gift, 32:13-21

Encounter at the Jabbok, 32:22-32
    32:22-23 Introduction
    32:24-29 Confrontation
        Struggle, 32:24-25
        Dialogue, 32:26-29
    32:30-32 Concluding Actions and Notes

Meeting with Esau, 33:1-17
    33:1-3   Action of Jacob
    33:4   Response of Esau
    33:5-11   Presentation
        Of Jacob's Family, 33:5-8
        Of Jacob's Gift, 33:9-11
    33:12-17 Resolution of Conflict
        Dialogue, 33:12-15
        Separation, 33:16-17

Conclusion, 33:18-20

EXPLANATORY NOTES

Encounter at Mahanaim 32:1-2

Genesis 28:10-22 narrates Jacob's encounter with the angels—
messengers of God—as Jacob journeyed to Haran. In 32:1-2 we find a
brief report of a corresponding encounter as the sojourner returns
home. This report is extremely brief and cryptic. In fact the encounter it-

self is told with only four Hebrew words: *God's angels met him.* By themselves the two verses function to explain the name of the sanctuary Mahanaim, as 32:2 shows. However, in the context of the larger narrative of Jacob's return home and meeting with Esau, these two cryptic verses may have a different function. One uses the word "may" advisably. Because the verses are so brief, we risk overinterpreting them, that is, making them carry too much weight.

Nevertheless, these two verses connect with the language and tone of the rest of this unit. The language of this Mahanaim encounter is confrontational, even martial. To say the angels *met* Jacob may translate the Hebrew word *paga'* too mildly. The word often carries the element of surprise, danger, and attack (Amos 5:19; Exod. 5:3; 1 Kings 2:25, 32, 34, 46). Jacob responded to divine encounter at Bethel with language of worship, *This is none other than the house of God* (28:17). However, here he uses military language: *This is God's army,* or perhaps better, "This is God's army camp" (Westermann, 1966: 612, cf. NASB, NIV).

The verses do not tell us what happened in this "meeting." We find no angels on stairs, no divine speeches. Such silence about the setting adds to the tone set by the language—surprise, danger, and conflict. We do not know who is in danger from God's army. Perhaps the episode signals that Jacob goes with God's protection. But the text does not say, and the brevity serves to increase the sense of danger in Jacob's preparations to meet Esau.

Preparations to Meet Esau, 32:3-21

32:3-6 Sending Messengers

Jacob prepares for his meeting with Esau by sending a message asking to be accepted by him, *find favor in your sight* (v. 5). The text casts the "sending" in the very familiar genre used for commissioning messengers and entrusting them with a message. We know this genre best from the prophetic literature in the Bible, but the same way of commissioning messengers was used in the ancient Near East (cf. Exod. 3:14-15; Isa. 37:6). The commissioning formula declared: *Thus you shall say to . . .* or "Go and say to. . . ." The messenger formula announced: "Thus says. . . ." Both formulas are found in Jacob's commissioning speech: *Thus you shall say to my lord Esau: Thus says your servant Jacob* (v. 4).

God's "messengers" had met Jacob unexpectedly (v. 1). Now Jacob sends messengers (v. 3). The same Hebrew word *(mal'ak)* we variously translate "messenger" or "angel." This time we know the message and the report back. However, the report of the messengers can be interpreted variously: *Esau . . . is coming to meet you, and four hundred men with him* (v. 6). Does Esau come with hostile intent? The messenger's words do not say for sure, but Jacob interprets the message that way.

32:7-21 Jacob's Response

Jacob immediately acts on his own interpretation of the messenger's report. First, he arranges his family in a way designed to maximize the possibility that some of them will survive an "attack" by Esau (vv. 7-8). Second, he petitions God for help (vv. 9-12). Jacob grounds his petition in God's previous promise of safe conduct for Jacob (v. 9). This appeal almost makes God responsible for Jacob's current danger. Then Jacob turns around in his prayer declaring that he, Jacob, does not deserve all that God has given him (v. 10). Following the petition in which he expresses his fear of Esau (v. 11), Jacob turns to God's foundational promise of descendants to further bolster his petition. The prayer illustrates the various feelings of one turning to God in time of danger: (1) You promised me, God; (2) I do not deserve your help; (3) I am afraid.

In Jacob's final act of preparation, he selects a gift to placate Esau's anger and perhaps win acceptance. The narrative shows Jacob as frantic, wanting to do everything to avoid the disaster he expects. The last verse seems like an exhausted breath after the frantic activity (v. 21).

Encounter at the Jabbok 32:22-32

But the meeting with Esau is not the next moment in the narrative. A "dark" encounter at the Jabbok River delays that meeting (32:23-24). The word "dark" expresses not only the time of day according to the tale (v. 22), but also the ominous feeling tones of the story. The power of this tale has been discovered by authors both inside and outside the community of faith. The meaning of the story can never be exhausted in one retelling, nor can any commentary hope to do more than point to some of the possibilities.

For the night Jacob arranges to be alone. The narrative emphasizes Jacob's aloneness first by the double introduction (vv. 22-23) and then reinforces it by a statement, "Jacob remained by himself" (v. 24).

32:24-25 Confrontation: Struggle

Suddenly Jacob is not alone but struggling with another figure. A very general word is used for this figure ('is) suggesting mystery, revealing nothing of the figure's identity (Fokkelman: 213). At the end of the narrative Jacob knows that his encounter has been with God. But that comes at the end. In the middle Jacob knows only that he is locked in struggle with someone. Jacob holds his own. According to the narrative, when the figure was not able to defeat Jacob, it struck Jacob in the hip, dislocating it (v. 25).

32:26-29 Confrontation: Dialogue

With the crippling the physical fight ends and the struggle turns to combative dialogue. The figure demands that Jacob let go as dawn approaches. Whether the assailant fears that the dawn would diminish its power or reveal its identity, we are not told. Jacob, for his part, refuses to let go unless he is blessed (32:26). Jacob has never let go until he was blessed. The adversary asks the name of his opponent. *Jacob,* comes the answer. Then the adversary renames Jacob *Israel,* understanding that name as an expression of Jacob's history of successful conflict with everyone, humankind and God (32:28). The origin of the name *Israel* may point in a different direction, e.g., "may El preserve" (Speiser, 1964: 255), but the meaning in this narrative has to do with Jacob's success as a sighter.

Jacob turns the question around, asking the name of his adversary. This speech unexpectedly introduces an element of politeness, almost deference on the part of Jacob/Israel: "Tell me, please, your name" (v. 27). This politeness could perhaps be read sarcastically, but more likely the dialogue has taken a turn. The mysterious figure refuses Jacob/Israel's request for a name, but instead blesses him and apparently departs. [Blessing in Genesis, p. 312.]

32:30-32 Concluding Actions and Notes

The tale then concludes with two etiologies, a place name and a ritual practice associated with the story. Jacob names the place "the face of God," Peniel, because he met God face to face. (Penuel in verse 31 is a slightly different spelling of the same Hebrew word.) The speech expresses the ancient understanding that only under exceptional circumstances can one see God and live.

Also an ancient dietary practice has been tied to this story (v. 32). We have no other biblical reference to this practice. The story ends with daybreak, the dawn of a new day, but one that finds Jacob now Israel and crippled.

The narrative presents so many possibilities that we must be careful not to claim too much for any line of interpretation. The story remains open and defies any attempt to close it by commentary. The text narrates a victory, but it is a "crippling victory" (Brueggemann, 1982: 270). The tale wants us to see that God engaged Jacob, genuinely encountered him. The Jacob saga as a whole seems to imply that combat was the only way to relate to Jacob. Jacob struggled with God, but there is no implication that God's power was thereby diminished. Nor can we say that God "let" Jacob win, to avoid facing the prospect of a relatively impotent God (Calvin, *Genesis*, II: 198). The story form does not encourage that sort of logical dissection. The narrative observes simply that Jacob fought with God. Jacob gave everything he had to the fight and won his way in the relationship. But Jacob did not escape untarnished by the meeting. "There are no untroubled victories with this Holy One" (Brueggemann, 1982: 270). But besides being crippled, Jacob leaves the confrontation blessed, empowered for a new day, however bleak its prospect.

Meeting with Esau 33:1-17

33:1-4 Jacob's Action and Esau's Response

The narrative now turns to Jacob's meeting with Esau. This scene opens with Jacob arranging his family so that if Esau attacks, the ones Jacob loves most will most likely survive (v. 1). Jacob himself goes toward his brother, acting in the traditional manner of the slave before the master, the defeated before the victor (Vawter, 1977: 353). The careful preparations of Jacob for this meeting (32:3-21) would indicate that this was mostly strategy born out of fear.

Esau's response is not what Jacob imagined. Instead of rushing to attack, Esau runs to embrace his brother (v. 4). This greeting, similar to the one which met the "prodigal son" in Jesus' parable (Luke 15:20), happens without comment in this story. Esau's initial action sets the tone for *his* responses in the remainder of the meeting.

33:5-11 Presentation

After presenting his family to Esau, Jacob turns to the gift. Esau asks about the purpose of the "parade" and Jacob responds that it is to win Esau's acceptance (v. 8). Esau refuses any present: *I have enough, my brother* (v. 9). Jacob immediately changes the purpose of the gift. He gives now not to *win* Esau's acceptance, but as thanks for Esau's reception of him. Jacob's speech (vv. 10-11) suddenly transforms the gift from a bribe to an expression of gratitude. Thus *urged*, Esau receives the gift.

33:12-17 Resolution of Conflict

The dialogue leaves the reader wanting to know what was going on inside each brother (vv. 12-15). Was Esau acting shrewdly, covering up his real feelings until another day? Nothing in the narrative gives us cause to assume that Esau's reception of Jacob was other than genuine. When he addresses Jacob he always calls him *my brother*. And in the meeting he acts as a brother.

Jacob is different, however. There is something deeply genuine about him too, but that is often so mixed up with the "master strategist" that one can hardly separate the two. Did Jacob change on seeing Esau's reaction, or was he simply protecting himself from any eventuality? When Jacob addresses Esau he always says, *My lord.* Does that come from fear, humility, or strategy? We do not know. The ensuing dialogue shows that Jacob is not willing to risk complete reconciliation with his brother.

In that dialogue Esau offers full reunion of the family, in effect, complete reconciliation with his brother (vv. 12-15) (Coats, 1979: 103). That reunion Jacob steadfastly, though not directly, refuses. To Esau's invitation that they journey on together, Jacob declares that the fragility of his family requires them to proceed so slowly that Esau's group should move on ahead. Jacob indicates that he will join Esau in Seir (vv. 13-14). To his brother's offer to leave some men to assist, Jacob replies that such assistance is not needed (v. 15).

The meeting closes with Esau going south to Seir (v. 16). But Jacob does not follow his brother. Instead, he turns west to Succoth. The narrative does not take us inside Jacob to let us know why Jacob did not join his brother in Seir or why Jacob stated that he would, if he never planned to do so. The narrative simply drops the story of Jacob and Esau at this point. The conflict between them seems resolved, but resolved by permanent separation, not by reconciliation. Resolution as separation came through Jacob's action. Esau offered reconciliation.

Conclusion 33:18-20

The return journey of Jacob which began in 31:18 ends, according to the narrator, with the sojourner's "peaceful" (*šalem,* i.e., shalom) arrival at Shechem (v. 18). Indeed the whole narrative of Jacob as sojourner which began with his departure/flight from home (Gen. 28:10) is successfully brought to a conclusion in "flight" back home.

But these concluding remarks have two other functions. Genesis 33:19 serves as a transition verse, to the tale about conflict between the families of Jacob and Shechem (Gen. 34). Verse 20 provides a point of connection between Israel's important sanctuary at Shechem and the ancestral tradition of Abraham, Isaac, and Jacob. Hence packed into these three verses we have the conclusion of one story and transition to the next, plus the connection with an important sanctuary in Israel's history (e.g., Josh. 24, Judg. 9).

THE TEXT IN BIBLICAL CONTEXT

Certainly the tale of Jacob's struggle at the Jabbok River stands out brilliantly in the saga of Jacob, like the near sacrifice of Isaac on Moriah in the Abraham saga. Hosea's brief mention of Jacob's life features this as the central event (Hos. 12:3-4).

Only infrequently in the biblical tradition does God act as the active antagonist of humanity. But other pages whisper about this experience of the dark side of the divine. It may be helpful to distinguish this experience from other dangerous moments in the divine-human drama. The "dark night of the soul" generally refers to the experience of feeling cut off from or abandoned by God. The quotation from Psalm 22 in the passion narrative illustrates that experience: "My God, my God, why have you forsaken me " (Matt. 27:46). Israel's prophets frequently speak of the anger of God, declaring that God will act out of that anger in the interest of divine justice (cf. Amos 1:2; 3:1-2; 4:1-3).

The experience of God as antagonist is not the same as being cut off from God or being the object of God's justified anger. The enigmatic anecdote of God's attack on Moses (Exod. 4:24-26) defies complete understanding. Job, more than any other biblical story or poem, explores the experience of feeling inexplicably "attacked" by God (cf. Job 6). Our thoughts race to explain such experiences, to justify God with our words. The biblical texts let such experiences stand without comment. Perhaps the encounter with the dark side of the divine cannot be talked about easily. Such encounters seem to be the experience of very few. But the tradition remembers that such moments do happen and preserves these few accounts. Because it does, subsequent generations can know that such experiences can be incorporated in a life pilgrimmage without destroying trust in God. Indeed, Jacob fought his way through such a moment, finally to be blessed.

We know that many names in the biblical tradition have specific meaning. Often the name contains a religious affirmation: Joel, "Yahweh is God"; Jonathan, "Yahweh gives"; and Daniel, "God is my Judge." Sometimes a specific meaning for the proper name will be used in the text: Moses, "he was drawn up"; Joshua/Jesus, "he will save"; Israel, "he has struggled with God." Similarly the renaming of an individual can have significance, as it did for Abraham and Jacob. That renaming marks a change of direction or context for the individual. It does not always mark a change in character or inner person.

The change in Abram's name to Abraham came with God's gift of covenant signified by circumcision (Gen. 17). The text does not encourage us to assume a significant change happened in Abraham's character. Rather, the name change was part of a changed context in which Abraham lived: now he lived in a covenanted community and carried in his name God's promise, "father of a multitude of nations." A similar name change often marked the coronation of a monarch in Israel and the ancient Near East. The person received a throne name together with the new position or context.

As much as we know about the biblical tradition of name change, we often presume that the name change of Jacob marked a transformation of his character. We interpret as if the Jacob of Genesis 33 was different from the pre-Genesis 32 Jacob. Certainly a transformation happened, but not necessarily in terms of Jacob's inner spirit or character. The change comes in the way Jacob's story is now to be read. This is the saga not just of a person, but of a people. In Genesis 35, the name change is repeated in an appearance of God to Jacob at Bethel. This likely represents a different retelling of Jacob's story now gathered into a single saga. But such retelling reinforces the affirmation that the whole of Israel is to see Jacob's saga as their story. Israel had received a blessing, blessing they did not altogether deserve. Israel's faith was born out of struggle, struggle with brothers and sisters and with the God of their ancestors. Israel's life had been one of opportunism and deception, victimization and political maneuver, journey and conflict, only occasionally returning home in peace.

THE TEXT IN THE LIFE OF THE CHURCH

With his flight from Laban, Jacob was forced to confront his past with his brother. Jacob had reason to fear that he would now face the consequences of his victimization of Esau. We are not surprised that Jacob expected ill as his brother approached, accompanied by *four hundred men*. Jacob carefully planned in hopes that he might appease his brother and soften the consequences of his past behavior. But in meeting his brother Jacob found not retribution but grace, not anger but acceptance, not revenge but reconciliation. This is the gospel, whether it be

Jacob and Esau or Jesus' parables of the prodigal son and the Good Samaritan (Luke 15:11-32; 10:30-36). Esau's response lived out the words which our stream of the Christian heritage has declared so central:

> Repay no one evil for evil,
> But take thought for what is noble and right. (Rom. 12:17)

> Love your enemies,
> And pray for those who persecute you. (Matt. 5:44)

Jacob was only partly able to receive what his brother offered. That too does not surprise the reader. A long relationship characterized by deceit and hatred probably needs more than one moment to heal. The reader wonders what would have been their future if Jacob had chosen long-term reunion, rather than separation. But the narrative does not press "what if's." Because relationship and reconciliation center the faith for our heritage, we wish that all faith narratives ended in reconciliation. But we recognize that even in the community of faith that reconciliation does not always happen. Jacob remains the carrier of God's promise even though he was never fully reconciled with Esau. Paul continues as an agent of the gospel even though Paul's split with Barnabas was final, so far as the New Testament record takes us (Acts 15:36-40). We may need to learn to rejoice when sharp conflict finds resolution which allows each disputant "space" to live, even if that resolution is not the reconciliation-reunion announced with the fulfillment of the kingdom of God.

Genesis 34:1-31

Conflict with the People of the Land

PREVIEW

The relationship between the herder-farmers of the countryside and the urban landowners and merchants who controlled the trade routes made conflict frequent in the ancient Near East (Halpern: 92). This tale reflects such conflict, portraying the mistrust and deceit that fueled the passions of both sides.

At the conclusion of his reunion with Esau, the saga narrates Jacob's move to the city of Shechem. However, in this tale, Shechem is not a place, but a Canaanite landowner or prince (34:2).

The place Shechem figures prominently in the history of biblical Israel as a political and religious center. Joshua 24 ascribes to Shechem the event of a significant covenant ceremony of the confederation of tribes called Israel. Judges 9 locates Shechem as the place of Israel's first experiment with monarchy. Archaeology tells us that Shechem was a very ancient Canaanite religious center. Although we can say little about the transition of the city from Canaanite to Israelite, Shechem sits in the central highlands where Israel developed.

The introduction to the tale narrates briefly the action and attitude of the prince of the land, Shechem, toward Dinah and then the response of Dinah's father and brothers and Shechem's father (34:1-7). The center of the tale reports the negotiations (34:8-18) and subsequent execution of the agreement between the two families concerning Dinah and Shechem (34:19-29). The tale concludes with Jacob at odds with sons over their actions (34:30-31).

OUTLINE

EXPLANATORY NOTES

The Setting for Conflict 34:1-7

34:1-4 Action of Dinah and Shechem

The tale begins with the action of Dinah. In fact the whole narrativ
reports only this single action of Dinah: she went out to visit the wome
of the land (34:1). Subsequently all the action happens to or abo
Dinah. The story moves immediately to the action of Shechem, calle
the prince of the land (v. 2). We can picture this farmer's daughter goir
to visit some of the women of the Canaanite town (von Rad, 1973: 53
when the son of the town's powerful ruler happened on the group
women. In four stacatto-like verbs, the text narrates Shechem's forcib
violation of the country woman (v. 2): saw, took, lay with, and violate
(*'anah* often translated *humbled,* RSV). Suddenly Shechem's attitu

toward Dinah changed. He was deeply drawn to her, came to love her, and *spoke tenderly to her* (vv. 3-4). He asked his father for permission to marry *the maiden.*

34:5-7 Response by Jacob, Hamor, and Jacob's Sons

The introduction continues by describing the response of the two families (vv. 5-7). Jacob's reaction introduces a new element to the story. He interprets Shechem's action as "defilement" *(tame),* a word designating ritual uncleanness, rendering one unsuitable to participate in the worshiping community (Lev. 13:3-25). But Jacob elects to do nothing at least for a while. This passivity is uncharacteristic of Jacob in the saga. Shechem's father, Hamor, approaches Jacob in response to his son's wish to marry Dinah. We are not told Hamor's feelings or how he viewed the matter. The sons of Jacob erupt instantly (v. 7). They understand the action to be *nebalah* (folly, disgrace), an angry word referring to serious violation of the community (Josh. 7:15; Judg. 19:23ff.; 2 Sam. 13:12).

Business Negotiations 34:8-18

34:11-12 Proposals of Hamor and Shechem

Exactly who negotiated with whom remains unclear in the text. This unclarity probably reflects different retellings of the story. Sometimes the story emphasizes the role of Hamor and at other times Shechem. For the most part Jacob's sons take precedence over the father, but that may not always have been the case as the story was passed on. In the text as we have it, Jacob is present but in a marginal and passive role.

Hamor proposes that Shechem be allowed to marry Dinah and indeed that intermarriage be permitted both ways. He suggests that such intermarriage would be economically advantageous to Jacob's family (v. 10). Shechem's proposal was more open-ended, giving Dinah's family the right to name the marriage present from the groom's family to the bride's (v. 12).

Israel's pre-monarchical legal tradition indicates that Shechem's willingness, even desire, to marry Dinah was preferable to his turning away from her (Exod. 22:16-17; Deut. 22:28-29). In a similar episode of violation by force, Tamar insists that Amnon's refusal to marry her magnified his violation still further (2 Sam. 13:16).

34:13-18 Completion of Counterproposal and Negotiations

The *sons of Jacob* make a counterproposal (vv. 13-17). The narrator warns us that they are speaking deceitfully (v. 13), motivated by the "defilement." The violation has disqualified Dinah for participation in the worshiping community. The brothers demand that Hamor's and Shechem's people make themselves "qualified" to participate in the Hebrew community by agreeing to circumcise all of their males. They can be one community and marriage would thus be an open matter (vv. 14-17).

The negotiations conclude with the agreement of Hamor and Shechem to the counterproposal (v. 18). The negotiations have produced an agreement, but the narrative has signaled dissonance between the overt agreement and actual intentions, especially of Jacob's sons. Their rage upon hearing of the rape does not match their action in the negotiations. Various words describing deep community violation have been used to interpret the event, and yet the brothers propose that the two become one people! The narrator has warned us: the brothers' plans are not what they seem.

Execution of the Agreement 34:19-29

34:19-24 Action of Hamor and Shechem

Hamor and Shechem carry out the agreement as negotiated. They "sell" the agreement to their people by insisting that the family of Jacob is "peaceful" šalem, 34:21), that enough land exists for both groups to live together, and that the agreement is economically advantageous to the Shechemites (v. 23). In addition the narrative points to the status of Shechem as Hamor's eventual successor, allowing the reader to include that as a factor in the "persuasion" of the people (v. 19). The circumcision of all the males completed Hamor and Shechem's part of the bargain (v. 24).

34:25-29 Action of Jacob's Sons

The reader then expects Jacob's sons to carry out their part of the bargain. But they act, not out of the negotiated agreement, but out of their rage. They attack the city, whose males are incapacitated by the circumcision, murdering the men and taking away Dinah. Some versions of the story may have featured all the brothers in the attack, while others focused on Simeon and Levi, two of the brothers. In the received text, Simeon and Levi murder all the men and the other brothers plunder the town (vv. 25-29). The brothers' action is narrated dispassionately without comment, except for reiteration of their motivation: *because their sister had been defiled* (v. 27).

Conclusion 34:30-31

The story concludes with Jacob moving back into an active role. He insists that the action of the brothers has severe consequences for the community. By dealing deceitfully with unlimited retribution, they have made their family an object of loathing ("odious") in their wider context (v. 30). The family does not have the power to survive such community hatred. The brothers respond with a biting question: *Should he treat our sister as a harlot?* (v. 31).

Jacob's statement may seem to us weak and "political," more concerned with survival than with ethical behavior. He does not rebuke his sons for their morality, the fact that they acted more like sons of Lamech (4:23) than like sons of Abraham. Instead, Jacob grounds his objection in the effect the attack on the city will have on the family situation. Perhaps that is so, and yet Jacob's rebuke may say more than appears at first. According to the tale, Shechem was an important urban prince and the family of Jacob farmers and herders. Quite often antagonism between two such communities played a central role in acts of violation and subsequent revenge. The need for the two communities to live together was a reality Jacob could not ignore. [*Occupation: Keeper of Livestock, p. 324.*]

The brothers' response does not acknowledge the complexity of their social context. For them it appears a simple matter. Their sister had been treated as a *harlot*, an interpretation of the violation which has not been made previously in the tale. The brothers' speech declares their rage as motivated only by the sexual and/or religious violation of their sister. That speech does not recognize that their anger may have had deep roots in the antagonism between two socioeconomic groups. Perhaps they used their sister's mistreatment as the "incident" to make "righteous" their deep antagonism toward the city people and their prince. Jacob's speech acknowledges that the community antipathy has been immeasurably deepened by the brothers' "righteous wrath." The future of both groups hangs in the balance of that antagonism. Jacob does not condemn his sons' violence in absolute terms, as perhaps we might prefer. Yet Jacob insists that the violence, whether justified legally or not, has been a disaster for any effort to live together with their neighbors. His rebuke suggests a preference for ways other than violent retribution, however justified that violence may seem in righting a wrong.

The narrative ends without resolution of the antagonism between Jacob's family and the "people of the land." It ends with no common understanding between Jacob and his sons. In this story no relationship is resolved, none reconciled.

THE TEXT IN BIBLICAL CONTEXT

The stories in the Jacob saga have left a trail of people victimized by Jacob and/or his family. Though not completely innocent of all wrongdoing, Esau, even Laban on occasion, and now Shechem elicit our sympathy. Calvin points to Shechem as a model of one who, having fallen, returns "to himself" (Genesis Commentary: 219). Calvin does not want to hold Shechem up too high but joins Luther in expressing guarded sympathy for Shechem when his action is placed alongside the "unspeakable barbarity" of the sons of Jacob (Luther's Commentary on Genesis: 213).

Placed beside the reunion between Esau and Jacob (Gen. 33), this tale displays in vivid color the problems of this "promise bearing" family. In the reunion scene Esau extends to his brother the opportunity for full reconciliation. Jacob accepts the reunion but covertly refuses the reconciliation, choosing instead permanent separation from his brother. In this tale Hamor and Shechem through negotiations attempted to right the violation of Dinah in a direction prescribed by the common legal tradition (Exod. 22:16-17; Deut. 22:28-29). The sons of Jacob respond to such effort with unlimited violence.

In the use of violence, the upcoming Joseph saga will change directions. That saga starts off with the violence of the brothers against Joseph. Indeed, the possibility of violence lies close at hand throughout the Joseph saga. But Jacob's family will finally choose reconciliation over separation and accommodation with other people over violent antagonism. The story of this family could hardly continue along the violent path of Genesis 34. As Jacob stated: "I shall be destroyed, I and my family" (34:30).

But inter-family conflict and inter-community violence were to follow the history of this people. Violation and violence were to threaten the family of David (2 Sam. 13—18; 1 Kings 1). Again the violence was intended to serve justice, and Solomon emerged victorious. But the violence which formed David's dynasty would eventually destroy it (2 Kings 23:29; 24:1; 25:1). Violence in the interest of faith and justice also engulfed the world in which Jesus of Nazareth lived. He had the opportunity to choose that path, but took another, one destined to offer not separation but reconciliation, not death but life to all humankind.

THE TEXT IN THE LIFE OF THE CHURCH

Genesis 34 begins with an incident of sexual abuse which the narrator condemns with words such as defile (vv. 5, 13, 27), disgrace/folly (v. 7) and violated/*humbled* (v. 2). Biblical legal texts recognize that such viola-tions have a clear element of individual responsibility. The word '*anah* (violated/humbled/forced, v. 2) recognizes that one person has used power to victimize another (Gen. 15:13; 16:6; 2 Sam. 13:12, 14). Most legal systems attempt to deal with the matter of individual responsibility and manage to do so with varying degrees of success and fairness.

But this tale suggests that the action of one individual against another does not fully explain Shechem's violation of Dinah. Shechem as prince of the land uses that power against the daughter of a less powerful group, unleashing the fury of the marginal shepherds from the hillside (Jacob: "We are few in number," v. 30, NIV). The only distinctive element in this scenario involves the prince falling in love with the woman of low estate whom he had violated. As marginal members of the society, Jacob's brothers may have "used" their sister as much as Shechem did. She seems to have become a "cause" rather than a person in their crusade against the "prince." We note that Dinah plays no role in the tale after the opening verse. She becomes a nonperson in the drama.

By trying to *limit* the focus to individual responsibility, i.e., the treat-ment of Dinah (v. 31), the brothers ignore other factors in the violation signaled by the narrator and Jacob. The brothers may "prosecute" this crime but do not deal with the antagonism between social, economic, and religious groups which Jacob insists threatens them all. The exercise of power *against* the disadvantaged, whether that be the hillside maiden or those sore from circumcision, is not questioned by the brothers in their passion for justice. Exactly that perversion of power, Jacob recog-nizes, may destroy them all (v. 30), the marginal groups ("we are few in numbers") *and* the princes of the land.

Genesis 35:1-29

Jacob's Concluding Journeys

PREVIEW

This chapter includes a wide variety of material gathered and held together as a narrative of Jacob's journey from one place to another. Even a quick reading shows death reports, a name list, a theophany—indeed a narrative marked by its distinct sections rather than a single story. The Abraham saga ended in a similar way with short segments of diverse material that did not fit easily together (25:1-18), and something of the same will show up again at the conclusion of the Joseph saga. Apparently such a gathering together of bits and pieces of traditional material was common to the ending of an ancestral saga. It describes the final tasks in life, the testamentary activities. Both the Abraham and Joseph sagas end explicitly with such "end of life" actions and words (testamentary actions). This saga does not end in that way because the main character, Jacob, does not die at the end of this saga. Instead, Deborah (Rebekah's nurse), Rachel, and Isaac die. Hence the concluding unit of the saga can be outlined by the destination of Jacob's journeys.

OUTLINE

Jacob's Journey to Bethel, 35:1-5

Construction of Altar, 35:7
Notation of Death, 35:8
Theophany, 35:9-13
Construction of Sanctuary, 35:14-15

Jacob's Journey to Ephrath and Beyond, 35:16-26
35:16-20   Death Report of Rachel
35:21-22a   Anecdote of Rebellion
35:22b-26   Name List

Jacob's Journey to Mamre (Notation of Death), 35:27-29

EXPLANATORY NOTES

Jacob's Journey to Bethel 35:1-15

35:1-4 Preparations for Journey

This section begins with a speech of God directing Jacob to go to Bethel and construct an altar (v. 1). Not until 35:7 does Jacob carry out these instructions. But as mentioned before, this unit includes a variety of material and so this "stop" on Jacob's journey includes more than the divine instructions and their execution.

As a part of the preparations for the journey to Bethel, Jacob instructs his "family" in a ritual of purification before the journey (35:2-3). Others have noted that the language and ritual of the speeches by God and Jacob remind us of ceremony that surrounds many pilgrimage festivals (von Rad, 1973: 336). A pilgrimage festival called the worshiper to journey to a sanctuary for a special service. The "pilgrims" often carried out special preparation rituals of purification and renewal before departure. Certain of the Psalms declare the reason for such ritual.

> Who shall ascend the hill of the Lord?
> And who shall stand in his holy place?

> He who has clean hands and a pure heart,
> who does not lift up his soul to what is false,
> and does not swear deceitfully. (Ps. 24:3-4)

We cannot say much about the details mentioned in the ritual. We are aware of the importance of such acts of purification and renewal in the later worshiping community.

35:5-6 Jacob's Journey

The text narrates the journey itself in 35:5 with a somewhat confusing statement: "The greatest terror (or 'divine terror') fell upon the surrounding cities and they did not pursue the family of Jacob."That language has more in common with the "conquest" narratives in Joshua than this context. But the function of the statement seems clear. Following their ritual of preparation and purification, the triumphant presence of God accompanied them on their pilgrimage. The altar at Bethel existed by the instruction and with the presence of God (v. 7).

35:7-15 Jacob's Stay at Bethel

However, the narrative does not conclude the journey to Bethel with the construction of the altar. Instead, we read of the death of "Deborah, the nurse of Rebekah" (v. 8). Genesis 24:59 mentioned a nurse of Rebekah, but not by name. The notation of her death here is quite unexpected. But this concluding unit incorporates several "floating" bits of tradition like this.

Immediately the text carries us to another theophany—appearance of God, 35:9-13. This theophany repeats elements from Genesis 28 and 32: the name change from Jacob to Israel and the promises given at Bethel. This context reports the name change and promises in a straightforward if not sterile way compared to the dramatic context of a dream (Gen. 28) and wrestling match (Gen. 32). The repetition of these elements in Genesis 35 may have come from a passing on of the story of Jacob among different groups in separate locations. If so, these different retellings have been incorporated into the present saga.

Jacob's whole family has left behind the old conflicts and come to the sanctuary. There God grants again the name Israel (v. 10) and entrusts to him/them the divine promises (vv. 11-12). In the context of the whole ancestral story, only here has the whole family come with the patriarch to an occasion of God's appearance. Even though the text says, "God appeared to Jacob," the context includes the whole family. There is a sense in which at the conclusion of the Jacob saga a family, not only an individual, is named Israel. A people, not a single person, will carry the promises into the future. So it will be in the saga of Joseph and beyond.

The journey to Bethel concludes (vv. 14-15) with the establishment of a sanctuary, a report that again duplicates Genesis 28 and to some extent even 35:7 especially in the naming of the sanctuary ("Bethel"). Bethel played an important role as a sanctuary in Israel until the conquest by Assyria in the eighth century B.C. (cf. Amos 7:12-13). Beyond that time it continued as an important city but did not have the preeminent role as a religious center of Israel that it had during the monarchy.

Jacob's Journey to Ephrath and Beyond 35:16-26

35:16-20 Death Report of Rachel

The report of Rachel's death illustrates much about the saga in few verses (vv. 16-20). Assurance, fulfillment, and life meet sorrow, anger, and death. At the birth of her first son, Rachel gave him a name which declared she wanted another (30:24). The midwife's words of assurance *fear not* announce the fulfillment of that desire. But the fulfillment brings with it a pain-filled vocabulary: "severe labor pain," "life draining away," the name "son of my sorrow," and finally death. The narrator tells us that the boy's father elects to feature his son's future, not the agony of the family's past. He renames the boy "son of the right side." Hence the heritage knows him as "Benjamin," not "Benoni (son of my sorrow)."

The burial of Rachel ends another thread of the saga. The beautiful woman, the one Jacob loved, struggled with barrenness until the end. But the saga has remembered her death. Leah disappears from the story altogether, reappearing only in the next saga with Jacob's final listing of those he has buried (49:31).

According to the narrative, Rachel was not buried in the family tomb of Sarah and Abraham. Indeed, the confusion and conflict of Rachel's life follow her even into this report of her death. First Samuel 10:2 and Jeremiah 31:15 point to a place (Ramah) just south of Bethel as the Ephrath where Rachel was buried. The parenthetical remark in Genesis 35:19 has Rachel buried at Bethlehem. This remark likely represents a later scribal addition to the text. This addition *(at Bethlehem)* "moves" her tomb to Ephrath that comes to be well known during the time of the monarchy.

This unit adds still more confusion to the matter of Rachel's death and Benjamin's birth. Genesis 35:24, 26 locates Benjamin's birth, not in the trauma of Rachel's death, but in Jacob's sojourn with Laban. Of course, lack of precision in such detail bothers us in a different way than it did earlier generations. Likely they were less bothered by a text which preserves, without comment, different traditions about the birth of Benjamin and the burial of Rachel.

35:21-26 Anecdote of Rebellion and the Name List

The new beginning symbolized by the ritual of purification (v. 4), renaming (v. 10), and renewal of promises (vv. 11-12) does not free the family problems. The note in Genesis 35:22 declares unexpectedly that Reuben moved to take over leadership of the family. The act of assuming Jacob's role with Bilhah marks such a coup by the eldest son (2 Sam.

16:22). The narrative does not evaluate Reuben's action, not here at least (cf. 49:3-4). This anecdote illustrates that Jacob has passed on to the next generation the struggle of preeminence and power so central to his own story. This legacy will furnish the tension in the next saga. Joseph will emerge the most powerful one in that story. But the naming of the family as "Israel" represents the future. The heritage will not be carried by just one person. The divine promises will be borne by all the children in the list (vv. 22b-26). None will be shoved aside, as Ishmael and Esau have been.

Jacob's Journey to Mamre 35:27-29

The saga comes to a close with the report of Isaac's death. The saga of Abraham ended with the death of that ancestor (25:8). The next saga ends with the death of Jacob and Joseph (49:33; 50:26). Those examples would suggest that this be called the saga of Isaac (Coats, 1983: 177ff.). But the figure of Jacob, not Isaac, has dominated this saga. So also the next saga will follow Joseph even though Jacob will remain a part of the story throughout.

The narrative brings Jacob and Esau together to bury Isaac (v. 29) as Isaac and Ishmael together buried Abraham (25:9). Like Isaac and Ishmael, these two brothers do not stay together, but they do have a common father. That unity no separation can deny. The death of Isaac completed his life as the Hebrew tradition wants life to end: *old and full of days . . . gathered to his people* (35:29).

THE TEXT IN BIBLICAL CONTEXT AND IN THE LIFE OF THE CHURCH

The saga of Abraham ended with that chapter of the family's life drawn to completion with the ancestor's death (25:8). The same sort of closure will happen at the end of the Joseph saga (49:33; 50:26). But this saga does not have a neat ending. The pilgrimage to Bethel provides a ritual of purification and renewal of the promise for the next generation (35:1-5), but the concern for preeminence which gave birth to Jacob's generation (25:19-34) continues to plague the family (v. 22). The beloved Rachel gives birth to a second son, but dies in the process. She names her son as a reflection of her sorrow-filled life, a name which Jacob changes after her death (vv. 16-20). The unloved wife, Leah, just disappears from the story. Isaac dies and is buried by his two sons Esau and Jacob, sons who will forever live apart. They live apart not out of Esau's deep hatred, as might have been the case, but by Jacob's choice (33:17), or perhaps because of economic considerations (36:6-7).

Not only the brothers but also other segments of the family as well, such as Jacob and Laban, remain divided (31:44-55). They have agreed not to kill each other or trespass on one another's space. But the relationship can not go much further (cf. Deut. 23:7). The saga of Jacob has no end to the conflict and alienation that followed this generation from the womb.

The saga is not only about anger and division, but also about promise and hope. At the most dangerous moments God appears. God comes to the thief fleeing from the justified anger of his brother (Gen. 28). God protects the refugee trapped between the angry world of the present (Laban) and the murderous hatred generated in the past (Esau) (Gen. 31—33). God calls again to the family, even after they have returned evil for evil against their neighbors (Gen. 34—35). The promises which had called the family into being seem almost lost in the drama of this generation—almost but not quite. The promises are heard again at night by the dreaming Jacob (Gen. 28) and in the worship of the pilgrim family (Gen. 35). God's unfinished story provides unending hope for the faith community. God cannot be silenced by conflict and alienation nor chased away by exploitation, deceit, and violence.

The faith community has realized what the saga says repeatedly, we read here not the story of one man, Jacob, long ago, but the story of Israel. Each new generation of the faith family seems born in struggle, divided by deceit and threatened by violence. Even so the promise cannot be destroyed though hopes lie shattered by violation and violence, and divine speech is drowned in a sea of angry voices.

> We have this treasure in earthen vessels,
> to show that the transcendent power belongs
> to God and not to us. (2 Cor. 4:7)

Genesis 36:1-43

Afterword

PREVIEW

This unit contains a collection of lists concerning the family of Esau. The material stands outside the Jacob saga per se, as signaled by the new "generations" formula: "These are the generations. . . ." We have met that formula several times in Genesis 1—11 and at the beginning of the ancestral sagas (11:27; 25:19; and 37:2). This formula is repeated a second time in these Esau lists (36:9). Even though separated by content and introductory phrase from the body of the Jacob saga, this unit about Esau functions in relationship to the saga as a sort of "afterword"—the opposite of a "foreword." An afterword provides material subsequent or peripheral to the main story line.

This afterword contains a variety of material mostly in list form concerning Esau/Edom. The unit begins in narrative form but this storylike way of writing does not really tell a story but gives us the wives and sons of Esau and the place where the family settled (36:1-8). The unit then turns to several different lists: sons of Esau (36:10-14), the "chiefs" of Esau (36:15-19), a genealogy from the land of Seir (36:20-30), a list of kings from Edom (36:31-39), and another list identifying Esau's chiefs (36:40-43).

230

OUTLINE

Introduction, 36:1

Report of Esau's Family, 36:2-8
  36:2-3 Marriages
  36:4-5 Births
  36:6-8 Settlement

List of Esau's Descendants, 36:9-19
  36:9   Introduction
  36:10-14 By Sons
  36:15-19 By Chiefs

Genealogy of Seir, 36:20-30

List of Kings in Edom, 36:31-39

List of the Chiefs of Esau, 36:40-43

EXPLANATORY NOTES
Report of Esau's Family 36:2-8

The unit begins with Esau's wives (vv. 2-3). The saga of Jacob tells of Esau's marriages to Judith, Basemath (26:34), and Mahalath (28:9). Two of those names have been replaced here by Adah and Oholibamah. Basemath is called the daughter of Ishmael in 36:3, whereas earlier Mahalath was Ishmael's daughter (28:9). Basemath was called the daughter of Elon (26:34); now Adah is designated Elon's daughter. To note those variations serves to remind us that we find here lists which have been preserved and passed along from different times and places. Differences can be expected and seem not to have troubled earlier readers.

The major surprise lies not in the differences in the names present in the various lists but that so much material about Esau has been preserved at all (Brueggemann, 1982: 285). Even though Jacob carries the promise, Esau does not disappear easily from the story. In fact by reporting Esau's move to Seir as his own choice based on economic consideration, this unit continues the benevolent portrait of Esau. The style of this Esau narrative features a stable instead of precarious family, a calm instead of stormy leader—certainly a contrast to the constant turmoil in the narrative portrait of Jacob.

List of Esau's Descendants 36:9-19

Again the genre list portrays Esau's family growing naturally, a model of a blessed family (Westermann, 1978). *[Blessing in Genesis, p. 312.]* Likely these lists make much less enjoyable reading than the dramatic narratives of the saga of Jacob. *[Reading Genealogies, p. 326.]* In fact we seldom read the Esau material except when demanded by circumstances or study. That shoves Esau out still further to the edge of the story. But Esau will not go away in spite of Jacob's chosenness. Always the tradition looks kindly on Esau, no matter how far out on the edge he sits (Coats, 1983: 247).

Additional Genealogies and Lists 36:20-43

The remainder of the unit contains a genealogy of Seir (vv. 20-30), a royal list from Edom (vv. 31-39, and a list of Esau's chiefs (vv. 40-43). Some of the names we can locate in the history of the area surrounding Palestine, especially to the southeast and south. But many of the names appear only in these lists (see the discussion of Vawter, 1977: 369-374).

The flow of the unit moves from Esau and widens to his family—wives and children (36:2-5). The next step extends the family still further by reaching into the third generation (36:10-14) and organizing the family politically according to the "chiefs" (*'allupim*). Genesis 36:20-43 broadens the family still further with a genealogy of Seir (vv. 20-30) and intensifies the political organization with an Edomite king list (vv. 31-39). The unit presents the reader with a very orderly picture of growth: (1) small family with Esau as the head, (2) extended family led by chiefs, (3) large nation ruled by kings.

The final verses return to the extended family led by chiefs, a literary move different from the ever broadening perspective which seems to guide the rest of the unit. The list of eleven "chiefs" may be intended to balance the list of twelve sons with which the Jacob saga ends (Coats, 1983: 257).

THE TEXT IN BIBLICAL CONTEXT AND IN THE LIFE OF THE CHURCH

With Ishmael in the Abraham saga and here with Esau, the Bible deals with the presence and the problem of the "other" child. Ishmael played no active role in the Abraham saga, but not so Esau. The tradition understands well the experience of being the "not chosen," the second of two. But it remains difficult to know what to do with that person.

The tale of Cain and Abel illustrates vividly the wrong way for the "not chosen" to react. According to the Jacob saga, Esau did not respond as did Cain, although he felt like killing his brother. His rage at his brother changed to the embrace of reunion, his alienation into the desire to live together. Esau did all one could ask of a person who expects to be first, and through a combination of divine decision and human deception ends up the second son. It is no wonder that the tradition has trouble letting go of this remarkable son of Isaac. We need not be surprised that the Bible remembers in this chapter that Esau grew and prospered even though relegated to the periphery of the main drama.

The community's later memory of Esau has not always been as kind in its treatment of this son as the Genesis saga (but cf. Deut. 2:4-8). This change happened in part because of antagonism which arose between Israel and its Transjordanian neighbor to the southeast, Edom. This antagonism grew into hatred, at the time of the destruction of Jerusalem by the Babylonian army (600-580, B.C. c.f. Obadiah). Slowly the community came to remember Esau not just as the son not chosen, but as the one whom God hated (Mal. 1:2-3).

Paul endeavored to help the new Christian community understand the mystery of divine election. In using the ancestral stories of Genesis, Paul quoted the tradition that Esau was hated by God (Rom. 9:13), but Paul did not reinforce that interpretation. Instead, Paul insisted that God chose Jacob and not Esau without reference to what each had done (Rom. 9:12).

We have experienced through the ages some of the problems with a "doctrine of election." Such a stance by different groups has complicated relationships between the Jewish and Christian faith communities. Ardent proclamation of election has similarly widened the gulf between the heirs of Jacob (Israel) and Ishmael (Islam). Our common heritage in its broad sweep includes Islam, Judaism, and Christianity in important ways as one family. Probably more useful to this "family" life than arguments about election is Paul's admonition in Galatians 5:25-26.

If we live by the Spirit, let us also walk by the Spirit. Let us have no self-conceit, no provoking of one another, no envy of one another.

Part 4

The Saga of Joseph

Genesis 37:1 – 50:26

The Saga of Joseph

PREVIEW

More than any of the other large units of Genesis, this saga reads as a single short story (novella). The story of Joseph, the centerpiece of this saga, is relatively complex when compared with other Hebrew narratives. Characters move in and out of the story. We get glimpses into the private emotions of Joseph. The life of the Jacob family mixes with the national politics of Egypt, providing danger and drama.

This carefully nuanced novella can provide the listener with new interest and excitement each time. Children enjoy the colorful coat, the mysterious dreams, and the suspenseful encounters between Joseph and his brothers. The complex nature of the novella makes it likely that a written form was always important in passing along this novella, even if different storytellers had a part in shaping this narrative as we have received it. Again the task here will not involve careful study of the history of the novella. That has been done elsewhere (e.g., Vawter, 1977). Rather, we want to encounter the narrative as Scripture in story form.

The story takes us from Joseph as teenager to his death. But the saga contains material not a part of the Joseph story as such. We have found sustained narrative interrupted by other material—tales, genealogies, episodes—in the sagas of Abraham and Jacob. Especially in the saga of Abraham, the heterogeneity of the material was more visible at times than the sustained narrative. Here the sustained narrative clearly controls the saga, but that only makes the disconnected material stand out more, e.g., the story of Judah and Tamar (Gen. 38) and the blessing of Jacob (Gen. 49). The outline of the saga will look at the way the whole unit flows, including the unexpected segments. Because the novella of Joseph controls movement of the narrative, the saga can be divided into "chapters," "acts," "scenes," or "episodes" following that story. Neither "chapters" nor "scenes" may be quite the right word. Chapters in the Bible refers to specific subdivisions of the biblical books, and "acts" or "scenes" refer to divisions in a work of contemporary drama. The word "episode" has been chosen here, hoping that will help open up the narrative.

The flow of the episodes in this saga moves from story of the separation and disintegration of a family (37:3-36) to its reconciliation and reunion (46:1—47:27). Between those moments two of the brothers, Judah (Gen. 38) and Joseph (Gen. 39—41), find themselves separated from the family. The road to reconciliation takes the family through intense conflict precipitated by a famine (Gen. 42). Circumstances force the family to stay engaged with one another even against the better judgment of the elderly father, Jacob (Gen. 43—45). The saga concludes, as does the Abraham saga, with a series of final actions or testamentary activities by both Jacob and Joseph (Gen. 47—50). The following outline will be supplemented by a more detailed one at the beginning of each episode.

OUTLINE

Introduction, 37:1-2a

Episode 1: Family Disintegration, 37:2b-36

Episode 2: The Separated Brothers, 38:1—41:57
     38:1-30   Judah
     39:1—41:57 Joseph

Episode 3: The Family in Danger, 42:1—45:28

Episode 4: The Reunification of the Family, 46:1—47:27

Concluding Episode:
     Testamentary Activities, 47:28—50:26

EXPLANATORY NOTES

Introduction 37:1-2a

We would expect the introductory formula, "These are the generations
..." to appear at the very beginning, as has been true of the two previous family sagas (11:27 and 25:19). The reason it comes in verse 2
remains unclear. Nevertheless, we can make some observations about
the function of these two sentences. As mentioned, the "generations"
formula marks the beginning of this family saga, incorporating it into the
general framework of the whole book. The genealogical framework for
Genesis casts the book as a family story. The three family sagas—Abraham, Jacob, and Joseph—follow a single branch of that family through
which God seeks to bring life/blessing to all the families and peoples.

Genesis 37:1 sets the location of the Joseph novella: *Jacob dwelt
... in the land of Canaan.* It also ties this saga with the previous ones:
"in the land where his father sojourned." In the course of the Joseph
story the location of the family will change. Genesis 47:27a serves as the
counterpart of this introductory phrase: *Israel dwelt in the land of Egypt.*
Genesis 37:1 and 47:27 form an envelope which incorporates the
family's story. This move from Canaan to Egypt prepares for the drama
of liberation which follows Genesis (Coats, 1975).

Perhaps a word should be said about the use of the names "Jacob"
and "Israel" in the saga. As was noted in the previous saga, the name
change from Jacob to Israel has not been carried through consistently as
it was with Abram—Abraham (32:28; 33:1; 35:10, 22, 27). Scholars
generally assume that the switch back and forth between Jacob and Israel in the Joseph story reflects different retellings of this story in the
process of its being handed on. Some traditions use Jacob, and others,
Israel. The story as we have it draws from the wealth of the tradition
about this ancestor of the family. Certainly the identification between
Jacob and Israel was sufficient to allow both names to appear in the final
form with no explanation. Because in the life of community "Jacob"
most often referred to the ancestor and "Israel" to the community of his
descendants, alternating between the two names could signal to later
listeners that this was earnestly their story and not just something that
happened to their ancestors.

Genesis 37:2b-36

Episode 1: Family Disintegration

PREVIEW

The tension driving this story arises from the disintegration of the family caused by favoritism, foolishness, jealousy, and deceit. This first episode in the story moves from an exposition which introduces the characters and the brokenness in the family (vv. 2b-11) to the separation of the family with Joseph carted off and sold as a servant in Egypt (v. 36). In the center of this episode lies a journey: Jacob sent Joseph to check on "shalom" in the family (v. 14). The actions of the brothers only serve to illustrate the absence of shalom in this troubled family.

OUTLINE

Exposition, 37:2b-11
    37:2b-4 Introduction of Characters
        Joseph, 37:2b
        Israel, 37:3
        Brothers, 37:4
    37:5-11 Report of Dreams
        Sheaves, 37:5-8
        Sun, Moon, Stars, 37:9-11

Report of Journeys, 37:12-36
  37:12   The Brothers' Journey to Shechem
  37:13-17   Joseph's Journeys
    Preparation, 37:13-14a
    To Shechem, 37:14b-17a
    To Dotham, 37:17b
  37:18-31   Encounter at Dotham
  37:32-35   The Brothers Return Home
  37:36   Joseph to Egypt

EXPLANATORY NOTES

Exposition 37:2b-11

37:2b-4 Introduction of the Characters

In 37:2b-4 we meet the characters who carry through the whole saga: Joseph, Jacob, and, as a group, the brothers. Joseph is introduced to the readers as a 17-year-old shepherd. This introduction pictures him working with his brothers. Subsequently, we find a somewhat different arrangement with Joseph as the youngest sent by his father to check on the brothers (so also David, 1 Sam. 17). With the introduction of Joseph as a separate character, we find the first element of tension in the family. He brought their father a "bad report" about the brothers. The narrator does not tell us whether the report was true or false, although the words used *(dibbatam ra'ah)* elsewhere refers to gossip, plotting, and misinformation (Prov. 10:18; Ps. 31:13; Num. 14:37).

Israel/Jacob is next introduced. He too has a hand in the alienation within the family. He favors Joseph over his other sons because Joseph is *the son of his old age* (v. 3). Jacob has made Joseph a "royal" coat (Speiser, 1964: 289-290). We do not know for certain what the coat, cloak, or robe looked like. The ancient Greek text translated the phrase "many colored." Our information from the literature of the ancient Near East suggests that the coat stood out because of its length and/or sleeves. At any rate Joseph is given a royal coat. In the "u" shaped flow of this saga, Joseph begins and ends in regal dress, but wears servants' and prisoners' clothes in between.

Readers often find confusing the narrative's lack of clarity concerning the presence and absence of Benjamin. Similarly the second dream seems to presume Joseph's mother, Rachel, is still living, whereas Genesis 35:16 reports her death. This probably reflects the long history of passing the Joseph story along in different ways and places. Perhaps some versions of the story had Joseph born in Jacob's old age, whereas the present context has Joseph born while Jacob was still living in Mesopotamia (30:23-24). In that understanding, Jacob would have preferred Joseph because he was born to Rachel, the favored wife. It seems likely that in some versions of the story Rachel was still alive and Benjamin not yet born at the start of this story. But in the narrative as we have received it, these matters are left unclear. The effect of this lack of clarity casts a further cloud of confusion over the family.

The brothers respond to their father's favoritism with hatred. The brothers can not say a peaceful (shalom) word to Joseph (v. 4). The absence of any trace of shalom expresses in summary fashion the alienation in the family. In the course of this section the dreams will serve to further aggravate the situation, but the narrator has told us with the introduction of the characters that Jacob's family is deeply troubled.

37:5-11 Report of Dreams

Throughout the narrative, dreams always come in pairs. In the dreams of Joseph (Gen. 37) and Pharaoh (Gen. 41), the two dreams are synonomous and reinforce one another. The dreams of the butler and baker (Gen. 40) are antithetical; they go opposite ways. Joseph, the one dressed in the royal robe, dreamed that he really was king. His family, represented as sheaves of grain and astronomical bodies, bow down to him. The brothers respond to the first dream with questions, as the father does to the second dream (vv. 8, 10). The accusatory form of the questions leaves no doubt about the outrage of the family at Joseph's dreams. Lest we miss it, the narrator reemphasizes that the dreams multiplied the brothers' hatred (v. 8). His father, although rebuking Joseph for his dreams, responded not with hatred or jealousy, but with wonder: "his father pondered the matter" (v. 11, NAB). Perhaps the royal coat symbolized more than Jacob knew. Dreams in the ancient world were seen as divinely given.

The one dressed like a king dreamed that he really reigned as king. Noteworthy in this report about dreams is that only Joseph is named, not the father, not the brothers. They are only referred to in relationship to Joseph, *his father, his brothers*. The narrative as written reinforces Joseph's dreams that he is the center of the "universe"; everything revolves around him. Perhaps no guile existed in Joseph's report of the dreams, although one who brings "gossip" or "misinformation" (v. 2) might also report dreams for a reason. Be that as it may, Joseph's retelling of his dreams at least certainly lacked diplomacy. Whether done by design or naïveté, the effect remains the same. Introducing this claim to dominance into an already alienated family will only raise the tension still further.

Report of Journeys 37:12-36

37:12 The Brothers' Journey to Shechem

The rest of this episode narrates journeys—by the brothers and by Joseph. The brothers go near Shechem to pasture the flocks. The picture given here is not likely of a family of nomads, but as we have seen before, agriculturists engaged in both cultivation of crops (so Joseph's dream, v. 7) and herding. The flocks were moved from place to place in different years and seasons, depending on the availability of grass. *[Occupation: Keeper of Livestock, p. 324.]*

37:13-17 Joseph's Journey to Shechem and to Dotham

While the narrator simply reports the journey of the brothers to care for the flocks, we hear about the trip of Joseph in more detail. The trip originates with Israel's commissioning speech to Joseph: *Go now, see* (vv. 13-14a). Israel's commission to Joseph is far more weighty than appears on the surface. Joseph is to see after the *shalom* of the brothers and the *shalom* of the flocks. Further, Israel directs Joseph to bring back a report. We recall from the introduction of the characters that Joseph has a history of bringing back negative reports from such visits (v. 2) and no *shalom* exists between the brothers (v. 4). Does Israel know what he asks? We cannot tell, but for the readers the tension rises still higher. One way to heighten suspense in a story is to send a person into what the listeners know is a dangerous situation.

Subsequently an unnamed man finds Joseph wandering around, unable to find his brothers (v. 15). Whether this serves to temporarily release the tension—maybe nothing bad will happen after all—or further heighten the suspense—delaying the inevitable—probably depends on the reader. But this unnamed helper very graciously directs Joseph right back into danger (v. 17). The stranger's act in itself must be understood as an act of hospitality, but in the context of the narrative the act of hospitality may serve to make disaster inevitable.

37:18-31 Encounter at Dotham

The brothers see Joseph coming. *Dreamer* or "Lord of dreams," the brothers call him in very biting language as they see Joseph in the distance coming toward them (v. 18). By killing the dreamer, perhaps they can destroy the dream (vv. 19-20). But Reuben objects, suggesting an alternate plan (v. 22). Spilling the blood of their brother would set off an uncontrollable chain of events, according to ancient tradition. The only thing certain is that the killers would somehow have to face the consequences of their action (4:10; 9:6; Deut. 19:11-13). Instead, they cast Joseph in a dry cistern. Perhaps they expected Joseph to die or be killed, the narrative doesn't say.

By parallelistic repetition the narrator emphasizes that Joseph could not have drowned in the cistern. Cisterns existed to catch rain so that there would be water for flocks during the dry season. Pasturing flocks where the cisterns are dry seems unusual. But the sterility of the cistern reflects the family situation. There is no life either place. The other information called to the attention of the readers involves Joseph's regal robe. The brothers strip away this symbol of favoritism and superiority. In the course of the narrative we will see that Joseph's clothing often changes at points of transition (Seybold: 63-64). We do not know yet what clothes Joseph will wear. The pit is a stopping-off place. Some brothers want the pit to be a temporary stop on the way to the grave (vv. 18-20); Reuben hopes to accomplish Joseph's restoration (v. 22); and Judah suggests something in between (v. 27). The middle course proposed by Judah prevails.

Nevertheless, not even Judah's plan works out, according to the narrative. Judah apparently hopes to sway his brothers by appealing to the profit motive *(beṣaʿ)*, even if it is unjust profit (v. 26; cf. Prov. 28:16).

Genesis 37:28 provides an ironic end to the brothers' plans. The brothers plot to kill Joseph; Judah convinces them to let Joseph live, but sell him to the Ishmaelites. Reuben wants to double-cross the brothers and rescue Joseph. None of those plans actually come to pass. The text is somewhat ambiguous at this point. Perhaps earlier retellings of the story had only Ishmaelites or Midianites, not both (Westermann, 1986: 41-42). Nevertheless, as we receive the story, it contains this ironic twist. Midianites come by, lift Joseph out of the pit, and apparently sell Joseph to the Ishmaelites. Despite all of their schemes, the brothers have managed no murder, no profit, no dramatic rescue, and they have no idea where Joseph is.

Reuben voices his own frustration, but it could as well be the frustration of all the brothers, *the lad is gone* (v. 30). The narrator has told us where Joseph is, but the brothers know nothing. Many suggest that Reuben's reaction perhaps came from his responsibility, according to custom, as the oldest sibling. The text does not say. Instead, not knowing Joseph's whereabouts, the brothers create an explanation for the missing brother (37:31).

37:32-35 The Brothers' Return Home

An unusual pair of verbs in the Hebrew text talks about the blood-splattered robe. The brothers *sent* and *brought* the robe to Jacob (v. 32). Perhaps the tension between these two verbs arose in the process of writing and copying the text. However, with the verbs fighting against each other, the narration expresses the ambivalence of the return home. Jacob had sent Joseph to see to the brothers' shalom, instructing him to bring back a report. What comes back is the brothers' report and Joseph's blood-splattered special robe.

Jacob recognizes that no shalom exists in this family (37:35). He goes into a grief so deep, no one can help him out. The good death in the Bible happens when a person completes a long life and goes to one's grave "in peace" (Gen. 15:15; 1 Kings 2:6; 2 Chron. 34:28). Sheol is not to be translated "hell," but either left as a proper name (RSV, NASB) or translated "grave" (NIV). Sheol designates the shadowy underworld to which all persons go. Jacob will go to Sheol in grief. The loss of his most loved son causes inconsolable grief. But in the context of the saga, Jacob's grief reflects the disintegration of the family—the family through whom all other families were to receive blessing.

37:36 Joseph to Egypt

Joseph has been taken to Egypt and sold to Potiphar, an officer in the royal guard (v. 36). The one who lost his royal coat now becomes the servant of royalty. We need to observe what has happened narratively in the journeys of the brothers and Joseph. The brothers travel to Shechem (v. 12); then Joseph follows with instructions to return home (vv. 13-14). After the encounter at Dotham the brothers return home (v. 32); Joseph is taken as a servant to Egypt (v. 36). [*Egypt, a River Nation, p. 318.*] On the surface everything has gone wrong. However, the very regular structure of the unit—brothers' trip, Joseph's trip, encounter, brothers' trip, Joseph's trip—may signal that all is not as hopeless as it at first seems.

Anything new will be a long time coming, however. The saga takes leave of the story of this family as a whole. Instead, it turns to look at two of the brothers who find themselves in danger not entirely of their own making, Judah and Joseph.

THE TEXT IN BIBLICAL CONTEXT

Again the biblical narrative faces tension among brothers and sisters caused by people or circumstances that favor one child over others. That favoritism comes from God, as in the Cain and Abel tale (Gen. 3), from the parent, like an Isaac and Rebekah (Gen. 25) and Jacob (Gen. 37), or even from a spouse (Gen. 29). The favoritism may be real, as here, or assumed, as in the story of the prodigal son (Luke 15). Whatever the circumstances, favoritism causes serious problems in the biblical narratives. How will the more favored sibling act? How will the less favored respond? The tales know the deep urge on the part of those left out to destroy the favored person in some way. The stories also realize the tendency of the favorite to exploit the situation as much as possible.

These several stories do not detail how one is to respond in the face of favoritism. Nevertheless, even if the anger is justified, further trouble comes when the less favored tries to solve the conflict by destroying the favored person. That destruction is to "intend evil" (50:20) to "give in to sin" (4:7). The speech of Reuben declares that those who act on hate have no place to hide from the destruction they have released: *The lad is gone; and I, where shall I go?* (37:30; cf. Gen. 50:25).

Other dangers attend the favored child, even if she or he should survive the destructive urges of the less favored one. In biblical stories the favored place is seldom based on merit. Whether we speak of Isaac instead of Ishmael, Jacob rather than Esau, Rachel over Leah, the people of Israel chosen over other people, or even the body of Christ grafted on the chosen tree, the favored ones did not earn their own place. They received their place as a gift. Even those closest to Jesus had trouble understanding that chosenness was a matter of gift and responsibility more than merit and honor (Mark 10:35-45).

THE TEXT IN THE LIFE OF THE CHURCH

This episode in the Joseph saga describes the anguish of deep alienation in the family. No family members are innocent bystanders, none are sheltered from the consequences: neither Jacob, who prefers his youngest son (Joseph); Reuben, who tries to initiate a secret move to counter the public plan of the brothers; Judah, who manages to divert the plot from murder to sale of a brother; nor perhaps even Joseph, who publicized his dreams. None of these stands unindicted by the narrative. Alienation in a family, be that of a biologically related community or "family" defined in other ways, includes everyone in the cause and the consequences. The tendency to locate the cause in one or a few persons and solve the problem by removing those "agents of alienation" usually misunderstands the complexity of the problem.

In this story, seeds of reconciliation lie hidden in the midst of the hatred. Jacob sends Joseph on a journey of shalom (peace and well-being). The shalom he intends is likely the immediate welfare of the brothers (37:14). But the journey proves far longer than Jacob intends and the shalom far greater than he likely imagines.

God does not intervene dramatically in this saga. God's presence is felt because the events of this story exceed human control. Jacob cannot publicly control the dynamics of the family. The family responds instead to his private preferences. Nor can the brothers in their hatred manage events. They cannot even accomplish their plot to sell Joseph to the Ishmaelites. Plots for evil and plans for good seem beyond human management, however much humankind participates in the action of the story.

Joseph is introduced to us as one who brings bad reports and dreams dreams—as complex a person as any we have met in the sagas of Genesis. The narrative then does a very interesting thing with Joseph. After he is introduced as a very active character in the alienation and the future of the family, Joseph completely drops out as an active character. We hear nothing of Joseph in his encounter with the brothers. Narratively, Joseph becomes the quiet victim of the family alienation, not the innocent victim, but the silent victim. Obviously, not all who are forced to bear the consequences of corporate alienation do so in silence, but some do (Isa. 53:7).

The chapter ends in disconsolate grief and deep separation. But the ending also contains, albeit hidden, the seeds of a different future. Joseph, a dreamer, has gone on a journey of peace. Joseph's dreams were not of peace but of power and not of reconciliation but of domination. The story knows life as too complex to have an obvious stream of innocence flowing from the beginning which finally wins in the end. Yet the presence of dreams and the mission of peace signal that the future will not be controlled by the alienating actions of the present.

Genesis 38:1-30

Episode 2a: The Separated Brothers —Judah

PREVIEW

Suddenly Judah, not Joseph, becomes the main brother in the saga. Tamar, rather than Joseph, becomes the primary victim. This "digression" allows for the passage of time in the primary story begun in chapter 37. The same narrative device functioned in the sagas of Abraham (14; 19) and Jacob (26; 34). In spite of the disjunction, some connections exist between the story of Joseph and this narrative of Judah and Tamar (Alter, 1981: 4-12). Some of those connections may have been intended by those who passed the saga on from one generation to the next. Others emerge as we closely read the saga in final form. Most importantly, both sections in this chapter deal with a brother who has been separated from the family. This first narrative looks at Judah, who chose separation from the brothers; the next, Joseph, whose separation was not voluntary.

In this story we first meet the principal characters, Judah and then Tamar (vv. 1-6). In the first scene, Tamar, who is introduced to us as Judah's daughter-in-law, married to his eldest son, Er, ends up as a childless widow (vv. 7-11). In the second scene, through an incomplete business deal, cloaked in mystery and intrigue, Tamar becomes pregnant with Judah's child (vv. 12-33). The third scene reports a legal process through which Tamar is quickly convicted of prostitution and sentenced to death. But in a dramatic reversal, Judah acknowledges his own guilt and exonerates Tamar (vv. 24-26). The conclusion of the narrative sees twins born amidst confusion over which child is the eldest (vv. 27-30).

OUTLINE

Introduction: The Setting, 38:1-6
Scene 1: The Childless Widow, 38:7-11
Scene 2: The Business Deal, 38:12-23
Scene 3: The Legal Action, 38:24-26
Conclusion: The Birth of Twins, 38:27-30

EXPLANATORY NOTES

The Setting 38:1-6

Set in the context of the Joseph saga we have in Judah a second brother separating from the family, this one by choice (v. 1). The separation of Joseph was an unnatural, forced separation. The separation of Judah happened consistent with the normal course of life, a visit to Hirah, a resident of Adullam southwest of Jerusalem. In fact, this entire introduction portrays a very normal family situation: Judah separated from the family to make his own home. He married and had three sons, providing for their next generation by arranging for the marriage of the eldest son. This peaceful picture of Judah's family stands in contrast to the family of Jacob from which Judah separated himself.

Probably many of the names found in the story have significance in the tribal history of Judah and related southern groups. However, in this text they appear as individuals in a drama in which Tamar and Judah play the main parts. The story describes considerable interaction between Judah and the Canaanite people: his marriage to an unnamed Canaanite woman—the daughter of Shua; his friendship with Hirah from Adullam: and his choice of Tamar as the wife for his eldest son. Both Hirah/Hiram and Tamar were common Canaanite names (Vawter, 1977: 393).

Scene 1: The Childless Widow 38:7-11

The normal course of Judah's family life is suddenly disrupted. With the narrator's explanation that he did what was *wicked in the sight of the*

Lord, Er, Judah's eldest, has died (v. 7). Judah instructs Onan, the second son, to assume the responsibility of impregnating Tamar and thereby provide offspring for the deceased eldest brother (v. 8). Onan accepts the mandate, but then sabotages the plan by interrupting his sexual relations with Tamar and spilling his semen on the ground. Because of that Onan too dies.

Judah's instructions both to Onan (v. 8) and to Tamar (v. 11) reflect the levirate custom. The levirate responsibility was a part of several next-of-kin responsibilities prompted by a death in the family. The next of kin *(go'el)* was to act to ensure that all property remain in the family (Ruth 4; Jer. 32), that justice happen when a family member had been murdered (Num. 35:19), and that the family produce a male heir in case of a husband's death in a childless marriage (Deut. 25:5-10). The levirate custom provided the process for obtaining the male heir, thus protecting the woman's place and inheritance in her deceased husband's family (Thompson and Thompson, 1968: 79-99). Onan, by covertly refusing to fulfill the levirate responsibility, apparently sought to protect his own access to the family inheritance.

With Onan's death the danger escalates. The quality of Tamar's life remains in jeopardy. She continues as a childless widow and as such has no place in her husband's family, and precious few other options as well. Now Judah, too, fears for the family. What is the connection between his two sons' intimacy with Tamar and their death? Does the same future await his youngest, Shelah? Perhaps Tamar, like Sarah in the intertestamental book of Tobit, was possessed by a jealous demon who killed any other man trying to touch her (Tob. 3; 8). The narrative does not tell us more than that Judah was afraid that Shelah would die also (38:11), thus leaving him childless. The scene leaves us with two persons with precarious futures: a childless widow living again with her parents and the head of a family who has mysteriously lost two of his three sons.

Scene 2: The Business Deal 38:12-23

In this scene both Judah and Tamar act to protect their future: one by refusing to risk and the other by risking reputation and even life. We learn about Judah's protective action only secondhand from the narrator. Shelah has grown up and apparently has not been instructed by Judah to fulfill the levirate responsibility. This has left Tamar in even greater danger and as far as we know with very little public recourse.

So Tamar acts unilaterally and privately. She learns from an unidentified source that Judah, after grieving over the death of his wife, has headed out to join his shepherds in "harvesting" the wool (v. 13). Seeing a woman dressed as a prostitute near the gate of Enaim, Judah stops. The narrative leaves us guessing why he stopped. The woman Judah sees is called a common prostitute (v. 15). Such a term might suggest that his stop was a matter of sexual gratification after the death of his wife. But later (v. 21) Judah's friend, when he searches for the woman, calls her a "temple" prostitute. That designation raises the possibility that Judah has sought to increase the yield of his wool by engaging in a Canaanite ritual of fertility.

In either case, Judah negotiates a business deal with the woman who, unknown to him, is his daughter-in-law. They negotiate an acceptable price: a young goat from his flock, secured by Judah's staff and his seal and cord (vv. 16-18). The seal, carried on a cord, bore a person's distinctive design. In the ancient Near East, an individual signed and sealed documents by pressing the seal in the tablet's wet clay. The seal as well as the staff were elements of personal identification and probably status (Speiser: 298).

Like the Joseph novella, within which this story is set, clothing plays a central role in this scene. Tamar enters and leaves the scene dressed as a widow. She takes enormous risk when she changes clothing. But in changing clothes for a brief time, Tamar acts to open a future different from that of a childless widow, a new future, as it turns out, for her, for the family, and for the faith community. Judah's clothes figure in that future also. He sends his Adullamite friend to reclaim his clothing in exchange for the agreed-upon goat. But the woman in prostitute's dress cannot be found. Rather than risk public embarrassment, Judah decides to let his clothing go.

Scene 3: The Legal Action 38:24-26

Again an "unnamed source" speaks in the narrative. First "it" told Tamar about Judah's actions (v. 13). This time "it" tells Judah about Tamar's (v. 24). It is unusual to have unnamed sources be as central in a Hebrew narrative as they are here (cf. 27:42). The source reports Tamar's pregnancy, accusing her of prostitution. Judah, apparently without the formalities of a trial, sentences Tamar to death (Coates, 1983: 274). As the sentence is about to be executed, Tamar produces clothing, stating that that person to whom the clothes belong has fathered her child (35:25).

We have met Judah in this narrative as the legal family head who mandates that his son shall carry out the levirate custom and who acts quickly to punish wrongdoing in the community. We have also seen Judah as a man who (like Abraham, Gen. 12; 20; 26) acts self-protectively out of fear in the face of the unexplained death of two sons. We have found that Judah, for unstated reasons, bought the services of a prostitute. Most of Judah's actions can be understood as the responsible actions of the head of a Hebrew family or actions growing out of natural human fears and inclinations. But when faced with Tamar's evidence, Judah finds himself confronted with a situation for which there existed no script. Nor is the reader prepared for Judah's response. This powerful head of the family not only pardons Tamar but publicly acknowledges his own guilt in not fulfilling his levirate responsibility (38:26).

Conclusion: The Birth of Twins 38:27-30

The narrative ends as it began, talking about the next generation in Judah's family. Twins are born to Tamar (v. 27). It seems the Genesis sagas never narrate a normal birth. Conflict, tension, and rivalry surround nearly every birth. The birth of Tamar's twins proves to be no exception. Zerah starts to come out and is marked as such. But Perez bursts through before Zerah. The question of the first- and secondborn is confused again. The matter ends there, however, and Perez and Zerah do not again figure in the Genesis sagas. Nevertheless, according to the genealogical tradition represented by Ruth 4; 1 Chronicles 2; Matthew 1; and Luke 3, David descended from the line of Perez, the first (or second) son of Judah and Tamar.

THE TEXT IN BIBLICAL CONTEXT

The story of Tamar and Judah causes discomfort in most who listen closely to it. Luther spends considerable time discussing why "God . . . was pleased to narrate such unspeakably atrocious things to be read and proclaimed in the church" (Luther's Commentary: 249). We can assume that the ancient readers were no more comfortable with some elements of the story, e.g., Tamar's deceptive prostitution, than we are. Although we may not feel compelled to justify the story's existence as Luther needed to, many do wonder about its value in the story of the faith.

The flow of the narrative focuses our attention on Judah's speech acquitting Tamar and convicting himself: She is more righteous than I. We have met other forms of the word "righteous" (ṣedaqah) in previous narratives in Genesis (15:6; 18:19; 30:33). We need to remember that the ṣedaqah, especially in Hebrew narrative, cannot be defined narrowly, by an abstract standard of moral or religious conduct, as our word "righteousness" has often been understood. Rather, the word describes actions which promote vitality and health within specific relationships. We cannot define "righteous" in the abstract, but only ask what is needed in specific relationships (von Rad, 1962: 371).

That being the case, let us look further at this situation. Several actions promoted death: Er's unknown offense, Onan's *coitus interruptus*, and according to Judah's own admission, his failure to instruct Shelah to carry out the levirate responsibility. Judah's action injured not only Tamar, but the whole family whom tradition celebrates as the ancestors of David and Jesus. Deception and especially prostitution are never approved as normative in the biblical tradition, not in either Testament. Nevertheless, Tamar's action, however problematic tradition might judge it to be, promoted life in a death-ridden situation. Tamar took responsibility to maintain the community at the risk of her life.

As one who risked her life in the interest of life for herself and others, the tradition can celebrate Tamar as an ancestor of Jesus. In so doing Tamar joins Ruth, who took a similar risk at the threshing floor of Boaz, and Jesus, who worked on the Sabbath, among the faithful witnesses who risked their lives by doing what was not acceptable. In doing what was deemed not acceptable in each context, they brought life and health to the community.

THE TEXT IN THE LIFE OF THE CHURCH

While recognizing the "righteousness" of Tamar's action, the believers church disciple still struggles with the suggestion that unacceptable means can be used to reach acceptable goals. We worry that this frees anyone to act in any way that the end might warrant. We experience that same tension whenever we face the necessity of civil disobedience. One of the tests we have required of all such "disobedient" actions is that they be brought in dialogue with the biblical tradition. Sometimes we have limited the discussion to the New Testament. In that way we might be tempted to dismiss Tamar as not important.

The New Testament report of Jesus' actions does not make it easy for us to dismiss the story of Tamar. Jesus' breaking of the Sabbath command in the interest of the life and health of the community members did not, so far as we can tell, destroy the commitment of the fellowship to the fourth commandment. Jesus did insist that the practice of any commandment promote life and health in the whole community.

Jesus, like Tamar, put his own life in danger in breaking the com-

mandment. He did not act in ways that forced others to pay the consequences for his actions unless they chose to stand with him. Most did
not. It may be unusual to find marginal persons willing to risk the future
to bring life and health to a death-ridden situation. Tamar did. Usually
the disobedient individual pays dearly. The price for Jesus was the cross.
However, the story of Tamar does not end with Tamar paying the price:
burned for prostitution. The almost unheard-of happens: the person in
power recognizes the righteousness of the powerless widow. Judah acknowledges the childless widow's righteousness. Thereby he admits his
own guilt.

We have only to remember other stories about the clash between the
powerful and the powerless to realize how remarkable Judah was.
Jeremiah was thrown into a pit because King Zedekiah (ṣidqiyyahu,
"righteous") did not recognize the rightness of the prophet's words (Jer.
38). Even when he recognized that Jeremiah was right, Zedekiah would
not publicly acknowledge it (Jer. 38:24-28). Jesus died of a cross because Pilate was unwilling to act on his public acknowledgment of Jesus'
innocence. Though Tamar could not anticipate the end when she took
the risk, because of Judah, the childless widow lived past the sentence of
death. Together, the powerless widow who secretively risked her life for
righteousness' sake and the powerful patriarch who publicly acknowl-
edged his guilt became the ancestors of David of Bethlehem and Jesus
of Nazareth.

Episode 2b: The Separated Brothers – Joseph

PREVIEW

This two-part episode of the saga began by narrating a story about Judah who *separated himself* from the family (Gen. 38). Now we have the story about the brother who *was separated* from the family. Together, these two stories create a considerable narrative delay before resolving the alienation in Jacob's family presented in chapter 37. Nevertheless, this digression is crucial for the saga. Especially Joseph, but even Judah, reenters the saga in a different role. Judah brings a family with him when he moves to Egypt and a willingness to place himself at risk in the interest and welfare of his brothers and father (Gen. 44:18-34). Joseph's situation in life undergoes several changes before the family is reunited. He rises from "sold into slavery" to become Pharaoh's vice-regent, but not before once again falling into the "pit."

This story of Joseph in Egypt divides itself into three scenes. The first scene takes place in the house of Potiphar, an Egyptian *officer of Pharaoh* (39:1-20a). After a narration telling about Joseph's rise to a responsible position in Potiphar's household (39:1-6a), the drama turns to Joseph's relationship with his master's wife and his consequent imprisonment (39:6b-20a). In prison Joseph rises to a place of overseeing the day-to-day operations of the prison (39:20b—23). Joseph's encounter with the royal cupbearer and baker turns out better for the cupbearer than for either Joseph or the baker (40:1-23). The final scene moves the action to the house of Pharaoh. The introduction to this scene does not narrate Joseph's rise to power, but the dreams of Pharaoh and his inability to obtain a satisfactory interpretation (41:1-13). This brings Joseph before Pharaoh (41:14-45). As a result Joseph rises in status to a position equal to that suggested by his initial royal cloak (37:3; 41:46-57). [*Egypt, the River Nation, p. 318.*]

OUTLINE

Scene 1: In Potiphar's House, 39:1-20a
     39:1-6a   Introductory Narration
     39:6b-12   Report of Encounters with Master's Wife
     39:13-20a Consequences

Scene 2: In Prison, 39:20b—40:23
     39:20b-23 Introductory Narration
     40:1-19   Report of Encounter with Cupbearer and Baker
     40:20-23   Consequences

Scene 3: Before Pharaoh, 41:1-57
     41:1-13 Introduction
           Report of Dreams, 41:1-7
           Interpretation Failure, 41:8-13
     41:14-45 Report of Encounter with Pharaoh
     41:46-57 Consequences

EXPLANATORY NOTES

Scene 1: In Potiphar's House 39:1-20a

The presence of God in this saga thus far has been confined to the background, there by implication, e.g., as the one who initiates dreams. However, in this story of Joseph in Egypt the narrator makes God more visible. God does not intervene in dramatic ways, controlling people and events, but we are told that God's presence with Joseph affected the course of events (vv. 2, 3, 5). God's presence brings success to Joseph and life to those whom he serves. Nevertheless, God's presence does not ensure that Joseph's life will be lived triumphantly day after day.

    The central action in this scene involves Joseph's encounters with the wife of his master. Neither the name of the master—Potiphar in 39:1—nor his wife is given in the remainder of the scene. The text introduces Joseph as one who has a handsome face and a good figure (v. 6b). To that the woman responds. She cannot be accused of seduction, just a straightforward, three-word (two in Hebrew) request, *Lie with me* (v. 7). We may read the woman's words as a proposition. However, the story defines the woman not by name, but only by position—Joseph's master's wife. The narrative has punctuated the imperative grammatical construction with raw power: *Lie with me.* As a servant Joseph must deal more with the reality of power than the danger of sexuality.

Joseph refuses to obey the command, citing his responsibility to his master as the reason for his refusal (vv. 8-9). Joseph makes his case on the basis, not of moral standard, but on his accountability to the master who has given everything to him except his own wife (Coats, 1975: 21). Such an act against his master would be evil, a violation against God (vv. 8-9). Joseph has said "no" to one with the power to destroy him and eventually must pay the consequences.

Again Joseph's clothing plays a key role. As the brothers stripped off his regal cloak, so the master's wife seizes this garment. Tamar used Judah's clothing to escape the death sentence, but Joseph's cloak silently witnesses against him. Again he faces death. For some reason Joseph is not executed, at least not immediately. This surprises us because both in Israel and Egypt this accusation deserved death as a violation of the servant's place and as adultery. Instead, Joseph is cast into prison. This episode has dropped him still deeper into the "pit," confined to the royal prison. For the second time Joseph stands on the edge of death.

Scene 2: In Prison 39:20b – 40:23

The introduction to this scene (39:20b-23) flows much like the introduction in Scene 1 (39:1-6a). Because God was with him, Joseph rose to a position of responsibility, albeit still as a prisoner (40:23). Some tension exists between Joseph's appointment as manager of the prison affairs (39:22) and his role as "servant" to the two important royal prisoners, the cupbearer *(butler,* RSV) and the *baker* (40:4). This may suggest differences in the Joseph story as it was passed on among separate groups (Vawter, 1977: 403-405). But in the text as we have it, the tension stands without comment, indicating nothing more than that two very important prisoners had arrived, ones requiring special treatment.

In spite of their official importance, the royal cupbearer and baker play a marginal role in this drama. We are not told their names. They serve primarily to enhance Joseph's stature still further. We first met

Joseph as a dreamer. The meaning of those dreams seemed self-evident, at least to Joseph's family. Now again Joseph's life will be changed by dreams, but this time he has a different role, the interpreter of dreams.

We have our own experience with dreams, at least as dreamers and perhaps some of us as the interpreters of dreams. Obviously, dreams play a quite different role in our society than in the ancient Near East. Even so, dreams have always had an element of mystery, dealing with the unknown or not consciously known. Whereas for us dreams most often touch the not remembered past or the unconscious present, in the ancient Near East dreams were understood as signals of the unknown future. Hence the practice of interpretation involved the ability to discern that future rather than to understand the hidden past, as is true of most dream interpretation in our context. Joseph declared through a rhetorical question: *Do not interpretations belong to God?* (40:8). Unlike the past, the future can not be discovered by analysis of the dreams. In the ancient Near East, the future and hence the interpretation of dreams belonged to God.

The introductory exposition again reminds the reader twice that God is with Joseph (39:21, 23). Because of that "presence" Joseph interprets the dreams of these royal officials. In chapter 37 Joseph had two dreams with a single interpretation. A similar structure will reappear with Pharaoh's two dreams (Gen. 41). But here the two dreams have two different interpretations. Joseph announces life for the royal cupbearer *(butler,* RSV), but death for the royal baker. A word play on the key phrase "lift up your head" binds the interpretations together and connects them with the resulting events. Joseph tells the cupbearer that Pharaoh will lift up his head, restoring him to his office (40:13). But for the baker, the head will be lifted *from you* (40:19). And he is executed.

This narrative presents Joseph as one gifted by God's presence, thus able to declare a future known only to God. But the scene has a countertheme, another picture of Joseph. This we find presented only in asides: at the end of Joseph's interpretation of the cupbearers dream and in the final sentence of the scene (40:14-15, 23). Joseph needs help. He needs to be remembered (Brueggemann, 1982: 324-325). He asked the royal cupbearer for *hesed—kindness* (40:14, RSV, NASB). *Hesed* is a voluntary act of assistance given to someone vulnerable and in trouble (Sakenfeld, 1978). In the introductory exposition of this scene, the narrator stated that Joseph had received *hesed* from God. But as the scene proceeds, Joseph's assistance must come concretely from this government official if Joseph is to have a different future. The scene ends with little hope. In a statement emphasized by repetition—*did not remember*, but *forgot*—the narrator reports that the future looks closed to Joseph. Joseph remains where he was when the scene began, wearing the clothes of prison. His position is neither better or worse, just endlessly the same.

Scene 3: Before Pharaoh 41:1-57

The introduction to this scene does not narrate Joseph's rise to a responsible position from which he will then fall, as has been the case in Scenes 1 and 2 (39:1-6a, 20b-23). Rather, this scene begins with Pharaoh's problems (vv. 1-13). Deeply troubled by dreams, he can find no one to interpret them. Dreams which cannot be interpreted hold the king hostage to an opaque future. The future is there, almost but not quite available. And none of the Egyptian experts can help their Pharaoh (v. 8).

Then the royal cupbearer remembers (v. 9). Remembering brings with it a change. As with Noah (8:1), Rachel (30:22) and the slaves in Egypt (Exod. 2:24), so also here "remembering" opens the future to one living in a sterile or dangerous present. In a long speech (vv. 9-13) the royal cupbearer introduces Pharaoh to "a young Hebrew" who can open the future to others by interpreting the dreams. The cupbearer's remembering changes everything for Pharaoh and subsequently for Joseph.

Clothing has been the signal of transition for the narrative, so we are not surprised that Joseph, when called before Pharaoh, changes clothes (v. 14). In the following dialogue Joseph presents explicitly the theology of dreams that we noted above. Dreams give access to the future. That future comes from God. Therefore, only God can interpret the dreams (vv. 16, 25, 32).

Pharaoh narrates his dreams to Joseph (vv. 17-24). The first-person narration of the dreams by Pharaoh contains more drama than the narrator's more matter-of-fact description earlier in the episode (vv. 1-7). Joseph's lengthy response to Pharaoh's dreams (vv. 25-36) takes an important turn in v. 33 (Brueggemann, 1982: 332). The word translated *now* or *therefore (we'attah)* frequently marks a call to special attention or action in Hebrew speeches (Exod. 19:5; 32:10; Isa. 5:3, 5; Amos 7:16). So it does here. Joseph stops interpreting the dreams and proposes action. Given the future as God will bring it to pass, Joseph instructs Pharaoh to implement a program of conservation in the fertile years to provide food for the lean years. The speech seems wordy and a bit redundant, but Joseph speaks loudly, showing none of the usual deference or timidity appropriate to a slave/prisoner standing before a monarch (vv. 25-36).

In the speech Joseph directs Pharaoh to appoint "a man of discernment and wisdom" to implement the program of food conservation (v. 33). Pharaoh observes that Joseph's speech is a model of discernment and wisdom (vv. 38-40). Hence through the display of perceptive discernment and forthright speech the narrative seems to allow a larger-than-life Joseph to emerge (Coats, 1973: 290-296).

The encounter with Pharaoh concludes with Joseph once more changing clothes (vv. 14-45). This time he is dressed even more royally than he was in the cloak given to him by his father (41:42). In addition, Joseph receives other items which mark installation to royal office: Pharaoh's own signet ring, a gold chain, the second position in the royal protocol, a new name, and marriage into the royal family.

Scene 3 concludes on a note far different from the one with which Scene 1 began. There the narrator described a young man sold into slavery by traders (39:1). Now we find Joseph as vice-regent in Egypt implementing a program of food conservation during the years of good harvests, and of distribution during the time of scarcity (vv. 47-49, 55-57). Sandwiched in the middle of the story about Joseph as public administrator appears a report of the birth of his two sons: Manasseh and Ephraim (vv. 50-52). Joseph's speech interprets the two names as a celebration of his new life at the end of this chapter, but also as an enigmatic signal that more drama awaits. Manasseh: "God has enabled me to forget all my trouble and my whole family." Ephraim: *God has made me fruitful in the land of my affliction* (vv. 51-52).

The key word *(Leitwort)* in this conclusion to the Scene 3 is *all (kol)*. In 41:46-57 we find the word *all* repeated a dozen times. In part the word serves as narrative binder, as key words often do. But in addition the word *all* emphasizes the scope of Joseph's control of the situation. In many ways it is a control rivaled not by Pharaoh, but only by God (Brueggemann, 1982: 328). The pilgrimage of this separated brother has led from the bottom to the top, from nothing to all.

THE TEXT IN BIBLICAL CONTEXT

The pilgrimage of Joseph from slave to vice-regent parallels the journey of Israel as escapees from Egypt to the nation under Solomon, the life of David from shepherd's helper to king, and the story of Jesus from manger to the right hand of God. The biblical tradition of the triumphant rise of a faithful person of low estate to a place of power and honor is not the only path the faithful travel, but it is the journey of God's promise. This story of Joseph, who through wisdom and patience becomes vice-regent, depends on the hidden presence of God (39:21, 23; 41:37). The presence of God brings life in the place of death, honor instead of humiliation, and fertility over sterility. The biblical stories of such triumph differ in the role ascribed to humankind. Sometimes the victory happens almost in spite of the individual's behavior, for example, with Jacob. In other stories the behavior of the individual is a model of virtue, as with Joseph. But in either case triumph in the story depends not on the prowess of the people, but the presence of God, Immanuel (Matt. 1:20-23).

We must not forget the danger of such triumphalism. Quite easily the triumphant community can presume on the presence of God or presume that divine presence guarantees success. Job knows a different road and Stephen a different result. Job receives honor, wealth, and position, but only after he realizes that God's visitation does not always bring good fortune (Job 7:17-19; 16:6-17). Stephen's life ends with stones, albeit with the faith that stones will not finally end his story (Acts 7:59-60). God's presence does not always bring triumph, nor does God bring good fortune only to the virtuous. *Lo, I am with you always, to the close of the age* (Matt. 28:20), whether life ends triumphantly on a throne or painfully beneath stones or on a cross.

THE TEXT IN THE LIFE OF THE CHURCH

Joseph must deal with the presence of imperial power as well as with the presence of God. Sometimes that power works for him, elevating him in the house of Potiphar and the royal court. At other times the imperial power enslaves him further, as in the episode with the wife of Potiphar. The temptation of that situation for Joseph, at least as the text comes to us, does not lie in sexual attraction. We are told that Joseph is attractive. But we know nothing about the woman, not her appearance, not even her name. We know only that she is the master's wife. She has the power that could destroy Joseph. Joseph chooses to disobey the illegitimate request of the powerful. He pays a high price, though not as high as others have paid.

The story does not cast imperial power in a one-sidedly negative way. Royal power can work for life as well as against it, can lift up as well as destroy. In our story it does both. For Joseph, royal power is dangerous, but not evil. He lives sometimes as victim and sometimes as agent of that power. Nevertheless, for all its force, royal power does not control the future. The power of dreams exceeds the power of Pharaoh (Brueggemann, 1982: 322-323).

Joseph appears in this story as one who lives the virtues celebrated in the ancient Near East, virtues that we too hold dear: patience in the face of unjust suffering, steadfast loyalty in the face of threat to one's position and even life, forthrightness before power. In that way the narrative presents Joseph as a model person, a hero figure. Such a presentation provides an excellent way to illustrate the virtues which the tradition wants to pass on to the next generation. Even while seeking to instill those virtues in God's people, the tradition knows that the heroes of the faith also hurt and stumble when they suffer or confront power. In the face of the threat from the powerful, sometimes the faithful lie and deny like Abraham (Gen. 12:11-13) and Peter (Mark 14:66-71). When forced to endure unjust suffering, God's people at times cry out of their pain like Naomi (Ruth 1:20-21) or rage against God like Job (Job 7:11-21), or even express their sense of abandonment by God like Jesus (Mark 15:34; Ps. 22:1). The patience of Joseph and the rage of Job, the steadfast loyalty of Ruth and the tears of Naomi, belong together in the community of faith.

In this narrative God's future impinges on the human present through dreams. The dreamers, Joseph, the cupbearer, the baker, even Pharaoh, know that the power of the present does not automatically control the future. The future belongs to God. The present must adjust to God's future, lest the fat cattle be eaten by the lean and there is no food.

Genesis 42:1 — 45:28

Episode 3: The Family in Danger

PREVIEW

A famine forced the family to re-engage one another in this third episode of the saga. Like the previous one, this episode can be divided into
separate scenes. The first scene (42:1-5) takes the reader back to
Canaan, back to the setting of the first chapter of the saga (Gen. 37).
Presently Jacob, the family father, must find a way to deal with the
famine that has afflicted the area. The second scene (42:6-26) shifts to
Egypt, where the sons of Jacob appeal to the powerful Egyptian ruler for
grain. [Egypt, the River Nation, p. 318.] The ruler's concern for their real
purpose creates a mysterious overtone to the meeting. This ominous
feel deepens when in the third scene (42:27-28) one of the brothers discovers money in his sack. The fourth scene moves back to Canaan and a
distraught Jacob (42:29-38). The family has food to eat, but the complete destruction of the family seems imminent.

In the fifth scene (43:1-14), the continuing famine forces a new decision regarding the family's future. Jacob sends his sons, including
Benjamin, to Egypt in spite of the danger. The sixth scene (43:15-34)
transports the reader back to Egypt, and all seems to go well. But the
seventh scene (44:1-13) proves nearly catastrophic when a stolen cup is
found on Benjamin. The eighth scene (44:14—45:24) stretches the
family danger to the limit, but then resolves it, when the Egyptian

governor introduces himself as a brother and receives them as family. The concluding scene (45:25-28) returns to Canaan to celebrate an end to both dangers, famine and separation of the family. The only matter left unfinished is the reunion of the family in one place. Clearly the episode follows the movement of the brothers. But narratively they are not the main characters in the chapter. The brothers function primarily in a passive role, doing what they are told, often in panic. Only rarely do they actively take a role that leads to the eventual resolution of the danger. The active agents in the narrative are the two men who never met: Jacob and Joseph. Jacob primarily reacts. He must respond to circumstances that he cannot control—the famine and the power of the mysterious Egyptian ruler. Joseph holds the power and attempts to use it toward one end, to see his full brother, Benjamin.

OUTLINE

Introductory Scene 1: Canaan
    The Brothers Before Jacob, 42:1-5
Scene 2: Egypt
    The Brothers Before Joseph, 42:6-26
Scene 3: At the Inn
    The Brothers Alone, 42:27-28
Scene 4: Canaan
    The Brothers Before Jacob, 42:29-38
Scene 5: Canaan
    The Brothers Before Jacob, 43:1-14
Scene 6: Egypt
    The Brothers Before Joseph, 43:15-34
Scene 7: Outside the Egyptian City
    The Brothers and an Egyptian Official, 44:1-13
Scene 8: Egypt
    The Brothers Before Joseph, 44:14—45:24
Concluding Scene 9: Canaan
    The Brothers Before Jacob, 45:25-28

EXPLANATORY NOTES

Introductory Scene 1: Canaan 42:1-5

In this scene, Jacob re-emerges in the saga. He comes back in essentially the same position in which he left it. Jacob had said that the disintegration of his family would dominate his life (37:35) and we find him still fearful of his family's future. Jacob must again deal with circumstances over which he has no control, but which threaten to further destroy the family. In the face of famine Jacob acts as best he knows to protect the family. He instructs his sons to go to Egypt to buy grain (vv. 1-6), but Jacob keeps Benjamin with him to protect this son.

The key to Jacob's actions throughout this chapter lies in his commissioning speech to his sons (v. 2). Jacob, on the basis of reports of grain in Egypt, instructs his sons to *go down and buy*. The elderly father then gives the reason: *that we may live, and not die*. In the face of famine, Jacob finds his sons completely impotent, standing around looking at one another (v. 1). The life and death of the family seems to rest on Jacob's shoulders. So Jacob acts to preserve the family, as he will throughout this episode. Jacob apparently wants most of all to protect Benjamin and insofar as possible the rest of the family. But Jacob's work of family preservation can only be reactive. The actual power of life and death rests in the famine and the vice-regent of Egypt. Jacob does what he can, but he has precious little room in which to maneuver.

The narration in vv. 3-4 very carefully expresses the mysterious relationships which complicate this chapter. Joseph has "brothers" and he has a "brother" (Alter, 1981: 161). Joseph and Benjamin have the same set of siblings, but in a different way Joseph and Benjamin are "brothers." Of course in the family saga they are the sons of the same mother, Rachel, the only two sons of Jacob's favorite wife. But much is left unsaid. The saga does not tell us of any relationship between Benjamin and Joseph prior to this chapter. Yet Joseph uses his imperial power always toward one goal, to bring his "brother" to him—an eventuality Jacob tries to prevent.

Scene 2: Egypt 42:6-26

With 42:6 the reversal pictured in Joseph's dreams (Gen. 37:7, 9) happens, the brothers bow down to him. And yet the reversal remains hidden, known only to Joseph. The interaction between "knowing" and "not knowing," "recognizing" and "not recognizing," flows throughout the saga. Joseph's power rests as much in "knowing" and "recognizing" as in his imperial position in Egypt. The previous episode related that his position came from his "knowing" and "recognizing." Jacob, the brothers, the cupbearer and baker, Pharaoh, remain relatively powerless because they do not know. Joseph, who does know, has the power to restore or destroy the family. He comes close to destroying it.

With 42:7-16 we come to the first of three major dialogues between Joseph and his brothers (43:27-31; 44:15—45:13). In all three, conversation happens at many different levels. Only at the end of the third dialogue do all the different levels become public. Joseph treats his brothers as strangers (v. 7). The narrator carefully informs us that this was intentional. Comments scattered throughout the dialogue reiterate that Joseph's attitude and statements are a deliberate result of his recognizing, knowing, and remembering (vv. 7a, 8-9a). The narrative does not tell us directly why Joseph acted this way. Perhaps Joseph seeks revenge or wants to test the brothers to see if they have changed. This scene only hints at the basic motive: Joseph uses all his knowing and power toward achieving one end—to bring Benjamin to him (vv. 15-16).

After the preliminary introductions, Joseph accuses his brothers of espionage (vv. 9, 12, 14). The brothers respond with denial, claiming to be honest brothers, sons of the same father (v. 11). Joseph reiterates the espionage charge, and again the brothers respond by claiming to be brothers: sons of one man, the youngest is with his father and one is no more (v. 13). These responses have little value as a defense against the accusation of espionage. But perhaps known only to Joseph, the brothers have repeatedly emphasized the basic theme of the saga—the integrity and solidarity of their family—a solidarity which had been destroyed. However fractured, that family remains all they have in time of danger. Unknown to them, family relationships, not protection for the empire, also motivates their accuser.

Joseph sets up a test for the brothers (vv. 15-16). This test has a national and a family purpose. In terms of national self-interest this test purports to determine whether the brothers are spies. This reason for the test Joseph makes public. However, as such it would have proven little if Joseph had not already known them. Spies could have easily passed the test. The family elements of the test, Joseph kept to himself. The test might have been motivated by revenge—Joseph might have thrown the brothers in the pit/prison as they had done to him. Or Joseph might have been testing their fraternal bond. Would they act like brothers this time? Apparently the test was not designed to serve any of those ends.

Joseph eliminates revenge as a motivating factor when he subsequently changes the rules of the test so that only one, Simeon, goes to prison (v. 19). Clearly, the brothers can pass the test out of self-preservation—need for food—rather than fraternal loyalty, as Judah later tells Jacob (43:3-6). The test proves inadequate to see if the brothers are spies, to get revenge, or to check their family loyalty. The test works well only to bring Benjamin to Joseph. That is its intended purpose. In the presence of the powerful Egyptian whose "test" is making their lives miserable, the brothers turn their frustration inward on one another. Some conclude that this trouble is the consequence of their violation of their brother Joseph (v. 12). Reuben angrily denounces his brothers, claiming that he had warned them of this eventuality (v. 22). In a way characteristic of the reticence in Hebrew literature, the narrator waits until this point to tell us that Joseph had pleaded with his brothers for help (v. 21). *[Characteristics of Hebrew Narrative, p. 313.]* When the selling of Joseph was narrated, he appeared silently passive (37:18-24). Similarly, only here do we find out that Joseph and his brothers have been communicating through an interpreter (v. 23). Joseph's knowing has exceeded even what the readers imagined. He has had access to the brothers' private conversation without their knowledge.

Joseph weeps (v. 24). The narrator does not say why he wept. We can only suspect that this powerful "Egyptian" is more vulnerable than he appears. When next Joseph weeps, he will see Benjamin (43:30).

Scene 3: At the Inn 42:27-28

The brothers stop at a *lodging place.* While caring for their pack animals, one of them discovers money in his sack (v. 27). The brothers panic in the face of another event which they cannot understand. Perhaps a terrible mistake has been made or, even more frightening, they have been trapped with "planted" evidence (Vawter, 1977: 421-422). By not "knowing," the brothers are powerless, caught by the terror of confused events with dangerous consequences. They respond only by crying out in complaint to God (v. 28). Again the brothers confront the ominous world of "not knowing." Events seem to happen at random and the *dark* side of their imagination senses a threat to their lives.

Scene 4: Canaan 42:29-38

On returning to Jacob the brothers relate their encounter with the Egyptian lord (vv. 30-34). Their report represents a composite of the dialogue they had with Joseph, except that the conversation, as they retell it, emphasizes the "youngest" brother who remained behind in Canaan. One other curious change happens in the report by the brothers. Joseph had declared that their life was at stake in this test (vv. 16, 21). The brothers, however, acknowledge only a threat to their ability to *trade* in the land. Indirectly, the two may be the same, because the inability to buy food would be life-threatening in the famine. Nevertheless, their circumstances appear life-threatening on many levels. They might die from famine, or execution for espionage, or in a final destruction of the family. In the context of the whole ancestral saga (Gen. 12—50) the destruction of the family of Jacob may be the biggest threat.

The mystery surrounding the situation mounts because of a second discovery of money in the bags (v. 35). Some would suggest that this repeated "discovery" may be the result of the growth of the saga as it was passed on from one generation to the next. However, in the story as we have it, this duplication serves to heighten the tension; it is another inexplicable event.

Jacob responds with anger, the family continues to disintegrate, and the brothers further jeopardize the family (v. 36). Reuben makes an absurd promise. Jacob can execute Reuben's two sons if he does not bring Benjamin home safely (v. 37). Jacob is to kill the next generation if this one is further damaged! The father decides to protect what he has left of his family: Benjamin, *my son*, will not go to Egypt (v. 38).

Scene 5: Canaan 43:1-14

The first sentence in this scene allows time to pass and accentuates the danger to the family: *The famine was severe in the land* (v. 1). Circumstances now force Jacob to send to Egypt for more food. Jacob directs his sons to make that trip (v. 2). Judah becomes the speaker for the brothers, insisting that their ability to buy food, indeed to see the face of *the man*, depends on Benjamin's presence (v. 3-5). Although Joseph's words can be interpreted differently, Judah's restatement accurately represents Joseph's determination to see Benjamin.

Jacob/Israel now complains that the brothers told *the man* about *another brother* (v. 6). The brothers deny having volunteered the information (v. 7). In view of the dialogue with Joseph as reported earlier (42:7-20), their denial portrays them as frightened individuals always trying to avoid trouble. They act as those who feel victimized from all sides. Indeed, caught between Jacob and Joseph, they are pawns in a mysterious power struggle.

Nevertheless, Judah's speech takes the initiative in a way that the brothers have not done until now (42:3-5). Judah is prudent in his analysis. He takes a risk in his willingness to promise to offer himself as bond for Benjamin's safe return. His offer marks the emergence in the story of a figure who will be important in breaking the deadlock in the struggle between Jacob and Joseph over control of Benjamin. Judah reintroduces the multiple levels of the drama, saying that the purpose of making the trip with Benjamin is that *we may live and not die* (v. 8; cf. 42:2, 18-20).

Jacob agrees to the trip (vv. 11-14). He will assist by sending gifts and returning the money which mysteriously appeared after the last trip. But he sends them, nonetheless, partly out of faith and partly out of resignation (Brueggemann, 1982: 339). May God *send back your other brother and Benjamin* (v. 14). In the multiple levels of the narrative the *other brother* is Simeon, but perhaps also Joseph.

Scene 6: Egypt 43:15-34

The narrator's transitional phrase immediately places the brothers before Joseph (v. 15). We should note that the style of the Hebrew in this transitional phrase emphasizes the presence of *Benjamin*. An expanded narration describes an initial encounter with Joseph's administrative assistant (vv. 17-23). Following Joseph's instructions (v. 16), the manager brings the brothers to Joseph's house. Continuing the motif of the fear produced by "not knowing," the brothers suspect trouble, imagining a present "threat" caused by the money discovered after their previous journey to Egypt (v. 18).

The ancient tradition of the "dangerous banquet" helps augment the brothers' fear of this invitation. In both biblical and extra-biblical literature, this motif creates an aura of foreboding; any invitation to banquet with a powerful enemy carries risk. One of the best-known stories from the Egyptian religious heritage tells of the death of Osiris in a trap set at a banquet by his brother Set. In Israel's own history, Abner was killed by Joab in a similar banquet trap (2 Sam. 3). Not surprisingly, when the brothers were directed to the Egyptian lord's house, not knowing what lay ahead, the dark side of their imagination suggested that the man intended "to attack us and seize us as slaves" (v. 18).

Immediately the brothers take the initiative, professing ignorance about how the money came to be in their sacks and stating their intent to return the money (vv. 19-22). The reply by Joseph's house steward again speaks on more than one level: "Be at peace (shalom); fear not. Your God, the God of your father, must have given you treasure in your bags" (v. 23). Certainly the statement intends to reassure the brothers that they are not in danger. In addition the statement introduces one whose presence has been hidden in the mystery of this drama in Egypt—"Your God, the God of your father."

At first the banquet proves not dangerous, even enjoyable (vv. 26-34). Protocol satisfies both Hebrew and Egyptian sensitivities. However, some surprising things happen. The Egyptian vice-regent knows the seating order of this Hebrew family, oldest to youngest. Benjamin receives the best portions, both in quantity and likely quality. But the visitors apparently dismiss these mysterious elements with a look of amazement and enjoy the banquet (v. 34). One moment at the banquet the brothers did not see: for the second time (42:24) Joseph weeps, but again only in private. This time the narrator gives us the reason for Joseph's tears, his affection for Benjamin (v. 30). Nevertheless, Joseph collects himself and carries on as the public situation demands. This powerful man's national and familial worlds remain split.

Scene 7: Outside the Egyptian City 44:1-13

The joy of the banquet abruptly ends as a result of another of Joseph's manipulations. He instructs his administrative assistant to hide a valuable cup in Benjamin's sack (vv. 1-2). When the brothers have traveled only a short way out of the city, Joseph sends his assistant to confront them about the missing cup (v. 4). The brothers vehemently deny the charge. The very construction of their speech expresses the brothers' fear and panic (Coats, 1975: 42). In desperation the brothers make a rash oath, promising death to the guilty one and enslavement to the rest if the cup be discovered in their midst. This ill-considered oath almost traps them (cf. Jacob's oath concerning his favorite wife, Rachel, 31:32-35, and Saul's oath in respect to his beloved son, Jonathan, 1 Sam. 14:24-46). Joseph's steward refuses to accept the conditions of their oath. Only the guilty one will be taken back to slavery (v. 10). The punishment appears surprisingly lenient. The cup may have been valuable not only because Joseph liked it, but also as a sacred vessel. Such a crime was punishable by death (von Rad, 1973: 392). However, punishment for the criminal is not the point of this plot—a fact the brothers do not "know."

The narration slows down as the Egyptian goes through the bags of each brother, beginning with the oldest. Abruptly the narrator reports that the cup has been found in Benjamin's bag (v. 12). The story provides no direct response by any of the brothers. The narrator simply describes the scene: they tear their clothes, load their animals, and head back to the city (v. 13).

Scene 8: Egypt 44:14 – 45:24

Two speeches dominate the final confrontation between the powerful Egyptian, Joseph, and the Hebrew famine victims, his brothers. Joseph speaks first with an accusatory question: "What is this you have done?" (44:15). Caught in a web of circumstances he cannot understand, Judah acknowledges the brothers' guilt and "sentences" them all to be slaves of this powerful Egyptian official (44:16). Joseph, however, refuses that punishment, as his administrative assistant had done earlier. Declaring only Benjamin guilty, Joseph frees the others "to go in peace to your father" (44:17). Joseph's plan to keep Benjamin with him now appears complete.

Changing the sentence from the enslavement of all the brothers to only the one individual might seem like clemency. But Judah appeals that sentence as unbearably harsh. In a long dramatic speech Judah offers himself as a substitute for Benjamin (44:18-34). Gone is the panic response to earlier accusations. Gone are the rambling, self-justifying speeches of other situations. What we find here is a judiciously constructed legal appeal. Legally, Judah grounds his appeal in the oath whereby he bound himself to guarantee Benjamin's safe return (44:32). But the passion of the speech is anchored in an humanitarian appeal: their father will be driven down to Sheol in sorrow (44:31). Indeed, evil (ra'a) will fall upon Jacob (44:34).

Judah's speech reads like a masterpiece of judicial appeal on humanitarian grounds. Judah did not know that he spoke also about Joseph's father. Joseph did know.

Apparently the appeal worked. We are not told why, simply that Joseph could not "control himself" ('apaq, 45:1). Perhaps Joseph suddenly saw that Judah would not betray a brother as had happened to him (von Rad, 1973: 397). Perhaps Joseph understood what his desire to keep Benjamin with him would do to his father (Vawter, 1977: 433). Maybe not even Joseph could explain why his control of the situation broke at this moment, but it did. The imperial power broker who had controlled the course of events in this whole chapter, with only an occasional and very private lapse, suddenly lost control of himself. The man who had been able to keep separate his family and national world could do so no longer.

The narrator insists that Joseph did not give up all control. He does not go completely public with his family life (45:1). He sends his Egyptian world out of the room. But he gives himself over to crying so entirely that even the Egyptians hear it. At that point Joseph introduces himself, not once but twice (45:3-4). However this duplicate introduction is to be explained, in the received text it adds to the intensity and perhaps confusion of the disclosure moment. After Judah's long speech about the effect on Jacob's life should Benjamin not return, Joseph asks if his father is *still alive* (45:3). The brothers' shock *(bahal)* is so great they cannot speak.

Joseph's self-disclosure speech (45:4-13) gives the whole drama a theological interpretation. He asserts three times that his coming to Egypt served the purposes of God. The speech does not remove the mystery about the presence of God in the treachery of the brothers or Joseph's rise to power. Joseph does not explain but simply proclaims that God acted to preserve life—life for the many (45:7). The second part of the speech commissions the brothers to return to Jacob with a message calling him to move the family to Egypt where they can be cared for (45:9-13). We can notice even in Joseph's speech the primacy of *my brother Benjamin* (45:12).

The narrator's description of the scene after Joseph's speech pictures a nearly out-of-control Joseph going first to Benjamin and then to the rest of the brothers, greeting them and crying (45:14-15). Joseph apparently still works within his initial goal, the reunion with Benjamin. Nevertheless, the previous picture of Joseph as a calculating imperial official, one who manipulates circumstances to control events, dissolves in the powerful passion of self-disclosure. It is not the calculating plans of the royal Joseph but the passionate self-disclosure of Jacob's son that heals the family (Brueggemann, 1983: 345).

The narrative speaks only one line about the brothers' response, three words in Hebrew, *his brothers talked with him* (45:15). That brief comment, characteristic of the reticence of Hebrew narrative, leaves unsaid as much as it says. Healing has happened. The brothers, who could not say a peaceful word to Joseph when the story began (37:4), now speak to him. But what do they say? Do they trust Joseph's interpretation of the past or his intentions for the future? The brothers emerge very rarely as speakers in the rest of the saga (45:26; 50:15-17). When they do speak, they remain apprehensive about whether the proclaimed new future can really be trusted.

The scene ends with Pharaoh instructing Joseph to do much of what he has already offered (45:16-20). The brothers head home loaded with gifts. All the drama of reunion has not changed one thing. Joseph still likes Benjamin best, and so the favorite returns home with more than anyone else (45:22).

Concluding Scene 9: Canaan 45:25-28

The brothers return to Jacob to report what happened in Egypt. The most important element is narrated by direct speech: *Joseph is alive and he is ruler over all the land of Egypt* (v. 26). According to the narrator, Jacob initially responded with numb disbelief (v. 26). But finally he could say, *Joseph, my son is still alive* (v. 28). He determines to see his son. That decision begins the transition between Jacob in Canaan and Israel in Egypt (Coats, 1975: 48). This move signifies more than just a new chapter in this saga. The shift marks the end of a biblical book and an era, the time of Israel's matriarchs and patriarchs in the broad story of the people of God. The journey to Egypt will reunite the family, but in the context of the larger story, unknown to the happy father, this reunion will come at the considerable cost of "Israel's" freedom *[Egypt, the River Nation, p. 318.]*

THE TEXT IN BIBLICAL CONTEXT

The tension between "knowing" and "not knowing" is one of the energizing motifs of this chapter in the Joseph saga (Alter, 1981: 163ff.). The first scene (42:6-26) begins with Joseph knowing and the brothers not knowing. Consequently, Joseph has more control over the present and the future than his brothers have. The phrase *know the truth, and the truth will make you free* has become a proverb quite apart from its place in the Gospel of John (8:32). Throughout most of this chapter, the story of the father and the brothers illustrates this proverb. The brothers and Jacob were not free because they did not know. They found themselves controlled by the "knower." The drama reaches its climax when Joseph lets his family "know." Control is given up and separation overcome.

The biblical tradition celebrates the joy and power that come with knowing. Ezekiel punctuates his prophetic words with a traditional liturgical formula: "You shall know that I am Yahweh" (Zimmerli, 1982: 29-98). The Gospel of John emphasizes knowing as the way to life (14:1-7). Such a life-giving disclosure happens in Jesus Christ:

> I am the way, the truth, and the life; no one comes to the Father, but by me. If you had known me, you would have known my Father also; henceforth you know him and have seen him. (John 14:6-7)

However, "knowing" also has a dangerous side. This episode portrays Joseph using his knowing as a weapon. Through his discernment Joseph was able to fulfill brilliantly his role as vice-regent in Egypt. Yet his managerial skill combined with his private knowledge of the visitors' identity brought the family to the brink of ruin. The tale of the garden

(Gen. 3) reminds us that the misuse of knowledge can bring disaster, even punishment.

In Genesis 45:5-8 Joseph interprets the whole story theologically as a part of the divine drama to "save lives." Luther describes Joseph's words as the biblical "theology of promise" *(Luther's commentary on Genesis:* 314-316). According to Luther, we live in the promise that God's providential presence follows us "whether the days are good or evil." Protestant theology usually turns to Calvin for an emphasis on God's providential action of salvation. Not surprisingly, Calvin calls this text "remarkable" *(Calvin's Commentaries:* 377-381). Indeed we find in Calvin's commentary, more than Luther's, an emphasis on the God who secretly directs the motions of human actions. Calvin struggles to discuss the way in which the brothers remain responsible in the face of secret divine control of events. But finally little can be said except that God's hidden presence in events turns "wicked designs" to good. The relationship between the providential power of God to control events and the God-given freedom of people to make history remains a mystery. That riddle can be stated, perhaps illustrated, in story form as here, but never finally defined.

THE TEXT IN THE LIFE OF THE CHURCH

This chapter in the saga of Joseph builds on the previous ones, showing a broken family in danger of complete destruction. Many issues emerge from the pages of this episode, too many to be taken up here. Some of the issues arise here but continue later and discussion of them will be held off, e.g., forgiveness and reconciliation (50:20). Just now we shall look at only one motif, one that has been building throughout the saga and reaches a crescendo in this episode—the situation of persons who find themselves not in control of the events that shape their lives.

In the introductory episode all the characters experience themselves in one way or another as victims. The brothers find themselves victimized by their father's favoritism (37:4) and their brother's dreams (37:8). Joseph and Jacob become victims as the brothers act out of their hatred. Both Judah and Tamar are victimized, Judah by the mysterious death of two sons (38:11) and Tamar by Judah's response to those two deaths (38:14). In Egypt Joseph is victimized by the anger of his master's wife and the forgetfulness of the imperial servant. Finally in this chapter the famine and the harsh Egyptian vice-regent victimize Jacob and his eleven sons.

In the course of portraying these persons, whose lives are shaped by events over which they have no control, the narrator pictures the whole spectrum of available responses. Jacob most often responds by dissolving into grief and self-protective actions. He refuses to be comforted following the reported death of his favorite son (37:35). He acts to protect a second son, clinging to him until famine forces his letting go. Jacob allows Benjamin to make the dangerous trip to Egypt only when the very life of the whole family depends on it, and then with a fatalistic resignation (43:14). Judah, the other responsible head of a family in this saga, acts in self-protective ways similar to Jacob's. Judah safeguards his only remaining son, refusing to allow him customary intercourse with a daughter-in-law who is perhaps implicated in the deaths of his other two sons (38:26). Very often, it seems, those in responsible positions act first to preserve and protect when confronted by the uncontrollable, the unexplainable.

The brothers usually respond to the uncontrollable with anger or panic. Seizing the opportunity, they attack Joseph, making him the victim of their hostility. However, in the face of famine and the power of the Egyptian official, they have little recourse. Reuben turns on his brothers with hostility similar to the hatred all of them visited on Joseph, "Didn't I tell you . . . ?" (42:22, NIV). But for the most part, the speeches of the brothers reveal confusion created in part by events they do not understand and by their own imaginations. The brothers, caught between famine and political power, seem victimized as much by the dark side of their imaginations as by the external events themselves.

The narrative shows Judah explicitly trapped by his own fear following the death of his two sons: "for he thought, 'Perhaps he will die as his brothers did' " (38:11). Caught in the unknown, the brothers, and even Jacob, find themselves gripped by fear, intensified by the dark side of their own imaginings. Judah finally breaks out of that "prison" when confronted with the evidence brought by his daughter-in-law (38:26). Later he expresses this "freedom" with his father (43:8-10) and finally face-to-face with the powerful Egyptian administrator (44:18-34). The course of the story changes with Judah's emergence as one who refuses to be victimized either by circumstances or his own fears. Instead he acts decisively toward the future, albeit within the constraints of circumstances.

Two other characters seize opportunities to respond "pro-actively" in dangerous circumstances. Genesis 39—41 presents Joseph as a model of such a person. Though servant and prisoner, Joseph manages as responsibly as possible, administering a household and prison, even interpreting dreams of others who are confused by the unknown. Tamar also refuses to be reduced to victim (Gen. 38). Even though circumstances give her no legal room to maneuver, she makes history happen, providing space for herself and a future for the family.

The narrative also portrays Joseph and especially Benjamin as completely passive victims of circumstances (Gen. 37; 43; 44). Later we are told that Joseph pleaded with his brothers not to kill him (42:21), but in the midst of the kidnapping, the narrative tells us nothing about Joseph. He remains a silent victim. As for Benjamin, he never speaks in the saga. He initiates no action. We learn nothing about his thoughts or feelings. He remains hidden from view, caught between the protective grip of his fearful father and the yearning desire of his powerful brother. Never does he break that silence. The only hint we have of a Benjamin beyond silence is his tears at Joseph's self-disclosure (45:14).

The narrative illustrates well the range of human response to the unknown and uncontrollable. Although the story depends on the active initiation of Joseph, Tamar, and Judah, those are not the only responses that the saga values. The hostility of the brothers delivers Joseph to Egypt. The grief of Jacob expresses the brokenness of the family. In the midst of all the hostility and grief, activity and passivity, lies hidden the presence of God, more inexplicable and mysterious than any other factor. Joseph can only name but never explain God's presence in these events. Undoubtedly many times we feel as victimized by God's hidden presence as we do by uncontrollable circumstances. Sometimes we can mirror Tamar, Joseph, and Judah, and follow the steps of the one who refused to be victimized even by the cross.

Episode 4: The Reunification of the Family

PREVIEW

The family was divided emotionally and physically in the first episode of the saga (37:1-36). Some of the narrative tension was resolved in the previous episode with Joseph's self-disclosure (45:3), the brothers' words to one another (45:15), and Jacob's revived spirit (45:27-28). This episode reunited the family, this time in Egypt rather than Canaan.

Genesis 46:1—47:27 presents us with a collection of material rather than the carefully woven narrative we have become accustomed to in this saga. Jacob's encounter with God (46:1b-4), the list of names in Jacob's family (46:8-27), and the report of Joseph's economic program (47:13-26) have a relatively minor function in the Joseph narrative itself but help tie this saga with the Jacob story before it and the Exodus narrative afterward. The broader narrative, more than the separate details, will command our attention here.

Notes about the journey (46:1a, 5-7) bracket the speech of God to Jacob (46:1b-4) with which the unit begins. Following that encounter with God comes a name list of the extended family of Jacob (46:8-27), then the reunion of Joseph with Jacob (46:28-30), followed by an audience with the Egyptian Pharaoh (46:31—47:1). The unit concludes with a long narration about Joseph's administration during the famine (47:13-26), sandwiched between two notes concerning the family's settlement in Egypt (47:11-12, 27).

OUTLINE

Report of Israel's Move, 46:1-27
 46:1a Note of Departure
 46:1b-4 Encounter with God
 46:5-7 Note of Arrival
 46:8-27 List of Names

Report of Reunion, 46:28-30
 46:28-29a Preparations
 46:29b-30 Meeting

Report of Audience with Pharaoh, 46:31—47:10
 46:31—47:1 Preparations
 47:2-10 Meeting
  Brothers, 47:2-6
  Jacob, 47:7-10

Report of the Family's Settlement, 47:11-27
 47:11-12, Note Concerning Settlement
 47:13-26, Administration by Joseph
 47:27, Concluding Note

EXPLANATORY NOTES

Report of Israel's move 46:1-27

The narration reporting Jacob/Israel's move to Egypt frames the only direct address by God in the entire saga. These journey notes (vv. 1a, 5-7) mention only scattered details about the family's move to Egypt, including one stop at Beersheba. The sentences make clear that the move was complete. Everything went to Egypt, all the movable property, especially all the people. Certainly the fact of the move to Egypt has to do with the flow of the Joseph story. But the narrative insistence on the completeness of the move probably pushes us into the story of the Exodus. A central affirmation of the Hebrew faith declares that all the people of Israel were children of God's deliverance from Egypt.

 The theophany (vv. 1b-4)—Jacob's encounter with God—at Beer

sheba ties this saga to the theme of promise which the Abraham saga bequeathed as the overarching theme of all the ancestral stories of Genesis. The encounter follows the very typical pattern we meet elsewhere in Genesis and other Hebrew literature: call by God, response of the individual, speech by God (cf. 22:1-3; 1 Sam. 3:10-14). Like some other addresses, this speech begins with a formula of divine introduction, *I am God,* followed by promise (cf. 28:13-15). The promise contains three elements, two of which tie this text to the great promise motif in the sagas of Abraham and Jacob: the promise of a great nation (12:2) and the promise of presence (28:15) (Westermann, 1980). But the third promise ties this moment to the future Exodus: *I will bring you up again* (v. 4). The narrative moves Jacob to Egypt, but the hidden element is Israel's move to Egypt and God's subsequent deliverance from Egypt. The lure of that future salvation pulls on the story from the very moment of Jacob/Israel's movement to Egypt.

The same tie to the past and the future can be seen in the list of names which concludes the report of Jacob's move (vv. 8-27). The name list organizes the family according to the mothers of the Jacob saga: Leah, Zilpah, Rachel, and Bilhah. It is not surprising that the tradition has handed on family lists that vary from one another. The list of names here differs in some particulars from the same basic list in Numbers 26:5-50 and 1 Chronicles 2:1-2. The list in Genesis 47:8 begins formally with the same words that start the book of Exodus: *These are the names of the descendants of Israel, who came into Egypt* (46:8; Exod. 1:1). Again we note the emphasis that the *whole* family of Jacob is a product of Egypt and the Exodus.

Reunion 46:28-30

We saw in the Abraham saga that the narrative awaited the birth of a son to Sarah and Abraham. When that birth finally happened, the narrative presented it in a very matter-of-fact way (21:1-3). The same dynamic happens here. This saga has yearned for a full reconciliation and reunion of Jacob's family. That reunion was accomplished in part by Joseph's self-disclosure (Gen. 45), but the full reunion awaits Jacob's move to Egypt.

Now the full reunion happens and the narrative makes relatively little of it. The narrator simply tells us that the reunion was an emotional one (v. 29). The only direct speech, Jacob's, declares that his life and with it the whole story is fulfilled (v. 30). The saga itself moves on quickly to the family's audience before Pharaoh.

Audience with Pharaoh 46:31 – 47:10

Perhaps the most curious element in the preparation for the audience with Pharaoh is the matter of the family's occupation. Joseph begins telling his brothers that *he* will introduce them to Pharaoh as *shepherds (ro'eh ṣon)* for they are "ones who care for livestock" *('anše miqneh,* v. 32). Joseph directs them not to use the word "shepherd" to identify themselves but just to say that they are "ones who care for livestock" (v. 34). The scene then turns to Pharaoh's presence. In introducing his family, Joseph does not use the word "shepherd" (47:1). However, the brothers, in response to Pharaoh, use exactly the word Joseph told them to avoid, without eliciting a negative response (47:3) *[Occupation: Keepers of Livestock, p. 324.]*

We have no evidence to suggest that a prejudice existed in Egypt against shepherds. It is wise counsel not to invest too much energy in trying to figure out this detail of the story (Brueggemann, 1982: 357). Other details in this meeting also cause problems. For example, Pharaoh speaks to Joseph as if he, Pharaoh, were informing Joseph of the arrival of his family (47:5). Perhaps some of the confusing details can be explained by the growth of the tradition as it was passed on.

Whatever the explanation of these ill-fitting details, we can talk about the effect they have on the narrative. The merging of this family into the Egyptian imperial culture exhibits dissonance from the start. The two worlds do not quite fit together. The picture of Jacob twice pronouncing blessing on Pharaoh (47:7, 10) further extends the incongruity of this family as a part of this empire. Blessing is a royal, priestly responsibility. This elderly refugee from Canaan has no position from which to pronounce blessing on the Egyptian monarchy. The odd elements in the narrative feed the reader's sense that this family in this land constitutes a mismatch. *[Egypt: The River Nation, p. 318.]*

Settlement of the Family 47:11-27

Notes concerning the settlement of the family in Egypt (vv. 11-12, 27) bracket this section. These sentences serve as brackets for a long narration about Joseph's administration during the famine. The effect of his administrative actions strengthens governmental control over the entire Egyptian population (vv. 16-19). Pharaoh ends up owning all the livestock and property, save only that of the priests. The narrative certainly shows the brilliance of Joseph's administration when judged by its control over the country, and perhaps even by the ability of Joseph to find a way through the catastrophic famine (von Rad, 1973: 410-411).

But in the results of Joseph's administration another ironic note may be heard, especially in 47:21. The Hebrew text (as it stands) reads that Joseph moved the people into cities (v. 21, NASB). But the more likely reading, found in the Greek and other texts, declares that Joseph followed the people's offer and made the Egyptian people *slaves* of Pharaoh (RSV, NIV). This pattern of pharonic ownership of all the land may reflect development in Egypt after 1600 B.C. It may also reflect the tension that existed between pharonic control and the power of the priestly groups who historically resisted that control (v. 22).

The irony of this anecdote must not be lost on us. This is written in the shadow of Exodus 1:8, where a Pharaoh arose over Egypt who did not know Joseph. That Pharaoh made slaves of the Hebrews. In Genesis 47:21 a Hebrew made slaves of the Egyptians. In a double twist to the story, Joseph has established an economic order that would subsequently enslave his own people (Vawter, 1977: 447). One senses that much of the history of the use and abuse of economic power is mirrored in this anecdote.

THE TEXT IN BIBLICAL CONTEXT

Most of the Joseph story has moved along without explicit relationship to the other ancestral sagas of Genesis, but that changes with this episode. This episode looks backward to pick up the promises that have bound together the previous sagas and forward to life and subsequent enslavement in Egypt. The family receives permission from Pharaoh to settle in Egypt without any restrictions. Indeed Pharaoh is blessed by Jacob. And yet the family does not quite fit in Egypt. There is a hint of prejudice against these shepherds, and the tightly centralized system of royal control which Joseph helped to foster appears ominous.

The biblical texts often reflect the faith's ambiguous relationship with royal organizations and traditions. This ambiguity shows up in the stories of the rise of Israel's own monarchy. The phrases, *In those days there was no king in Israel; everyone did what was right in his own eyes"* (Judg. 17:6; 21:25) characterize pre-monarchical Israel as a time without proper controls and limits. On the other hand, apparently, those same historians concluded that evil in the royal office was responsible for the nation's defeat by foreign powers (2 Kings 23:26; 24:3). The speech of Samuel anticipates a king who will nearly enslave the people (1 Sam. 8). But the psalmist celebrates the king as the agent through whom justice and righteousness, peace and fertility, come from God to the people (Ps. 72). The powerful efficiency of a monarch attracted Israel and was understood as a divine gift to a threatened and troubled people. But the faith warned also of the danger that lay in centralized royal administration.

The same ambivalence appears in the New Testament as the Christian church sought to understand Jesus. He was the King of the Jews, but different from other kings. Jesus inherited David's royal office but combined that with the tradition of the suffering servant to create a new figure.

Joseph administered the economy with royal authority. The family lived on the edge of complete "royalization" (Brueggemann, 1982: 352-358). But the faith community of the God of Abraham, Isaac, Jacob, and Jesus can never quite fit into a kingdom as this world understands it. The kingdom of God is like none the rulers of the nations have ever seen (Matt. 27:11-12; Luke 18:18-25; John 10:22-24; 18:36).

THE TEXT IN THE LIFE OF THE CHURCH

Danger attends any economic system (Brueggemann, 1982: 357). From a faith perspective, danger exists whether one wields economic power or is the victim of economic forces. This saga understands very well both sides of the danger. Joseph's initial introduction into this arena was as a victim, sold into slavery. At the end of this episode in the saga, Joseph functions as the most powerful figure in Egypt's royal economy. The economic pilgrimage of the brothers took them from being shepherds to famine victims to settled refugees. In this story the economic path of the Egyptian populace followed still another route, from being independent landowners, to slaves, to heavily taxed farmers.

The victims of economic power live always at the behest of those in control. The question of basic survival dominates their life. In the New Testament no writer understands that danger better than Luke. In beatitude form Jesus announces God's realm with the sort of economic adjustments that will satisfy the needs of those struggling for survival.

> Blessed are you poor,
>   for yours is the kingdom of God.
> Blessed are you that hunger now,
>   for you shall be satisfied. (Luke 6:20-21)

We cannot abstract a normative economic system from the Bible, but the biblical texts constantly reinforce a commitment to fairness in economic matters. We find a critique of economic malpractice from both the prophets and Jesus, as well as an attempt to redress unfair economic situations through the Sabbath and Jubilee programs outlined in the Hebrew Bible and the sharing of resources recorded by the early church (Lev. 25; Acts 2; 4; Rom. 15).

In the course of this saga, Joseph came perilously close to using economics as an oppressive tool to accomplish other goals. He used economic muscle to force his father to give up control of Benjamin. Joseph also managed Egypt through the famine, but at the cost of introducing a heavily centralized economic system. The narrative does not evaluate Joseph's performance directly. Pharaoh believes Joseph to be a brilliant manager. As we shall see, the brothers remain wary of Joseph's power (50:15-17).

This saga knows that economic systems pose a danger not only for the poor, the hungry, the enslaved, but also for the rich, the satisfied, the managers. The danger of too much economic power is only suggested by this narrative, but comes into sharp focus in the Exodus saga that follows. The biblical tradition knows that it is hard for the rich to manage in the kingdom of God—not impossible, just hard (Mark 10:23-27).

Genesis 47:28 — 50:26

Concluding Episode: Testamentary Activities

PREVIEW

The saga has centered around two figures—Jacob and Joseph. The story began with the two of them sharing a parent-child bond that excluded and troubled other members of the family. The narrative moved through a time when, against one another, they each tried to gain or maintain protective custody of Benjamin. Finally Jacob and Joseph were tearfully reunited. Following that reunion, the story and the lives of the two main characters came to an end. As does the Abraham saga (Gen 24—25), this narrative concludes with the testamentary activities (i.e., the final words and actions) and death of Jacob and Joseph. The biblical tradition preserves the testamentary activities of many of its major figures—Moses (Deut.), David (1 Kings 1—2), and Jesus (the Passion narrative). These testamentary activities involve the passing along of tradition, responsibility, authority, and sometimes property from one generation to the next.

This concluding chapter in the saga gives major space to the testamentary activities and death of Jacob. The material preserved about Jacob's death reads like a puzzle that does not quite fit together. The narrative gives the readers different feelings about how long Jacob lived after moving to Egypt. Some phrases, including Jacob's speeches, sug gest that events moved quickly from the reunion with Joseph to the elderly father's death. The genealogical note says 17 years (47:28). The "blessings" on the brothers (Gen. 48) are written in the manner of ancient tribal sayings. In some of them the Hebrew text is so confusing that the translations can vary widely. When translators cannot clear up difficult places, they continue the past translations. That has happened through many of these sayings. Nevertheless, we can see some of the textual problems by looking at the footnotes in the translations of Genesis 49.

We find an additional puzzle in this unit. Was Jacob buried near the threshing floor of Atad in Transjordan (50:10-11) or the cave of Machpelah in Canaan? (50:13). Explanations and understandings of these confusing elements vary, but the overall effect is a roughness uncharacteristic of much of the rest of the saga.

While the bulk of the unit reports the testamentary activities and death of Jacob, the last few verses do the same for Joseph (50:22-26). Both sections begin with a genealogical note (47:28; 50:22), but the narrative concerning Joseph moves swiftly through his last words with his brothers (50:24-25) to his death and at least temporary burial in Egypt (50:26). The fact that his older brothers seem not to have aged compared with Joseph provides an unusual note to this section similar to the one we found in the report of Jacob's last activities and death.

A concluding confrontation between Joseph and his brothers lies between the two reports of testamentary activities and death (50:15-20). In spite of its brevity, this encounter provides an important theological conclusion to the saga, corresponding to the final activities and death of the two main characters.

OUTLINE

Narration of Jacob's Testamentary Activities
and Death, 47:28—50:14
47:28   Genealogical Note
47:29-31   Oath Ritual (Burial Request)
48:1-7   Ritual of Adoption
48:8-20   Blessing of Ephraim and Manasseh
48:21—49:32 Farewell Speeches
    To Joseph, 48:21-22
    To All the Brothers, 49:1-28
    Jacob's Burial Request, 49:29-32
49:33   Death
50:1-14   Mourning and Burial

Report of an Encounter Between Joseph
and His Brothers, 50:15-21
   50:15-17 Preparations
      Speech of the Brothers, 50:15
      Action by the Brothers, 50:16-17a
      Response of Joseph, 50:17b
   50:18-21 Meeting
      Speech by Brothers, 50:18
      Speech by Joseph, 50:19-21

Narration of Joseph's Testamentary Activities
and Death, 50:22-26
   50:22-23 Genealogical Note
   50:24-25 Farewell Speeches to the Brothers
      Concerning the Future, 50:24
      Burial Request, 50:25
   50:26 Death and Burial

EXPLANATORY NOTES

Narration of Jacob's Testamentary Activities
and Death 47:28 – 50:14

47:29-31 Oath Ritual

The final actions, testamentary activities, of Jacob begin and end
with his request that he be buried with the family (v. 30; cf. 49:29-32). As
mentioned above, the narrative leaves the exact burial site uncertain.
Here Jacob requests to be buried *with my fathers* (47:30). The later burial request again uses the phrase *with my fathers,* but goes on to specify
the cave as Machpelah from the Abraham saga (v. 30). Joseph, addressing Pharaoh, speaks of Jacob's request to be buried in the tomb *which I
[Jacob] hewed out for myself* (50:5). Later the narrative locates the
funeral east of Jordan (50:11) and then returns to Machpelah (50:13).

The effect is to emphasize the deep uncertainty surrounding Jacob's
burial. That uncertainty fits with Jacob's anxiety about his burial in his
speech first to Joseph, then to all his sons. By means of oath, Jacob tries
to control his relationship to the future, when he can no longer act for
himself (vv. 29-31). His request to Joseph for *ḥesed* (loyalty, love, kindness) reminds us again about the power of that word. *Ḥesed* involves the
voluntary action of one in response to the serious need of another.
Jacob can appeal for *ḥesed,* even try to secure the promise by oath. But

once he dies, Jacob's request for ḥesed depends on the voluntary action of Joseph (Sakenfeld, 1978). Jacob's tie to his ancestors and his place in the family's future rests in the hands of Joseph and his brothers. Can Jacob trust those hands?

48:1-7 Ritual of Adoption

In some genealogical lists, Joseph appears as the primary name (Gen. 49: Deut. 33). But in others Ephraim and/or Manasseh are listed as the tribal units, either with or without mention of Joseph (Num. 1; Judg. 5). This ritual of adoption brings those two traditions together. According to this text Ephraim and Manasseh become sons of Jacob, rather than Joseph (vv. 5-6). This displacement of the favored Joseph constitutes another jarring element at the end of the saga.

Jacob's comments concerning Rachel's death further add to the confusion in this final scene, confusing at least to an onlooker (v. 9). Again one might explain in different ways the reason for the verse or its connection with its context. But the effect of 48:7 is to give a vividness to the deathbed scene. Unexpectedly, as Jacob tries to set the family matters in order before his own death, he mentions the death of his wife, Rachel, a memory still very present to the dying father.

One suspects that this speech of Jacob reflects accurately the last moments of those for whom rational consistency is no longer of primary importance. The thoughts of those dying often move according to their own logic. They selectively choose moments from their past, not to chronicle their life but to ease the family into a future without them or to pass on items from their life that remain important at their death. It is the living that demand an explicitly logical progression to speech and think odd or senile conversation whose logic lies in the memory of the dying.

48:8-20 Blessing of Ephraim and Manasseh

We encountered the motif first with Cain and Abel—the younger child favored over the older. We have found the same motif throughout the family stories: Isaac rather than Ishmael, Jacob instead of Esau, Joseph over all his brothers. Here again Jacob's primary blessing goes to the younger, Ephraim, over Manasseh.

This episode begins in a way similar to the blessing of Jacob (Gen. 27). Again the scene is the bed of the dying patriarch. The nearly blind man cannot recognize the ones who stand before him. Unlike Jacob himself, however, Joseph undertakes no deception, telling his father who stands before him, even positioning the sons so the blessing ritual is correctly carried out (v. 13).

Jacob blesses his grandsons (now his sons) but not correctly as Joseph has positioned them. By laying the right hand of blessing on the younger son and the left hand on the older, he favors the younger. Joseph tries to stop this "error," interrupting the ritual (v. 18). But Jacob keeps his hands where they were, giving preference to Ephraim, the ancestral name of the tribe that became the dominant group in the Northern Kingdom, Israel.

The words of blessing themselves do not show preference of Ephraim over Manasseh (vv. 15-16, 20). Only the ritual and Jacob's response to Joseph's objection favor Ephraim. The blessing words tie the family's past to the future of both sons. The same God who carried the family throughout this story is invoked to prosper the family in the future. The name "Israel" and the promise of fertility for the family now becomes the heritage of a new generation. The boys receive a promise which is an extension of the promise of blessing woven throughout the ancestral stories of Genesis. Ephraim and Manasseh are empowered to become a model of a community blessed by God (48:20). [Blessing in Genesis, p. 312.]

48:21—49:32 Farewell Speeches

The narrative of Jacob's testamentary activities concludes with a series of three speeches by the patriarch. The first speech is addressed to Joseph (48:21-22). This speech reiterates the promise of God's presence, an element added in the Jacob saga to the flow of "promise" through Genesis (26:3). Usually the promise of God's presence comes to the recipient in connection with a journey (Westermann, 1980: 141-143). For example, the promise came to Jacob as he traveled to the family's homeland (28:15). But this narrative connects the promise of presence with a future journey, the Exodus. Jacob's farewell speech signals again that the pilgrimage of this family will not end where Genesis does, in Egypt.

Farewell speech to Joseph, 48:21-22. Jacob's farewell speech to Joseph ends on an enigmatic note (v. 22). Jacob bequeaths to Joseph a "shoulder" *(šekem)* which he took from the inhabitants of the land. The Hebrew word could be the proper name, Shechem (see *The Jerusalem Bible),* or it could refer generically to any *mountain slope.* A veiled reference to a Hebraic conquest of Shechem may also stand behind the story of the violation of Dinah in Genesis 34. However, in Genesis 34 Jacob condemns the deceitful conquest. Nevertheless, we do not know any other hillside or slope that might have been conquered by the Jacob tribes early in the Hebrew settlement in Canaan. Jacob's bequest of *šekem* to Jospeh leaves the reader with an element of mystery, perhaps even confusion.

Farewell speech to all the brothers, 49:1-29. Jacob's speech to his sons also has some confusing elements. Part of this comes from problems that we have translating some of the verses (e.g., vv. 4, 21, 22, 24, 26). The introduction leads us to expect oracles about the family's destiny (v. 1). Some of the oracles appear in that form (e.g., concerning Judah, vv. 8-12 and Joseph, vv. 22-26). But in other of the blessings we find not an oracle but a proverb (e.g., Naphtali, v. 21 and Benjamin, v. 27). Several points of tension appear between this farewell speech and the saga in which it is found. For example, Ephraim and Manasseh are not mentioned in spite of the fact that they have been adopted as sons. Perhaps this old poem was passed on separate from the saga into which it has been incorporated.

Nevertheless, the poem set in the context of Jacob's death further forces the attention of the reader on the future, beyond even the Exodus to Israel's nationhood. As such, the sayings emphasize the ones whose descendants will become the dominant groups in the North (Joseph) and the South (Judah). For Judah the saying looks toward a time of wealth and power, indeed royal (messianic) power. For Joseph the word *blessing* is repeated six times in six lines (vv. 25-26): fertility from the heavens, the deeps, and the womb will carry the posterity of Joseph. *[Blessing in Genesis, p. 312.]*

The poem expresses that the family's future includes trouble as well as blessing: scattering, violence, violation, and turmoil follow the family as well as blessing and power. Through all this, the family remains the carrier of God's blessing into the future, as it was in the past (49:28).

Jacob's burial request, 49:29-32. The testamentary words of Jacob call the reader back to the dying ancestor's initial request (vv. 29-31)— that he be buried in Canaan with his ancestors. The desire to be buried with one's ancestors was central to the Hebrew approach of death. Generally this involved burial in family tomb or property. And yet the need to be buried with the ancestors touched a need that ran deeper than the geographical location of the burial. Burial was invested with the hope that not even death could break the family bond (Kaiser and Lohse, 1981:51). To be buried with the ancestors helped solidify that bond.

Jacob grounded his burial request in the promise of land which had carried the family from the beginning of these ancestral sagas (12:7). The promise which held together this community in some way involved land, Canaan. By the providence of God the family's future lay in

Canaan, the land of famine and promise, not in Egypt, the country of food and Pharaoh. Jacob's burial request, twice reiterated (47:29-31; 49:29-32), appears as a statement of faith in God's future rather than just the nostalgic demand of an old man to be buried on the homeplace.

49:33–50:14 Death and Burial

Jacob's last breath, which the reader has expected since 47:31, happens after the second burial request (49:33). The weeping of Joseph has marked all the moments of tension and transition of the family in Egypt (42:24; 43:30; 45:15; 46:29; 50:1, 17) and so it too marks his father's death.

The burial and mourning become a joint Hebrew and Egyptian affair (50:1-3). Archaeology suggests that Egypt took more care in the preservation of the corpse than any people of the ancient Near East. Their burial customs included elaborate rituals designed to prepare the deceased for a future at least as comfortable as the past. Hebrew burial tradition seems far more simple, but even Israel insisted that the corpse be handled properly, not just in honor of the person's life, but out of concern for the future. It was important for the living and dead that the deceased rest peacefully in Sheol (Kaiser and Lohse, 1981).

The death of Jacob results in a very elaborate mourning ritual. The Canaanites looked with astonishment at the funeral cortege and ceremony (50:11). Usually the biblical narrative of death and burial describes that moment with great restraint (cf. Abraham, 25:8-10; Moses, Deut. 34:5-8; David, 1 Kings 2:10). But not here. Jacob, who fought his way into life, departs life just as dramatically. The life of Jacob, which has stretched over half the book of Genesis, has seen the family through moments of trust and betrayal, sterility and fertility, feast and famine, separation and reunion, all within the promise and providence of God. Whether in trust or in treachery, Jacob/Israel was never far from the center stage.

Report of an Encounter Between Joseph and His Brothers 50:15-21

The leaving of the central character creates uncertainty in any social structure. Not unexpectedly, apprehension strikes this family at Jacob's death. We do not have to think of the brothers as unchanged and petty to understand their fear at their father's death. The resolution of past family issues had happened in a specific social context. The brothers' guilt and Joseph's use of power had been reconciled in a context which included Jacob as the head of the family. But with Jacob's death the family is dramatically changed; the social context within which the resolution happened no longer exists. The unexpected resignation of a pastor, the sudden removal of a political figure, can have the same effect on those contexts as the death of a central figure has on a family. All of the relationships within the community are affected. When the family gathers at the death of a member, they must deal with their apprehension concerning the family's future. For example, how will the brothers and sisters get along when the parents are gone?

Joseph's speech begins the process of redefining their relationships (50:19-21). Before the speech the narrative again marks this moment of family tension in Egypt with Joseph's tears (50:17b). After the formula of assurance, fear not, Joseph's speech continues with an enigmatic question: *Am I in the place of God?* (50:19). The rhetorical question expects to be answered, "No." On the surface, a simple "No" does little to clarify matters for the brothers, who are unsure about where they stand. And yet it might also be a way for Joseph to lay aside his royal power, declaring that he will not assume or resume that role he exercised in their first meetings. Even though ambiguity remains in the rhetorical question, the element that carries the speech is the twice repeated formula of assurance: *Fear not* (50:19, 21) (Brueggemann, 1982: 372-373). Joseph declares that his actions in the future can be trusted to promote life, not to avenge past wrongs.

The family can trust the future because of God's intention. Joseph's speech places the "intention" (NIV) of the brothers over against the "intention" of God (50:20). The brothers intended evil; God intended good. The brothers intended death to one; God intended life to many. The intention of God prevailed over, worked through, circumvented the intention of the brothers. Joseph's speech does not tell us exactly how God's intention works its way, something we all would like to "know." The speech of Joseph does not offer us this knowledge, but calls forth praise of the God who works the divine intention amidst the human drama. This one statement from Joseph's speech captures much of the theology of Genesis—creation beyond violation, blessing overtaking sterility, reconciliation easing conflict: "You intended evil against me; God intended it for good, in order that the life of many might be preserved as is the case this day" (50:20).

Literarily, the Joseph saga comes to an end. Two elements in this final scene recapitulate the first chapter of the saga. The brothers bow down before Joseph, reminding the reader a final time of the dream with which the narrative began (37:7; 42:6; 43:26; 44:14; 50:18) (Gunkel, 1910: 490). The brothers are comforted, a comfort not possible in the saga's first episode (37:35; 50:21) (Brueggemann, 1982: 377). The words which control the family's future come still from the heart, but are quite different from the evil words with which the story began (37:2; 50:21). Through this web of phrases the narrative artistically unites and brings to a close the saga of this family.

Joseph's Testamentary Activities and Death 50:22-26

But the story of the family is not over yet. This short epilogue closes this chapter and at the same time opens the next generation. The blessing of God which enables one generation to follow upon another has undergirded the narrative from the orderly presentation of creation (Gen. 1) to this final genealogical note (v. 23). God's blessing has survived the raging flood of divine anger and the unexplained sterility of Sarah and Abraham. That quiet blessing, which makes it possible for the human story to continue beyond a single chapter, will carry the family still further into the future.

Joseph's farewell speeches also look toward the future (vv. 24-25). For the only time in this saga, the speech of Joseph appropriates the tradition of promise which led the ancestral stories from the beginning (v. 24) (Brueggeman, 1982: 379). For all the fertility of Egypt, this land was not home. Egypt was not the land of promise. The promise of a home is not fulfilled in this "beginning" book. That promise will carry Israel *out of the land of Egypt, out of the house of bondage* (Exod. 20:2) and bring them *to a good and broad land, a land flowing with milk and honey* (Exod. 3:8).

Joseph's burial request separates him from the land which brought him wealth and power, food and honor (v. 25). He too wants his moment in the family story to be connected with the people's future (cf. Jacob's burial request, 49:33). Joseph spent his life faithfully living his dreams (37:5-11). The dreams end when Joseph is embalmed in Egypt. But those dreams were but a part of the larger promise, and Joseph calls the community to wait for God's visit in behalf of the promise.

THE TEXT IN BIBLICAL CONTEXT

The biblical tradition knows very well the relationship between acts and consequences. The wisdom teachers in Israel, like their colleagues in the ancient Near East, transmitted volumes of advice for everyday living grounded in the experience that good acts bear good fruit—friendship, health, and honor; evil acts bring trouble—illness, misery, and poverty.

One of the most remembered proverbs preserved in the New Testament says the same thing: "whatever one sows, that shall one reap" (Gal. 6:7).

However basic that proverb to everyday living and even to one's relationship to God, the story of God's people and indeed all people cannot be reduced to that simple formula. The proverb does not make sense to Job when the disaster of the moment cannot be explained as the consequence of any of his actions. Joseph's words to his brothers—"You intended evil . . . but God intended good"—provide another experience in which the act-consequence pattern is broken. Job experienced undeserved disaster, the Jacob family unmerited grace.

Luther, writing on Genesis 50:20-21, worries that the people of God will misread this text as excusing or even promoting evil action in the expectation that good will result *(Commentary,* II: 364). Calvin too is concerned to maintain that the good act-good consequence, bad act-bad consequence pattern be understood as the basic premise of life *(Commentaries on Genesis,* II: 488). One must always expect, as Joseph's brothers did (Gen. 42:24; 50:15), that a direct relationship between acts and consequences will eventually work out.

Nevertheless, once in a while the community finds itself confronted by God's surprise (von Rad, 1973: 73, 125). However a just order to life is deeply ingrained in the biblical faith. Nevertheless, Israel had no counterpart to the Egyptian *Maat,* which *guaranteed* justice and order, the act-consequence relationship. Within biblical faith, the matter of consequences belongs to God (Rom. 12:19). Hence when they least expect it, God's people find themselves surprised by God's grace. The world cannot be reduced to an inherent law of crime and punishment, but must reckon with the elusive presence of God (Terrien, 1978).

Good Friday and Easter represent the model in the Christian faith of the surprise factor in God's world. The consequences of Jesus' life should not have led to the cross. But he was nailed there, surprised by evil: "My God, my God, why have you forsaken me" (Mark 15:34). On the third day God surprised all humanity with good: *God was in Christ reconciling the world to himself, not counting their trespasses against them* (2 Cor. 5:19). The brothers of Joseph were surprised by the same God who surprised us on Easter Sunday: "You meant it for evil, but God meant it for good . . ." (v. 20).

THE TEXT IN THE LIFE OF THE CHURCH

The testamentary work of Jacob and Joseph displays a variety of activity having to do with passing onto the next generation the heritage of a life just coming to a close. Jacob speaks to each son. He appears utterly realistic about the future, expecting violence and violation as well as prosperity and promise. Joseph's speech, on the other hand, deals with the family as a whole, handing on to them hope for God's visitation and the family's return home. Testamentary activities provide a moment of transition, officially giving the next generation a heritage from which to address their new moment.

Such a process benefits not only the succeeding generation but also the one whose time is ending. It functions as a way of accepting the conclusion of the nearly completed life. By intentionally drawing life to a close, Jacob's own life is validated. He has something to pass on, even from a life that was lived in unending family conflict, first with his brother and then among his sons. Still Jacob bears the unmistakable mark of God's blessing, and he has that blessing to hand on to his descendants.

Joseph's life has been lived in an alien land with infrequent references to God and none of the dramatic divine revelation that his father encountered. Still, in his final speeches Joseph can teach the next generation to read life as a manifestation of God's presence with a willingness to await God's visitation, however hidden and delayed that visitation might be.

We find the same gathering up and passing on in the testamentary activities of Jesus which we call the Passion narrative (e.g., Mark 11:1—16:8). An ongoing community bound together by his presence, the redemptive value of suffering, a legacy of service mark just a few of the elements which Jesus explicitly passes on to his "descendants" in his final speeches and actions. In these testamentary activities Jesus' life reaches for validation even in the face of the cross, the event which threatens to render invalid his entire ministry. That validation is completed on the first day of the week when Mary Magdalene can report to the disciples, *I have seen the Lord* (John 20:18).

But testamentary activities of Jacob and Joseph do not control the future. They give over control to the next generation. However secure the oath, Jacob cannot guarantee his burial, his place in the family's future. In fact the narrative of Jacob's death and burial is confusing at just that point. Joseph too has no power to control the disposition of his heritage either in Egypt or in Canaan. A generation grew up in Egypt that did not know about Joseph, and the result was oppression. Jesus could not ensure the acceptance of his ministry. Many, even among the disciples, doubted whether that ministry could survive the verdict of the crucifixion. We find in the testamentary activities, not only the work gathering up and passing on, but words of deep anxiety about the future:

Jacob's repeating twice his burial request; Jesus' sense of being left by God. The testamentary activities include also loss, anxiety, and grief.

Many of us live in a culture in which we do not know how to die: a world of machines and sterile rooms, where the final actions are likely to be a frantic hospital alert and a hasty family gathering. The world we leave is not the family world left by Jacob and Joseph. But perhaps by listening closely to the accounts of the testamentary activities of our ancestors, the church can find alternative ways by which the Christians can draw their lives to a close. There should be no expectation that we can recover an idealistic ancestral past, but perhaps we can discover ways in which we can gather up our own lives and assist the next generation as they step into God's future.

Outline of Genesis

Part 3: THE SAGA OF JACOB
Genesis 25:19 – 36:43

VI. Concluding episode:
Testamentary activities . . . .**47:28 – 50:26**

Summary Essays

'ADAM   The Hebrew word *'adam* appears 24 times in Genesis 2—3. The word *'adam* uses the same Hebrew letters as a very closely related Hebrew word, *'adamah*, "earth," "ground," which is found eight times in these two chapters. A check in the Hebrew concordance shows that the word *'adam* in the Bible regularly refers to humanity as a collective group. Occasionally *'adam* can refer to the male as distinct from the female. But we see common generic or collective use of *'adam* in Genesis 1:26 and 9:6 as well as in 3:22, 24.

If we repeat the same word over and over in our stories, the grammar teachers among us would urge that we find synonyms so as not to become repetitious. But repetition is common in Hebrew narrative. *[Characteristics of Hebrew Narrative, p. 313.]* Repeated key or leading words *(Leitwort* in German) function as the glue that holds the narrative together. The use of this narrative technique may have been a legacy of oral storytelling where such repetitions carry the listener along to the end of the story, as well as call attention to a special focus in the story (Alter, 1981: 88ff.).

A narrative may make use of only one specific meaning for its key words, but usually a word has a range of possible meanings. Often the story draws from this variety of meanings throughout the narrative, using different nuances as the word appears and reappears.

Genesis 2—3 makes use of several meanings of *'adam.* We find the "person" *('adam)* who is made from the "ground" *('adamah).* This ground is then cursed because of the disobedience of *'adam* (humanity). In addition, the narrative moves back and forth between the collective use of *'adam* and the use of it to refer to a male. The story begins with a use of the word that does not emphasize a male: God formed a person *('adam)* out of the ground *('adamah)* (2:7). As the narrative moves along, the meaning of this key word shifts so that where the two sexes are distinguished, *'adam* designates male (at least by 2:22). Nevertheless, the collective meaning comes back later (3:22, 24). Even though the speech in 3:19 is directed to the man, it is not just he who will return to the ground. Rather *'adam,* all humanity, will return to the ground.

311

BLESSING IN GENESIS   We often think of promise as the dominant motif in Genesis. But the motif of blessing may in fact be just as central. Genesis begins with God energizing creation through blessing: blessing on humanity, animals, and the seventh day (1:22, 28; 2:3).

> And God blessed them, and God said to them,
> "Be fruitful and multiply, and fill the earth
> and subdue it." (1:28)

The story closes with the last will and the testamentary activities of both Jacob and Joseph. Both include a speech of blessing:

> All these are the twelve tribes of Israel, and this is what their father said to them when he blessed them, giving each the blessing appropriate to him. (49:28, NIV)

Blessing winds its way through the narratives, sometimes surfacing as a crucial element in the story, for example, the story of Jacob and Esau. At other times the motif of blessing is hidden or absent. But the stories of Genesis never put aside for long the motif of blessing.

The bestowing of blessing regularly empowers the receiver, bringing fertility, prosperity, and vitality. Blessing strengthens the solidarity of the persons within a group, bringing life to a community as well as an individual (Scharbert: 303). The picture of Isaac and Jacob blessing their children just before their death apparently reflects a common practice in the ancient society. However, in Israel and elsewhere the bestowal of blessing becomes a special responsibility of the priest in the sanctuary. Because blessing is the power for growth of all kinds, it has a natural association with birth, death, weddings, coronation, planting season, and harvest. But blessing is also at home in the common greeting when persons gather and separate. It is a blessing from God, whether the blessing is bestowed by the companion, the parent, or the priest. Blessing designates God's constant empowering presence in nature and in the human community.

Because blessing is such a prominent motif in Genesis, it appears in a variety of different texts and situations, some of them quite surprising. The act of bestowing blessing as a part of one's last testament is common, but having only *one* blessing to bestow is unusual (Gen. 27). More commonly we find the practice of Jacob where each child is blessed and a mistake can be corrected (Gen. 48—49). The blessing of the seventh day in Genesis 2:6 is a very unusual use of blessing: the Sabbath day is given the power to renew and restore life. In Genesis 32 Jacob wins a blessing in combat. Traditionally, blessing is given or bestowed, not won or earned.

Precisely the tradition of bestowal makes unusual another use of blessing in Genesis, the *promise* of blessing. In our familiarity with Genesis, the blessing as a promise may not seem surprising. But the tradition of blessing leads us to expect blessing as a gift for the present, not as a promise for the future. Yet the saga of Abraham begins exactly with the promise of blessing (12:1-3). Abraham does not begin as one blessed, but as one promised that in his life, and the life of those around and after him, blessing will happen. For Abraham vitality and fertility, security and rest are not immediately bestowed but promised.

Through the promise of blessing, benediction becomes a part of the history of God's people. Blessing is received not only in greeting, worship, and last will and testament, but all through everyday life. Living in the *promise* of blessing means that one enters each day knowing that one will find benediction, if not today, then perhaps tomorrow, or at least someday. We walk into the future with the promise that the God who blesses will meet us there.

CHARACTERISTICS OF HEBREW NARRATIVE   From the stories of our childhood to the memories of the elderly, narrative prose follows us through life. In fact, most of us, when asked to tell our life pilgrimage, do it using stories in narrative form. Such stories enable us to learn, cause us to laugh and free us to cry. Television has added a visual dimension to narrative but does not replace the importance of oral and written narrative. Narrative is so much a part of our common life that we have to stop and think if asked to name the characteristics of our stories. Basically, narrative combines description (narration) with dialogue (direct speech) to portray figures in particular times, places, and situations (Coats, 1983: 4). We might list other specific characteristics of our narratives, but our stories have at least those elements.

An interpretation of Genesis depends in part on our ability to understand narrative literature. Some understanding comes easily because of our acquaintance with narratives in our culture. Nevertheless, many specific characteristics of Hebrew narrative differ from those of narratives in our culture. That can be expected, because those who read narrative literature in modern languages other than our own recognize differences there as well. That being the case, in order to better understand the narratives of Genesis, we need to be aware of some of the elements which go into a Hebrew story that make it different from our narratives.

Hebrew narratives have a beginning and ending. Usually the beginning sets up a problem (a tension) which is resolved at the end of the story. The simpleness of that observation hides a bigger problem than we often realize. When we have a series of stories, as we find in Genesis, we must take care to identify the beginning and ending of each, understanding the basis for that decision (Muilenburg, 1979: 362-380). Sometimes the chapter divisions will help us identify the beginnings and endings of narratives, but more often we must make that decision based on a close reading of the story itself. Before we can understand a story, we need to pay attention to where that story begins and ends.

Direct Speech. In Hebrew narrative direct speech plays a primary role (Alter, 1981: 63-87). In our literature, description or narration often has the dominant place. We have large blocks of description—description of setting, situation, action, even thoughts and feelings of the actors in the story. In Hebrew narrative description or narration plays a relatively less important role, most often serving to introduce, reinforce, and tie together the speeches. Frequently description of a situation will be a brief phrase, such as *there was a famine in the land* (12:10; 26:1). The description of action may be equally brief: *Jacob was left alone; and a man wrestled with him until the breaking of the day* (32:24). The description of a person or figure in a story is often limited to few words: *Dinah, the daughter of Leah, whom she had borne to Jacob* (34:1); *Esau was a skilful hunter, a man of the field* (25:27); "the snake was smarter than any other wild animal Yahweh God had made" (3:1). These descriptions, although important, are brief and leave much to the imagination of the reader. In fact, the brevity of descriptive material invites, perhaps even necessitates, that the listener imaginatively enter the narrative and participate in telling the story.

Hence Hebrew narrative most often centers not around description, even description of action, but around direct speech. An accurate reading of Hebrew narrative must note carefully what the principals say to one another. Normally there are only two actors on stage at a time. The two principals speak to one another, rather than several persons in a group speaking at various times (Olrik: 135). Sometimes in a more complex narrative like the story of Joseph, several people can be together. But even then Joseph's brothers speak as a single person (43:7ff.), or a single individual acts as spokesperson for the group and the others fade into the background.

Hence as we seek to understand the individual stories, one avenue into the narrative is through the speeches. We must pay close attention to the way a person speaks as well as the context of what is said. A narrative might seek to say something by setting a long speech right next to a short one. Gentle language of one speaker may contrast with harsh words of another, or flowery speech with earthy. Not all of us may interpret such elements of the speeches in the same way, but discussing our various understandings becomes part of the interpretive process. One cannot understate the value of knowing Hebrew for this task, but much can still be learned by comparing different translations of the same narrative.

Repetition. Besides the priority of direct speech, repetition plays an important role in Hebrew narrative. The easiest repetition to see in English translations involves key words that are used over and over throughout a single story. We need only notice how many times the related Hebrew words *ground/person* (*'adam*) are used in Genesis 2 and 3, the word *bless* in Genesis 12:1-3, and *birthright* in Genesis 25:29-34. In English narrative, that kind of repetition is usually discouraged, except perhaps in literature for young children.

Repetition of key words, however, is an important literary device in Hebrew narrative perhaps because of its deep roots in oral tradition (Olrik: 132-133). Even after the stories were written down, storytellers continued to pass on the tradition in the sanctuaries and in the town squares. In any case, we can suggest some of the functions of such a repeated word. In some stories repetition of a word may serve simply as a thread to carry the narrative along, to keep the listener following the chosen path. But at other times the repeated word has more interpretative significance, perhaps representing one important emphasis of the story. Occasionally the word might represent the interpretative key that helps the listener understand the whole narrative. Each time we find a word, noun or verb, that appears over and over again in one narrative, we need to explore its function in that story. Other kinds of repetitions appear in Hebrew narrative, such as motifs and themes. Those take a lot of study and testing before one can be sure whether they are useful in understanding the text.

Understatement. In many ways Hebrew narrative features the art of understatement. The narratives often express humor with a very light touch and seldom picture personalities using adjectives of exaggeration. The personality traits are hinted at and the characteristics left to be inferred. The narrator seems reticent to give too much information. For example, in Genesis 22, the story of Abraham, the two characters, God and Abraham, just start talking. We are not told their relationship to one another either spacially or temporally. Nowhere does the narrator tell us what Abraham feels about Isaac, about God, or about his own situation. Indeed Hebrew narrative implies but leaves unexpressed a large background of information which we might consider important or necessary for a story (Auerbach: 7-9). Most of what the reader learns about the people comes from what they say and from what they do. Occasionally the narrator provides us direct information about a person. For example, Esau was born with a lot of hair. Even then we have to decide if that is meant to be funny, pejorative, or just a contrast with Jacob.

Because Hebrew stories tell us about people by their words and actions, we, the readers, must participate actively in the narrative, making decisions and drawing conclusions. For example, we must be the ones to decide whether Jacob was a clever opportunist, a naive young man, and so on. The narrator does not tell us. Through understatement Hebrew narrative asks us to join the story, reminding the listener that mystery and wonder surrounds every person (Alter, 1981: 114-130). No one can ever be fully described. Our best understanding of persons comes not by remaining outside and being told about them, but by joining the story and living it with them.

Chiasmus. We could note many additional stylistic elements present in Hebrew narrative. However, the use of *chiasmus* to shape the Jacob saga (Gen. 25—35) necessitates that we mention at least that one. In literature with a chiastic organization, the opening element and the closing element in a unit are parallel in clearly discernible ways, e.g., content and/or word choice. The next element in the unit parallels the next to last. This parallelism continues until one reaches the central section of the literary unit. Symbolizing chiastic parallelism with letters would look like this: A, B, C, D, C¹, B¹, A¹. Of course chiastic literature may have any number of parallel sections (for instance, see the outline of the Jacob saga, p. 166).

No doubt, chiasmus functioned as a literary device, shaping both poetry and narrative literature in the Hebrew Bible. However, we have problems identifying exactly when chiasmus clearly affected the organization. It is easy to select elements from the different sections of the literature and thereby identify chiastic structure. Such imposition by the reader may ignore other literary devices more instrumental in shaping the particular story or poem. Nevertheless, chiasmus, along with repetition and understatement, had a role in giving shape to some Hebrew literature.

COVENANT The word *covenant* has provided the biblical tradition an important way of talking about the relationship between God and humankind, and among people. Whether covenant is the central theme of the Bible, as some suggest (Eichrodt, 1961), or one of a number of key metaphors describing relationships, its importance cannot be doubted. In Genesis, covenant appears in the text speaking of the relationship of God to all humanity after the Flood (Gen. 9), God and the family of Abraham (15:17), Abraham and Isaac with Abimelech (Gen. 21; 26).

In any discussion of covenant we run the risk, indeed the necessity of oversimplifying the term just to understand it. Covenant is not a concept that can be described by listing a series of characteristics. Rather, covenant involves a way of understanding relationships. The characteristic elements of that way, or perspective, on relationships could and did change as God's community continued its pilgrimage.

Sometimes biblical "covenant" borrowed its language from the way in which treaties were made in the ancient Near East. At other times covenant language comes from the world of family organization: husband and wife, brother and sister, parent and child. Still different language could be used to describe covenant: language from other forms of social organizations, such as kingship, or even from nature.

One common way of organizing the discussion of covenant in the Old Testament is to speak about two different streams or paths of the tradition of covenant. One of these streams finds its key expression in the Exodus material about Sinai. The Sinai narrative understands covenant as a two-party agreement emphasizing the responsibilities (laws) which the community assumes as the people of Yahweh. God has rescued the group from bondage, made them a people. This community covenants with its Deliverer to live responsibly as God's people. A serious breach in the agreed-upon responsibilities of the covenant people will result in a rupture in the relationship. The people may become *not my people* (Hos. 1:9).

A second stream of the covenant tradition finds its expression in the texts concerning David and Abraham. This covenant tradition emphasizes God's unconditional commitment to be with and for the people. To be sure, this covenantal perspective knows that responsibilities are incumbent on the people of the covenant. But the emphasis lies on God's gracious gift of relationship, a relationship which no one can "put asunder."

In Genesis 21 and 26 we see the two-party or bilateral covenant in operation between Abraham/Isaac and Abimelech. The two men "cut a covenant" which stipulated their behavior concerning the wells which herdsmen of the two were guarding (Gen. 21), and perhaps more general interaction as well (Gen. 26). The bilateral covenant in this case was sealed with an oath and perhaps a meal (Gen. 26) or a symbolic gift (Gen. 21). Primary emphasis in this covenant falls on the responsibilities and obligations of the parties involved and in that way reflects the perspective on covenant present in the Sinai material.

Genesis 15 and 17 (the Abraham story) and Genesis 9 (the Flood story) reflect a covenant tradition similar to the Davidic material (2 Sam. 7). In various ways the texts emphasize God's "forever" commitment to the relationship. In Genesis 9 the sign or symbol of the covenant, the rainbow, functions as reminder of the covenant, lest God forget. In Genesis 15 only one party, God, passes between the split animal in the covenant ritual, thus taking on the obligation of covenant. In Genesis 17 the gift character of the covenant is emphasized by the words chosen and by the structure of the unit, in which Abraham has not even a chance to speak.

To be sure, each of these covenantal texts (Gen. 9; 15; 17) realizes that human response, perhaps even specific behavior, is a part of the covenant. Genesis 9 speaks about behavior which respects the gift of life, mentioning specific actions which the early church continued, according to Acts 15. Genesis 15 speaks about Abraham's response in terms of trust or faith. Genesis 17 calls the Abrahamic family to participate in a ritual of inclusion for its male members as the sign of covenant. Nevertheless, these covenantal texts do not speak of God's commitment to the relationship as dependent on even these responses by God's covenant partners. The steadfast love of God, not the ambivalence of human response, grounds the security of the covenant.

Both perspectives of covenant in the Old Testament remain important for the church. If the unconditional-gift emphasis of the Davidic-Abrahamic covenant disappears, covenant can dissolve into a legal contract dependent on the right behavior of the people for its future. Misbehavior looms as a final threat to the future of the relationship. But should the Sinaitic emphasis be lost, covenant can provide a false sense of security, allowing the covenant people to assume that God is for them regardless of what they do. Covenant initiated by God involves both gift and responsibility. Sometimes we need to sound one note, sometimes the other.

CREATION AND EVOLUTION   Periodic controversy between the scientific and religious communities focuses attention on Genesis 1. Long ago Copernicus (1473-1543) and Galileo (1564-1642) found themselves caught in the tension between the science and religion of their age. The controversy surrounding the Italian Galileo culminated in the fact that both his work and that of the earlier Polish astronomer Copernicus were banned by the Roman church. In the nineteenth and twentieth centuries, similar attention has turned to Charles Darwin (1809-1882) and his book, *Origin of the Species* (1859).

Although such controversy presents itself as the claim of the truth of the Bible versus the truth of empirical science, it does not take much exploration to discover that the tension usually involves issues other than just those truth claims. In Galileo's time, argument within the Roman hierarchy and between Protestant and Catholic Christianity made Galileo more a scapegoat than the cause of the problem. Political and sociological causes may be harder to see in our day because we are too close. But we need to watch that Genesis 1 does not become again a victim, as it so easily can if we use it to "take up arms" to defend the faith.

Polarization is almost inevitable in a "Bible-science" clash, if both sides assume only two options—either the Bible or natural science. The heat of battle cannot admit a variety of possibilities. Yet rigid dogmatism does not do justice to the thought of either the scientific or religious community. The early evolutionary theory of post-Darwinian biology is not the only scientific theory which sees the development of life as a process rather than a static order of discrete species. In fact, a rigid evolutionary theory against which some in the religious community fight may be more a result of the controversy than of scientific consensus. Similarly, the Bible does not require as a test of faith that one understand the beginning of human and natural history as a sudden, spontaneous event. The Bible does use idolatry as a test of faith, idolatry which includes absolutizing any theory about life and God's work in the world. Warfare between the religionists and scientists tends to limit possibilities and create idolatrous clinging to specific theories. Efforts toward understanding and reconciliation seem to give truth its best chance.

Knowledge comes to us in different ways. Natural science provides us data indispensable for daily life. But natural science can help us in only a very limited way to "know" another person, and helps us almost not at all to "know" God. The social sciences, for example psychology and sociology, can tell us additional things about people and discuss God in some helpful ways. But even that does not provide the "knowing" that comes with and is necessary for human relationships and relationship with God. Knowledge in the religious community has more in common with the knowing of the artist than that of the natural or social scientist, however much we lean on science. Artistic knowing can enable us to join with other people and God in ways the sciences do not. Not accidentally, when the Bible seeks to express its knowing about God, it does so through art—narrative, poem, and song. In those ways the texts can talk most clearly about meaning and purpose in life. Genesis 1 knows about meaning and purpose in God's world and wants us to know it too. Knowing is not reducible to arguments over scientific data.

DATING OF THE PHILISTINES   Genesis 20:1-18 and 21:22-34 portray Abraham in conflict with Abimelech of Gerar, the land of the Philistines (cf. 21:32, 34). Genesis 26 pictures Isaac in conflict with Abimelech, "the king of the Philistines." This connection of the ancestors with the Philistines causes major dating problems. Archaeology has dated the presence of the Philistines and

Beersheba as an inhabited city from about 1200 B.C. on. The ancestral families are normally dated to the so-called Middle Bronze period, about 1700-1500 B.C. These date discrepancies cause some to suggest moving the date of Abraham, Isaac, and Jacob to 1200 B.C. (e.g., Cornfeld). That creates difficulties for other dates in the Hebrew history, e.g., the Exodus. Others suggest that both the Abraham and Isaac stories use the names, Beersheba and Philistines, to locate the story for the later listeners who know the area in terms of those cities and peoples, but that the city and people did not exist in Isaac's time. Still others suggest that isolated colonies of Philistines appeared in Palestine early in the second millennium. A fourth option would suggest a reconstruction of the early history of the Hebrews. We have been used to thinking of this early history as a rigid sequence of events. That may not be the most adequate way to understand Israel's earliest history. Perhaps the ancestral sagas retell in linear story form events involving different times, places, and groups of Hebrews.

EGYPT, THE RIVER NATION   Much of the Joseph saga is set in Egypt *(miṣraim* in Hebrew). Even though the narrative identifies the place of the story as Egypt, we are given no specific time. The same can be said about the narrative of Abraham's visit to Egypt (Gen. 12). Archaeology has provided us ample evidence of economic and diplomatic intercourse between Egypt and Canaan as well as temporary and long-term settlement of groups from Palestine in Egypt. Archaeology does not identify a time when situations such as the Joseph novella or the story about Abraham must have occurred. Many scholars place the stories, at least the Joseph saga, at a time when Egypt was controlled by the Hyksos. The name "Hyksos" designates a mixed population group who had migrated into the river nation from areas north of Egypt. These "foreign rulers" controlled Egypt for most of the eighteenth and seventeenth centuries B.C. If one looks for a historical time when the Egyptian Pharaoh might have accepted and employed people from Canaan, the time of the Hyksos marks one possibility.

Nevertheless, any decision concerning the date of Joseph originates mostly in our desire to have material located chronologically. Those who passed the saga along to us apparently cared less about such dating than we do. Indeed the one time-limiting name found in the Joseph narrative, "the land of Ramses" (47:11), would point to a time much later than the normally assumed Hyksos period. Actually the events narrated concerning the ancestral families in Egypt, both Abraham and Sarah (Gen. 12) and Joseph (Gen. 37—50) could fit in many time periods.

More important to these ancestral stories than any precise time period in Egyptian history is the tradition of Egypt as a politically strong and food-rich country. Egypt's political and military strength often posed a danger to the inhabitants of Canaan. However, at other times the peoples of Canaan would look to Egypt for help from the threat of other even stronger nations, for example northern neighbors. Occasionally, one city-state in Canaan would appeal to Egypt for help from a threat posed by another city-state.

Egypt's primary resource, the Nile River, was the locus of both its strength and weakness. Because the population was all gathered along this one river, the Nile provided a source of unity for the people. But because the Egyptian segment of the river stretched for some six hundred miles (a little less than one thousand kilometers), the people along this river tended to divide and go their own way. Especially tense was the struggle between the powerful city of Thebes in Upper Egypt (southern Egypt) and Memphis in Lower Egypt (the Delta or northern Egypt). In spite of its internal problems, Egypt often presented itself to the people of Canaan as a powerful, imperial nation (cf. Ezek. 29:3). When Israel passed on traditions about its relationship to Egypt, this was the element that mattered.

Besides power, Egypt also meant food in the ancestral stories of Genesis. The Nile provided a relatively constant source of water for food, very constant compared to the tenuous water situation in Canaan. In addition, heavy rain in the mountains south of Egypt would cause periodic flooding of the river, covering the farmland with rich soil from upriver. Even though only a thin band of land along the Nile was arable, that ribbon of farmland provided food far more regularly than the farming areas of Palestine, where the amount of rain each winter determined in large part the size of the harvest.

When the inhabitants of Canaan looked south toward Egypt, they saw imperial power and regular harvests. The preserved stories of Israel's encounter with that country center on those two factors. From Israel's standpoint the particular time did not greatly affect those elements. Hence as we listen to the Egypt stories, it will be less beneficial for us to try to locate the stories chronologically than to experience Israel's attraction to, and dread of, the powerful, fertile land of Egypt.

GENRES OF HEBREW LITERATURE The terminology used to describe the material in Genesis sometimes looms as the most important decision which the interpreter makes. Because of the way language functions in our everyday life, the words we use will not mean exactly the same thing to any two individuals, let alone groups. Nevertheless, because of the deep investment in the Bible by Christians and especially those in the believers church tradition, the interpreter must take care with the language employed in biblical study in describing genres of forms of biblical literature.

"Poetry" and "prose" commonly describe very broad categories of Western literature. While this distinction seems obvious at first glance, further exploration shows that it provides us only limited help. Immediately we notice that in Hebrew literature many of the characteristics of Hebrew poetry show up in material we designate as prose. Hence the two categories quickly blur. Second, some literature does not fit neatly into either category. In Genesis we find several lists, most commonly genealogical lists. Are they poetry or prose? Well, neither actually. Third, both poetry and prose constitute categories so broad as to tell us only a little about the literature we are reading. Nevertheless, if we use those categories, Genesis includes mostly prose, with some snatches of poetry.

While biblical scholars use the term "poetry," they do not use "prose." The term lacks precision to identify any particular form of Hebrew literature. More commonly they use the word *narrative* to describe Hebrew literature, which we normally think of as prose. Narratives include such literature as short story, chronicle, saga—literature written to describe a series of events in a given time and place (Coats, 1983: 4). The common word we use to refer to narrative literature is *story*. Throughout the discussion of Genesis, this commentary uses "story" as a functional synonym for narrative.

Most of the literature in Genesis is narrative. We will meet some poetry (Gen. 49) and frequently a genre (literary form) which is neither poetry nor narrative, the list. As mentioned, genealogy is the list genre that we meet commonly in Genesis. [*Reading Genealogies, p. 336.*]

The tale and the *saga* appear more frequently in Genesis than other narrative genres. The tale is a short simple story, not necessarily simple in its meaning, but in its structure (Olrik: 129-141; Coats, 1983: 7-8). The reader meets only a few characters, quite often in one location and a brief time span. Usually a single tension controls the movement of the tale, and that reaches some type of resolution at the end (Westermann, 1980: 29).

The saga is a longer narrative usually telling the story of a family, individual hero, or the beginnings of humanity (Coats, 1983: 5-7). The saga can include many genres of literature: tales of the hero or family, genealogical tables or notes, poems, and the like. The family saga commonly narrates internal family strife (Gen. 28), tension with non-family members (Gen. 34), encounters with God (Gen. 15), the final activities and death of a family member (testamentary activities, Gen. 48—50), among other things. Sometimes the saga will have a single tension which controls the movement from beginning to end (e.g., the Joseph saga, Gen. 37—50), but often it does not (e.g., the primeval saga, Gen. 1—11). In such cases the saga comes to us more as a series of tales, poems, genealogies gathered around a particular time, family, or person. The fairly long narrative which does possess a clearly defined arc of tension from beginning to end is the novella or "short story" (Coats, 1983: 8).

The narrative genre which we sometimes assume when we come to Genesis is history. The genre, history, intends to report events as they happened for the purpose of giving the reader data about people, places, and events. Its value currently lies almost entirely in the accuracy of the data provided. The narratives of Genesis frequently use data that historical investigation can study, but clearly, providing historical data is not the primary goal of the narratives. They want to narrate the story of these faith families and of humanity in general as a divine and human drama. The value of the narratives lies not in the degree that they can be verified by modern historiography, but the way in which they accurately describe God's story with humankind.

The problem of the historicity of the events narrated stirs a lot of controversy. Regrettably it is a matter that can neither be dismissed nor resolved. The literature of Genesis comes to us as traditional narrative. The stories have been received from the ancestors and retold from generation to generation. Such transmitted narratives were not memorized and passed on verbatim but "reenacted." Nevertheless, each retelling was expected to preserve the basic content of meaning (Noss: 301-318).

Indeed "meaning" remains an important word. Hebrew narrative's prime interest lies less in reporting data than in understanding God and Israel. The story functions as a vehicle for such understanding. When we focus our energy on arguing whether the data were reported accurately, we move away from the heart of Hebrew narrative.

HISTORICAL STUDY OF GENESIS   Proposals concerning the origin and growth of Genesis have generated considerable, often heated, debate. One well-known proposal gained general recognition through the work of Julius Welhausen in the last half of the nineteenth century (1899). Welhausen suggested that the Pentateuch (Genesis, Exodus, Leviticus, Numbers, and Deuteronomy) as we have received it, is the final product of a literary process that stretched over four centuries.

According to Welhausen, the earliest of these Pentateuchal narratives developed in connection with the Judean kingdom in about 850 B.C. This material has been called "J" for the characteristic use of the divine name, Yahweh (Jahve in German). A northern Israel strand of narrative was joined to this after its capital, Samaria, fell to an Assyrian invasion in about 721 B.C. This Israelite or

Ephraimite material has been designated "E," following its use of Elohim for the divine name in Genesis. Other Ephraimite material, largely legal, formed the basis of a fourth source "D" (for Deuteronomy). This Deuteronomic material was connected with the reform of Josiah about 621 B.C. (cf. 2 Kings 22). The latest narrative source to be included in the Pentateuch originated in priestly circles in and after the Babylonian Exile (586-538 B.C.). This sixth- or fifth-century "P" source pulled together a large body of cultic law and some narrative material not preserved in the other sources.

This source or documentary hypothesis has undergone rigorous review and significant criticism in the century since its presentation by Welhausen and others. Some have criticized this and any proposal that Genesis resulted from a process of growth and development, maintaining instead a unitary author hypothesis, e.g., Mosaic authorship (e.g., Young; and Harrison). Others have accepted the general hypothesis of a literary development. But some insist that little of the material of the Pentateuch can be firmly dated before the Babylonian Exile (e.g., Van Seters, 1975), or they organize the literary material not by general documents, but around specific themes, such as those used by Martin Noth (1972; e.g., Rendtorff). Still others have insisted that oral transmission of the tradition played a very important role in the development of the Pentateuch, suggesting that much of the material was passed on in the sanctuary, the home, and the village square long before and even after it took literary shape (e.g., Gunkel, 1910 and 1964; cf. Knight, 1975).

Gerhard von Rad and Martin Noth have focused the discussion for our time by presenting a comprehensive picture of the oral and literary development of the Pentateuch. Besides their fundamental discussion of the issues (von Rad, 1966; Noth, 1972), between them Noth and von Rad have written commentaries on all five of the books in the Pentateuch. Their basic work, which now is a half century old, has come under increasing criticism, but no comprehensive proposal has yet succeeded in obtaining general acceptance (cf. Knight, 1985).

Alongside the debate over the origin and growth of Genesis, others have been at work exploring the literary character of the Genesis as we find it now (e.g., Alter, 1981; Coats, 1983; Fishbane; and many others). They lay aside at least temporarily the question of the growth of the tradition to explore the shape of the final form of the book. While such literary analysis is by no means new, the recent use of that methodology in biblical study opens up new possibilities, providing not only fresh ways to interpret Genesis, but also a common task for groups that have long argued about the origin and development of this first book of the Bible.

IMAGE OF GOD God created humanity in the "image of God." For centuries the community of faith has tried to define the meaning of that simple phrase. The most assured result of this discussion shows that the phrase "image of God" cannot be reduced to just one simple definition which we can extract from the texts. One must understand the phrase in several different ways to remain true to its use in the Bible.

In the broadest perspective, image of God in Genesis defines the way in which humankind differs from the animals. The phrase *nephesh ḥayyah*, "living creature" (1:20-21) distinguishes animal life from plant life. Then *ṣelem ʾelohim*, "image of God," separates the human being from the animal. So in part the phrase functions to distinguish one group in God's world, humankind. Recognizing that function warns us against anxiously trying to decide exactly *how* humanity is or acts in the image of God. We have little indication that a single attribute of a person makes one more or less in God's image, e.g., reason or spirituality. The human species together images God (Vawter, 1977: 56). All of us, rich and poor, Christian and non-Christian, male and female, together, are created in the image of God. In so being, we differ from all other elements in God's creation.

We recall that Israel was forbidden to make any image of God (Exod. 20:4; Deut. 5:8). In creation God has done what the community must not do. As we live out our humanness, God's image is present in creation (Brueggemann, 1982: 32).

The word *selem*, "image" in the Old Testament, usually refers to statue, often in contexts concerning forbidden idols. However, in Genesis 5:1-3 we find even a closer parallel to Genesis 1:27. There Seth is said to be in the "image" and "likeness" of Adam. The phrase reappears in Genesis 9:6, where no one is allowed to take the life of another because everyone is made in the image of God. Therefore, we must watch our inclination to spiritualize the image of God. Although the image of God cannot be reduced to humanity's physical shape and appearance, neither can we choose a non-physical attribute of a person and call that the image of God.

Genesis 1:27; 5:3; and 9:6 also remind us that the image of God is a deeply relational term. The phrase incorporates both horizontal and vertical relationships. Even as Seth stands in close relationship to Adam, creation has provided a distinctive bond between God and humankind. Something special may happen between people and God (Westermann, 1974: 60).

The image of God bonds us in a special way to God but also to one another. The poetic lines in Genesis 1:27 weave the "image of God" together with humanity as "male and female."

> In the image of God he created him;
> male and female he created them. (1:27b)

Phyllis Bird rightly reminds us not to make this phrase a foundation on which to build a biblical understanding of the male/female relationship. The phrase will not carry all that weight (Bird: 129-159). Nor can one assume from the poetic parallelism that sexual differentiation belongs to the person of God. Nevertheless, the phrase "image of God" refers to the whole of humanity in relationship, not to male more than female. Those made in the image of God are bonded uniquely to one another and to the one who gave us this image.

The image of God speaks not only of relationship but also of responsibility. Genesis 1:26-28 uses royal language in connection with the image of God: the strong, controlling language of a king. The king receives "dominion" from sea to sea (Ps. 72:8). David subdues and brings nations under his control (2 Sam. 8:11). Psalm 8 joins Genesis 1 in proclaiming that God has given humanity royal dominion over creation. The psalmist gives us a picture of such a "royal manager."

> May he be like the rain that falls on the mown grass,
> like showers that water the earth!
> In his days may righteousness flourish,
> and peace abound, till the moon be no more!
> (Ps. 72:6-7)

Such a one manages the world, so that help comes to those who need it.

For he will deliver the needy who cry out,
        the afflicted who have no one to help.
He will take pity on the weak and needy
        and save the needy from death. (Ps. 72:12-13, NIV)

Nevertheless, not for the benefit of human life alone do those in God's image manage the world, but for the benefit of all life on earth.

You set springs gushing in ravines,
        running down between the mountains,
        supplying water for wild animals,
        attracting the thirsty wild donkeys;
        near there the birds of the air make their nests
        and sing among the branches. (Ps. 104:10-12, JB)

Humanity has been given tremendous power over the creation. Rulership, dominion, control in the image of God brings with it an awesome trust.

In the Bible the image of God functions as a broad metaphor referring to all human beings. It speaks about our relationship to God and to one another. This symbol defines our management task in God's world. The Reformation and Anabaptist Christians sometimes understood the image of God as something that was badly distorted, if not completely lost in the Fall (*Martyrs Mirror*: 39; Friedmann: 59). Karl Barth rightly observes that the image of God was not lost (Barth: 200). Genesis 9:6 reminds us that God continues creating humanity, including each person, in the divine image. That is our gift and our responsibility.

MALE AND FEMALE IN GENESIS 1–3   John Calvin (1509-1564) understood the narrative in Genesis 2—3 to describe a relationship between the man and the woman that one might call benevolent subordination. Interpreting this text in connection with New Testament passages (e.g., 1 Cor. 11), Calvin saw a hierarchy in Genesis which put God at the top and then the man and finally the woman. The disobedience, or Fall, introduced hostility and harshness into the hierarchy (*Calvin's Commentaries*: 129-130). Calvin's position reflects the understanding of many in the church.

Martin Luther (1483-1546), however, understood the text differently. Prior to the disobedience the man and the woman were "equal in all respects" (*Luther's Commentary*: 55, 82). A relationship of domination and subordination followed as a consequence of disobedience and was not a part of the vision of creation. The church has only occasionally remembered Luther's interpretation (cf. Menno Simons: 113). Currently, Luther's perspective has been rediscovered, albeit with modifications.

Among the reasons for moving away from Calvin's understanding of this text are the following.

1. Nothing in the phrase *helper fit for him* suggests priority given to the man. Elsewhere the word "helper" (*'ezer*) describes God as "helper" (Ps. 121:1-2). In fact the use of the term in synonymous lines of Hebrew poetry has suggested to some that the word here means "power" (Deut. 33:29; Ps. 115:9-11) (Friedman: 56-58).

2. The statement that woman was made from material taken "from the man" does not imply that the woman is "lower than" the man. The phrase "from the man" describes a close relationship between the man and woman. In a

similar relationship, 'adam is formed out of material taken *from the ground* (2:7). The woman and the man correspond to one another. The animals, however important, cannot be co-respondents in that way. The story of the creation of human community is followed by statements of mutuality and intimacy, not of structure and hierarchy.

3. Genesis 1:26-27 does not understand the relationship between the man and the woman differently than Genesis 2—3. Genesis 1 talks other language, *male and female he created them* (1:27). However, it is the same community which God created and which is recreated through Jesus Christ—a community of correspondence (Rom. 5:17).

OCCUPATION: KEEPER OF LIVESTOCK   In Genesis 46:32-34 Joseph tries to help his family learn the customs of Egypt. He advises them not to describe themselves as "shepherds." Instead they should introduce themselves as "keepers of livestock" (NASB). We continue to struggle to describe the occupation of the early Hebrews. Keepers of livestock, shepherds, may be the best we can do.

In the past we have used "nomadic" or even "semi-nomadic" to describe them. The term "nomad" presents problems. Our Hebrew ancestors can be dated in several different eras in the second or perhaps even the third millennium B.C. We know very little about nomadism as a way of life in any of those centuries (Dever and Clark: 70-148). Perhaps at the very least, nomadism implies a group regularly on the move looking for water for their herds. The Genesis narratives do not present us with the picture of these Hebrew families that allows us to conclude that they were nomads in this sense (Matthews: 215-218). It would seem prudent to drop the word "nomad" or even "semi-nomad" as the term to describe the way of life of these ancient families and search instead for more adequate terms.

"Pastoralist" describes people who derive their primary living from herding. Pastoralism may take many forms. Quite commonly, pastoralists had sedentary roots in one location but would send some of the members to herd the flocks in other locations. The location of the grazing would change depending on the seasons and rainfall. Some scholars suggest that these pastoralists would go quite a distance from their homes, perhaps even putting down roots in a new location. Normally, however, they would stay closer to home, returning home periodically. The families of Joseph (Gen. 37) and Judah (Gen. 38) seem to reflect this type of pastoralism. Likely the home territory of these pastoralists was near or in small villages. Often they would engage in some agriculture in the land around the village. At least some of the Genesis narratives mirror hostility between these village pastoralists and nearby urban areas (Gen. 34).

It may be that some pastoralists were more mobile than that, moving from one location to another, perhaps forced to by climatic or political circumstances. The Abraham saga talks about moves occasioned by famine (Gen. 12:10-20), while the story of Isaac attributes moves to the hostility of some neighbors (Gen. 26). Other moves may have been caused by family quarrels, population explosion, or even personal choice. But the occupation of herding, rather than a constantly mobile way of life (nomadism), appears to be the primary characteristic of the pastoralism reflected in the Genesis narratives.

Perhaps we should take Joseph's advice and call these Hebrews keepers of livestock. When we think about them, we ought to picture an extended family (tribe) living primarily in one location. Some family members went to other places for a time to pasture the herds. Others probably engaged in subsistence agriculture. The tribe as a whole likely formed a village or attached themselves to one that already existed. To us it would seem a precarious existence—always living on the edge of drought. Indeed such was the life of the Hebrew keepers of livestock.

PROMISE IN THE FAMILY STORIES The motif of promise spans the whole of the stories of Abraham, Jacob, and Joseph. Promise launches the story in Genesis 12:1-3:

> I will make you into a great nation
> and I will bless you;
> I will make you name great,
> and you will be a blessing. (12:2, NIV)

Promise reappears throughout the narratives, often in quite unexpected ways and places, until it is reiterated finally in Joseph's speech before his death.

> I am about to die; but God will visit you, and bring you up out of this land to the land which he swore to Abraham, to Isaac, and to Jacob. (50:24)

The relationship of each person to the promise plays a decisive role in the life direction of each character in the sagas. Abraham, Isaac, and Jacob enter each episode as carriers of the promise. Lot, Ishmael, and Esau, on the other hand, live in these stories as ones who are not bearers of the promise. No reason is given why the promise has been entrusted to one and not the other. That remains a mystery of God's choice.

One risks overgeneralization of the motif when speaking of promise as the umbrella covering the whole of Genesis 12—50. "Promise" is quite specific and in fact plural rather than singular. We can identify at least four promises that occur either alone or in various combinations (Westermann, 1980: 1-30). The promise of land is often found alone (12:7), as is the promise of a son (18:10). However, in some texts the promise of one son is augmented by the promise of many descendants (15:4-5). The combination that occurs most often puts together the promise of many descendants with the promise of blessing (17:6; 22:17). The association of blessing with the promise of offspring as "numerous as the stars" emerges naturally out of blessing as the bestowal of fertility.

Land, a son, descendants, and a blessing are all promised in various texts. We might even want to single out other promises such as an aid or escort (26:3, 24; 28:15; 31:3) and covenant (17:7-8). These latter do not occur throughout. Nevertheless, we dare not forget that the motif of promise is not present in an abstract or simple way. Instead we find different promises pulled in together under the one umbrella.

Remembering the variety of the promises becomes important when we consider fulfillment. The sagas end without realization of the promise in all its specifics (Heb. 11:13). Central to the Abraham saga lies the promise of a son. Fulfillment came with Isaac's birth. With the birth of the sons of Jacob we find the realization of the promise of "many" descendants. Several individual stories acknowledge that the promise of blessing has been realized (26:12-13). Only the promise of land lacks some measure of being fulfilled (50:24). Hence the arc of promise and fulfillment stretches beyond the sagas of Genesis. Fulfillment happens within the ancestral stories as well as pointing beyond these narratives.

READING GENEALOGIES   We do not normally read the genealogies in the biblical texts. The names are difficult to pronounce and the repetition boring. We struggle to know how to read the genealogies, how we should understand them. Sometimes we find tension between different genealogical lists. For example, the names found in Genesis 4:17-26 appear also in Genesis 5:1-32, but in different order and with slight variations on some of the names. Usually we do not read the genealogies closely enough to notice such variations.

In our culture we record genealogies to tell exactly who is related to whom by blood and marriage. We develop elaborately branched genealogies with complex relationships between their various segments. We seldom find such elaborately segmented genealogies in the Bible. The function of genealogy in ancient Israel was less to record data than to talk about groupings. Genealogies were lists that grouped and ordered different aspects of Israel's domestic, political, and religious life (R. R. Wilson, 1977: 38-45). If we require biblical genealogies to be like ours, we will find ourselves pushing and tugging to get all the relationships to fit in so they come out "right." Doing that will cause us considerable frustration and likely cause us to miss what is available in the genealogy.

Perhaps we can learn to ask different questions as we read biblical genealogies. Suppose we begin by asking why each genealogy appears in its particular place. Often we find such a list at the end or sometimes the beginning of a narrative section. Positioned there, the genealogy may function to bring a narrative to a close or serve as a transition to the next narrative (e.g., Gen. 36). The list may group some persons together, distinguishing them from other persons that have been or will be important in the narrative (e.g., Gen. 25:12-18). Or the genealogy may function to tie a person or group to its roots: family, religious, or political roots (e.g., Jesus' genealogy in Matthew).

Second, we need to look inside the genealogy to see what stands out as important in the flow of the list. Even in the most repetitious genealogy, we can search for variations and pay close attention to those. Not always, but often those variations signal important elements in the genealogy as it comes to us.

Third, we need to look closely at the genealogy to find out why this list was passed on. For example, Genesis 4:17-22 served to group together various occupations, and Genesis 10 organized different national groups. The genealogies can tell us much about how Israel understood the order of its world and its community.

Genealogies may never become favorite texts. However, as we learn how to read them, we can find different kinds of information than simply who gave birth to whom.

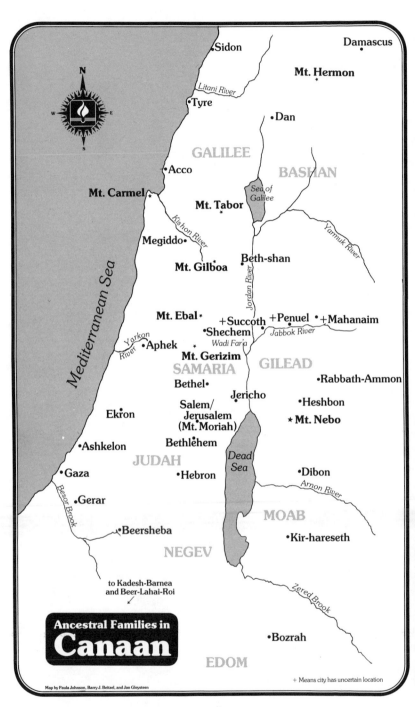

Ancestral Families in **Canaan**

Map by Paula Johnson, Barry J. Beitzel, and Jan Gleysteen

+ Means city has uncertain location

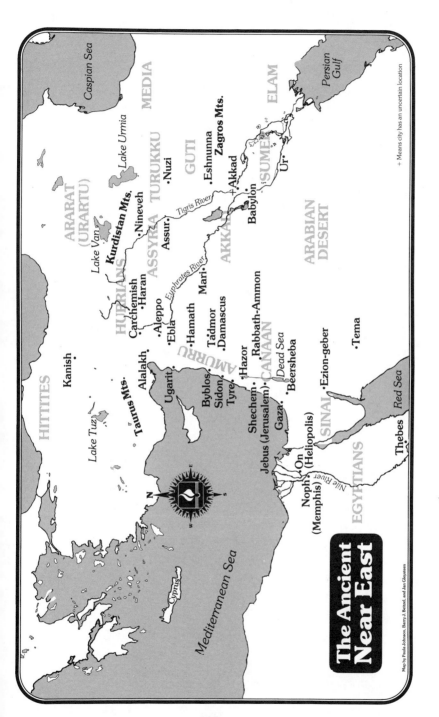

The Ancient Near East

+ Means city has an uncertain location

Map by Paula Johnson, Barry J. Beitzel, and Jan Gleysteen

329

Reference Bibliography

Aharoni, Yohanan
    1982   *The Archaeology of the Land of Israel.* Translated by A. F. Rainey. Philadelphia: Westminster Press.

Alter, Robert
    1981   *The Art of Biblical Narrative.* New York: Basic Books, Inc.

    1986   *The Art of Biblical Poetry.* New York: Basic Books, Inc.

Anderson, Bernhard W.
    1977   "A Stylistic Study of the Priestly Creation Story." *Canon and Authority.* Edited by G. W. Coats and B. O. Long. Philadelphia: Fortress Press.

    1978   "From Analysis to Synthesis: The Interpretation of Genesis 1—11" in *Journal of Biblical Literature* 97:23-29.

    1982   "The Problem and Promise of Commentary." *Interpretation* 36: 341-355.

Anderson, Bernhard, Editor
    1984   *Creation in the Old Testament.* Philadelphia: Fortress Press.

Augustine
    1955   *Confessions and Enchiridion.* Translated by A. C. Outler. [Library of Christian Classics, 8]. Philadelphia: Westminster Press.

    1958   *The City of God.* Translated by G. Walsh, et al. Garden City, N.Y.: Image Books.

Auerbach, Eric
    1953   *Mimesis.* Translated by R. Trask. Garden City, N.Y. Doubleday.

Barker, Verlyn
    1983   "Creationism, the Church, and the Public School." United Ministries in Higher Education Conference.

Barth, Karl
1958-1962   *Church Dogmatics.* Edited by G. Bromiley and T. F. Torrence. Vol. III/1-4: *The Doctrine of Creation.* Edinburgh: T and T Clark.

Bassett, F. W.
1971   "Noah's Nakedness and the Curse of Canaan." *Vetus Testamentum* 21: 232-237.

Beachy, Alvin
1977   *The Concept of Grace in the Radical Reformation.* Nieuwkoop: B. De Graaf.

Betz, H. D.
1979   *Galatians* [Hermeneia]. Philadelphia: Fortress Press.

The Bible in Art: Miniatures, Paintings, Drawings and Sculptures Inspired by the Old Testament.
1956   New York: Phaidon Publishers, Inc.

Bird, Phyllis A.
1981   "Male and Female He Created Them: Genesis 1:27b in the Context of the Priestly Account of Creation." *Harvard Theological Review* 74: 129-159.

Blass, Thomas
1982   "The tenacity of impressions and Jacob's rebuke of Simeon and Levi." *Journal of Psychology and Judaism* 7: 55-61.

Blenkinsopp, Joseph
1981   "Biographical Patterns in Biblical Narrative." *Journal for the Study of the Old Testament* 20:27-46.

1983   *A History of Prophecy in Israel.* Philadelphia: Westminster Press.

Blenkinsopp, Joseph, and John Challenor
1971   *Pentateuch* [Scripture Discussion Commentary, 1]. Chicago: ACTA Foundation.

Bloody Theatre or Martyrs Mirror
1950   Scottdale, Pa.: Mennonite Publishing House.

Bonhoeffer, Dietrich
1959   *Creation and Fall. Temptation.* New York: Macmillan.

Booij, T.
1980   "Hagar's words in Genesis XVI,13B." *Vetus Testamentum* 30: 1-7.

Booth, Wayne C.
1979   *Critical Understanding, The Power and Limits of Pluralism.* Chicago: University of Chicago Press.

Botterweck, G. J., and Helmer Ringgren, Editors
1977-   *Theological Dictionary of the Old Testament.* Translated by J. T. Willis. Grand Rapids, Mich.: Wm. B. Eerdmans.

Brueggemann, Walter
  1977   "A Neglected Sapiential Word Pair." *Zeitschrift für die Alttestamentliche Wissenschaft* 89: 234-258.

  1978   *Prophetic Imagination.* Philadelphia: Fortress Press.

  1982   *Genesis.* Atlanta: John Knox Press.

  1982a   "'Impossibility' and epistemology in the faith and tradition of Abraham and Sarah." *Zeitschrift für die Alttestamentliche Wissenschaft* 94: 615-634.

Brueggemann, Walter, and H. W. Wolff
  1975   *The Vitality of Old Testament Traditions.* Atlanta: John Knox Press.

Calvin, John
  1948   *Commentary on the First Book of Moses Called Genesis.* Translated by J. King. Grand Rapids, Mich.: Wm. B. Eerdmans.

Campbell, Edward F.
  1974   "The Hebrew Short Story: A Story of Ruth." Pp. 83-102 in *A Light unto My Path.* Edited by H. Bream, et al. Philadelphia: Temple University Press.

  1983   "A People in Covenant." Zenos Lectures at McCormick Theological Seminary, Chicago.

Cassuto, U.
  1964   *A Commentary on the Book of Genesis.* Translated by I. Abrahams. Jerusalem: The Magnes Press.

Childs, Brevard S.
  1962   *Memory and Tradition.* [Studies in Biblical Theology, 37]. London: SCM Press.

  1962a   *Myth and Reality in the Old Testament.* [Studies in Biblical Theology, 27]. London: SCM Press.

  1974   "The Etiological Tale Re-examined." *Vetus Testamentum* 24: 387-397.

Clark, W. Malcom
  1969   "A Legal Background to the Yahwist's use of 'good and evil' in Genesis 2—3." *Journal of Biblical Literature* 88: 266-278.

  1971   "The Flood and the Structure of the Pre-patriarchal History." *Zeitschrift für die Alttestamentliche Wissenschaft* 83: 184-211.

  1971   "The Righteousness of Noah." *Vetus Testamentum* 21: 261-280.

Clines, David J. A.
  1978   *The Theme of the Pentateuch* [Journal for the Study of Old Testament Supplement Series, 10]. Sheffield, England: University of Sheffield.

Coats, George W.
1972   "Widow's rights: a crux in the structure of Genesis 38." *Catholic Biblical Quarterly* 34: 461-466.

1973   "The Joseph story and ancient wisdom: A reappraisal." *Catholic Biblical Quarterly* 35: 285-297.

1975   *From Canaan to Egypt: Structural and Theological Context for the Joseph Story* [Catholic Biblical Quarterly Monograph Series, 4]. Washington: Catholic Biblical Association.

1975   "The God of Death." *Interpretation* 29: 227-239.

1979   "Strife without reconciliation—a narrative theme in the Jacob traditions." *Werden und Wirken des Altes Testaments.* Festschrift: C. Westermann; edited by R. Albertz, et al. Göttingen: Vanderhoeck und Ruprecht.

1983   *Genesis* [Forms of Old Testament Literature, I]. Grand Rapids, Mich.: Wm. B. Eerdmans.

Cohen, N.J.
1983   "Two that are one—sibling rivalry in Genesis." *Judaism* 32: 331-342.

The Complete Writings of Menno Simons
1956   Translated by J. C. Wenger. Scottdale, Pa.: Herald Press.

Cornfeld, Gaalyah, and D. N. Freedman
1976   *Archaeology of the Bible: Book by Book.* New York: Harper and Row.

Crenshaw, James
1969   "Method in determining wisdom influence upon 'historical literature.'" *Journal of Biblical Literature* 88: 129-137.

1975   "Journey into Oblivion." *Soundings* 58: 243-256.

Cross, F. M.
1973   *Canaanite Myth and Hebrew Epic.* Cambridge, Mass.: Harvard University Press.

Dahlberg, Bruce T.
1977   "On recognizing the unity of Genesis." *Theological Digest* 24: 360-367.

Daube, David.
1947   *Studies in Biblical Law.* Cambridge: University Press.

1981   *Ancient Jewish Law.* Leiden: E. J. Brill.

Davies, P. R.
1979   "The Sacrifice of Isaac and Passover." *Studia Biblica* (1978) [Journal for the Study of the Old Testament Supplement Series, 11]: 127-132.

Davies, P. R., and B. D. Chilton
1978   "The Agedah: A Revised Tradition History." *Catholic Biblical Quarterly* 40: 514-546.

Delitzsch, Franz.
1899   *A New Commentary on Genesis.* Translated by S. Taylor. Edinburgh: T and T Clark.

Dever, W. G., and W. M. Clark
1977   "The Patriarchal Traditions." *Israelite and Judaean History.* Edited by J. H. Hayes and J. M. Miller. Philadelphia: Westminster Press.

Eichrodt, Walther
1961   *Theology of the Old Testament.* Translated by J. A. Baker. Philadelphia: Westminster Press.

Ellington, John
1979   "Man and Adam in Genesis 1—5." *The Bible Translator* 30: 201-205.

Ellis, P. F.
1968   *The Yahwist. The Bible's First Theologian.* Notre Dame, Ind.: Fides.

Exum, J. Cheryl, Editor
1985   *Tragedy and Comedy in the Bible [Semeia, 32].* Decatur, Ga.: Scholars Press.

Fishbane, Michael
1979   *Text and Texture: Close Readings of Selected Biblical Texts.* New York: Schocken Books.

Fokkelman, J. P.
1975   *Narrative Art in Genesis.* Assen, The Netherlands: Van Gorcum.

Francisco, Clyde T.
1973   *Genesis.* The Broadman Bible Commentary. Revised by C. J. Alen. Nashville: Broadman Press.

Freedman, R. David
1983   "Woman, A Power Equal to Man." *Biblical Archaeology Review* 9: 56-58.

Fretheim, Terence E.
1969   *Creation, Fall and Flood.* Minneapolis: Augsburg Press.

1972   "The Jacob traditions: theology and hermeneutic." *Interpretation* 26: 419-436.

Friedmann, Robert
1973   *The Theology of Anabaptism.* Scottdale, Pa.: Herald Press.

Frye, Northrop
1957   *Anatomy of Criticism: Four Essays.* Princeton, N.J.: Princeton University Press.

Gaston, Lloyd
    1980   "Abraham and the Righteousness of God." *Horizons in Biblical Theology* 2: 39-68.

Geisler, Norman L.
    1983   "Creationism: A Case for Equal Time." *Christianity Today* 26 (March 19): 26-29.

Gevirtz, Stanley
    1981   "Simeon and Levi in the 'blessing of Jacob.'" *Hebrew Union College Annual* 52: 93-128.

Gibble, Kenneth L.
    1981   "The Preacher as Jacob: Wrestling with the Daimonic." Unpublished D. Min. Project. Bethany Theological Seminary, Oak Brook, Ill.

Gilkey, Langdon
    1982   "Creationism: The Roots of Conflict." *Christianity and Crisis* 42: 108-115.

Gottwald, Norman
    1979   *The Tribes of Yahweh: A Sociology of Liberated Israel 1250-1050 B.C.E.* Maryknoll, N.Y.: Orbis Books.

Grant, Robert M., with D. Tracy
    1984   *A Short History of the Interpretation of the Bible.* Philadelphia: Fortress Press.

Gunkel, Hermann
    1910   *Genesis.* Göttingen: Vandenhoeck and Ruprecht.

Halpern, Baruch
    1983   *The Emergence of Israel in Canaan.* Chico, Calif.: Scholars Press.

Harrison, R. K.
    1969   *Introduction to the Old Testament.* Grand Rapids, Mich.: Wm. B. Eerdmans.

Hartman, Geoffrey H.
    1980   *Criticism in the Wilderness.* New Haven: Yale University Press.

Hauge, M. R.
    1975   "The Struggles of the Blessed in Estrangement." *Studia Theologica* 29: 1-30, 113-146.

Hayes, J. H., and J. M. Miller
    1977   *Israelite and Judean History.* Philadelphia: Westminster Press.

Hayward, Robert
    1981   "The present state of research into the targumic account of the sacrifice of Isaac." *Journal of Jewish Studies* 32: 127-150.

Helyer, L. R.
    1983   "The Separation of Abram and Lot." *Journal for the Study of the Old Testament* 26: 77-88.

Hershon, P. I.
1885   *A Rabbinical Commentary on Genesis.* London: Hodder and Stoughton.

Horst, Friedrich
1961   *Gottes Recht. Gesammelte Studien zum Recht im Alten Testament.* Munchen: Chr. Kaiser Verlag.

Houtman, C.
1977   "What did Jacob see in his dream at Bethel? Some remarks on Genesis xxviii 10-22." *Vetus Testamentum* 27: 337-351.

Jacob, B.
1974   *The First Book of the Bible: Genesis.* Translated and abridged by E. Jacob and W. Jacob. New York: KTAV Publishing House.

Jenks, Alan W.
1977   *The Elohist and North Israelite Traditions* [Society of Biblical Literature Monograph Series, 22]. Missoula, Mont.: Scholars Press.

Johnson, M. D.
1969   *The Purpose of the Biblical Genealogies with Special Reference to the Setting of the Genealogies of Jesus.* Cambridge: Cambridge University Press.

Kaiser, Otto and E. Lohse
1981   *Death and Life.* Translated by J. Steeley. Nashville: Abingdon.

Kaiser, Walter C., Jr.
1982   "What Commentaries Can (and Can't) Do." *Christianity Today* 25 (October 2): 24-27.

Käsemann, Ernst
1980   *Commentary on Romans.* Grand Rapids, Mich.: Wm. B. Eerdmans.

Kidner, Derek
1967   *Genesis.* London: Tyndale Press.

Kierkegaard, Soren
1983   *Fear and Trembling. Repetition.* Translated by H. V. Hong and E. H. Hong. Princeton, N.J.: Princeton University Press.

Kikawada, I. M., and A. Quinn
1985   *Before Abraham Was.* Nashville: Abingdon Press.

Kilian, R.
1966   *Die vorpriesterlichen Abrahams—Überlieferungen literarkritisch und tradtionsgeschichtlich untersucht* [Bonner biblische Beitrage, 24]. Bonn: Hanstein.

Knierim, Rolf
1966   "The Problem of an Old Testament Harmartiology. Considerations to the book of Stefan Porubcan." *Sin in the Old Testament. Vetus Testamentum* 16: 366-385.

1981   "Cosmos and History in Israel's Theology." *Horizons in Biblical Theology* 3: 59-124.

Knight, D. A.
1975   *Rediscovering the Traditions of Israel.* Missoula, Mont.: Scholars Press.

1985   "The Pentateuch." *The Hebrew Bible and Its Modern Interpreters.* Edited by D. Knight and G. Tucker. Chico, Calif.: Scholars Press.

Knight, D. A., Editor
1977   *Traditions and Theology in the Old Testament.* Philadelphia: Fortress Press.

Koch, Klaus
1969   *The Growth of the Biblical Tradition.* Translated by S. M. Cupitt. New York: Charles Scribner's Sons.

Koester, Helmut
1982   *Introduction to the New Testament,* I and II. Philadelphia: Fortress Press.

La Sor, W. S., and D. A. Hubbard, and F. W. Bush
1982   *Old Testament Survey.* Grand Rapids, Mich.: Wm. B. Eerdmans.

Landes, George M.
1974   "Creation Tradition in Proverbs 8:22-31 and Genesis 1." *A Light unto My Path.* Edited by H. Bream, et al. Philadelphia: Temple University Press.

Landy, Francis
1981   "The Name of God and the Image of God and Man: A Response to David Clines." *Theology* 84: 164-170.

Leach, E. R.
1969   *Genesis as Myth and Other Essays.* London: Cape.

Lehmann, Paul
1975   *The Transfiguration of Politics.* New York: Harper and Row.

Levin, Saul
1978   "The More Savory Offering: A Key to the Problem of Genesis 4:3-5." *Journal of Biblical Literature* 98: 85.

Lind, Millard
1980   *Yahweh Is a Warrior.* Scottdale, Pa.: Herald Press.

Long, Burke O.
1968   *The Problem of Etiological Narrative in the Old Testament* [Beihefte zur Zeischrift für die alttestamentliche Wissenschaft, 108]. Berlin: A. Topelmann.

1976   "Recent Field Studies in Oral Literature and Their Bearing on Old Testament Criticism." *Vetus Testamentum* 26: 187-198.

Luther, Martin
1958   *Luther's Commentary on Genesis.* Translated by J. T. Mueller. Grand Rapids, Mich.: Zondervan.

Mailloux, Steven
1982   *Interpretive Conventions: The Reader in the Study of American Fiction.* Ithaca: Cornell University Press.

Marsden, George M.
1982   "A Law to Limit Options." *Christianity Today* 26 (March 19): 28-30.

Martyrs Mirror
         See *Bloody Theater.*

Matthews, Victor
1981   "Pastoralist and Patriarchs." *Biblical Archaeologist* 44: 215-218.

Mauldin, F. Louis
1983   "Singularity and a Pattern of Sin, Punishment and Forgiveness." *Perspectives in Religious Studies* 10 (Spring).

May, Rolla
1969   *Love and Will.* New York: W. W. Norton.

McEvenue, Sean E.
1971   *The Narrative Style of the Priestly Writer* [Analecta Biblica, 50]. Rome: Biblical Institute Press.

1975   "A Comparison of Narrative Styles in the Hagar Stories." *Semeia* 3: 64-80.

Mendenhall, George E.
1974   "The Shady Side of Wisdom." *A Light unto My Path.* Edited by H. Bream, et al. Philadelphia: Temple University Press.

Meyers, Carol L.
1983   "Gender Roles and Genesis 3:16 Revisited." *The Word of the Lord Shall Go Forth.* Edited by C. Meyers and M. O'Connor. Winona Lake, Ind.: Eisenbrauns.

1983   "Procreation, Production, and Protection: Male-Female Balance in Early Israel." *Journal of the American Academy of Religion* 51: 569-593.

Miller, J. M.
1974   "The Descendents of Cain: Notes on Genesis 4." *Zeitschrift für die Alttestamentliche Wissenschaft* 86: 164-174.

Miller, Patrick D. J.
1978   *Genesis 1—11: Studies in Structure and Theme* [Journal for the Study of the Old Testament, S. S. 8]. Sheffield: The University of Sheffield.

Miscall, Peter D.
    1983   *Workings of Old Testament Narrative*. Philadelphia: Fortress Press.

Mowinckel, Sigmund
    1964   *Erwargungen zur Pentateuchquellenfrage*. Oslo: Universitetfor-
              laget.

Muilenburg, James
    1979   "From Criticism and Beyond." *The Bible in Its Literary Milieu*.
              Edited by J. Maier and V. Toller. Grand Rapids, Mich.: Wm. B.
              Eerdmans.

Naidoff, Bruce D.
    1978   "A Man to Work the Soil: A New Interpretation of Genesis 2—3."
              Journal for the Study of the Old Testament 5: 2-14.

Nickelsburg, G. W. E.
    1981   *Jewish Literature Between the Bible and the Mishnah*. Phila-
              delphia: Fortress Press.

Niditch, Susan
    1985   *Chaos to Cosmos: Studies in Biblical Patterns of Creation*. Chico,
              Calif.: Scholars Press.

Neff, Robert W.
    1970   "The Birth and Election of Isaac in the Priestly Tradition." *Biblical
              Research* 15: 5-18.

    1972   "The Annunciation in the Birth Narrative of Ishmael." *Biblical Re-
              search* 17: 51-60.

    1976   "Saga." Unpublished paper presented to the Society of Biblical
              Literature Annual Meeting.

Noss, Philip
    1981   "The Oral Story and Bible Translation." *The Bible Translator* 32:
              301-318.

Noth, Martin
    1972   *A History of the Pentateuchal Traditions*. Translated by B. W.
              Anderson. Englewood Cliffs, N.J.: Prentice Hall.

Oden, R. A.
    1983   "Jacob as father, husband, nephew—kinship studies." *Journal of
              Biblical Literature* 102: 189-205.

Olrik, Axel
    1965   "Epic Laws of Folk Narrative." *The Study of Folklore*. Edited by A.
              Dundes. Englewood Cliffs, N.J.: Prentice Hall.

Orlinsky, H. M.
    1972   *Understanding the Bible through History and Archaeology*. New
              York: KTAV Publishing House, Inc.

Pedersen, John
  1926   *Israel: Its Life and Culture, I - II.* London: Oxford University Press.

Polzin, Robert
  1975   " 'The Ancestress of Israel in Danger' in Danger." *Semeia* 3: 81-98.

Porten, B., and U. Rapport
  1971   "Poetic Structure in Genesis IX 7." *Vetus Testamentum* 21: 363-
            369.

Pritchard, J. B.
  1958   *The Ancient Near East: An anthology of texts and pictures.*
            Princeton, N.J.: Princeton University Press.

  1969   *The Ancient Near East: Supplementary texts and pictures relating
            to the Old Testament.* Princeton, N.J.: Princeton University Press.

  1975   *The Ancient Near East, v. 2: A new anthology of texts and pictures.*
            Princeton, N.J.: Princeton University Press.

Rad, Gerhard von
  1962   *Old Testament Theology, I.* Translated by D. Stalker. New York:
            Harper and Row.

  1966   "The Joseph story and ancient wisdom." *The Problem of the
            Hexateuch and Other Essays.* Translated by E. W. T. Dicken. New
            York: McGraw-Hill Book Company.

  1973   *Genesis, A Commentary* (Revised Edition) [Old Testament Li-
            brary]. Philadelphia: The Westminster Press.

  1973a   *Wisdom in Israel.* Nashville: Abingdon.

Redford, Donald B.
  1970   *A Study of the Biblical Story of Joseph* [Supplements to *Vetus
            Testamentum,* 20]. E. J. Brill.

Rendtorff, Rolf
  1977   *Die überlieferungsgeschichtliche Problem des Pentateuch.* [Beiheft
            zur Zeitschrift für die alttestamentliche Wissenschaft, 147] Berlin:
            Walter de Gruyter.

Resseguie, James L.
  1984   "Reader-response criticism and the synoptic gospels." *Journal of
            the American Academy of Religion* 52: 307-324.

Riemann, Paul A.
  1970   "Am I My Brother's Keeper?" *Interpretation* 24: 482-491.

Roberts, A., and J. Donaldson, eds.
  1956-57   *The Ante-Nicene Fathers.* Revised by A. C. Coxe. Grand Rapids,
            Mich.: Wm. B. Eerdmans.

Robertson, David
  1977   *The Old Testament and the Literary Critic.* Philadelphia: Fortress
            Press.

Robertson, O. P.
    1980   "Genesis 15:6: New Covenant Exposition of an Old Covenant
              Text." The Westminster Theological Journal 42: 259-289.

Roth, Wolfgang
    1972   "The Wooing of Rebekah." Catholic Biblical Quarterly 34: 177-
              187.

Sakenfeld, Katharine D.
    1978   The Meaning of Ḥesed in the Hebrew Bible: A New Inquiry.
              Missoula, Mont.: Scholars Press.

Sarna, Nahum
    1966   Understanding Genesis. New York: McGraw-Hill Book Company.

Scharbert, Josef
    1977-   "brk" in Theological Dictionary of the Old Testament, pp. 279-
              308. Edited by G. J. Botterweck and Helmer Ringgren. Translated
              by J. T. Willis. Grand Rapids, Mich.: Wm. B. Eerdmans.

Seybold, Donald A.
    1974   "Paradox and symmetry in the Joseph Narrative." Literary In-
              terpretation of Biblical Narratives. Edited by K. R. R. Gros Louis, et
              al. Nashville: Abingdon.

Simons, Menno
    1956   Complete Writings of Menno Simons. Scottdale, Pa.: Herald Press.

Smith, Huston
    1982   "Evolution and Evolutionism." The Christian Century 99: 755-757.

    1982   "Scientism in Sole Command." Christianity and Crisis 42: 197-198.

Snyder, G. F.
    1976   "Repentance in the N.T." Interpreter's Dictionary of the Bible Sup-
              plementary Volume. Nashville: Abingdon Press.

Speiser, E. A.
    1964   Genesis [The Anchor Bible]. Garden City, N.Y.: Doubleday and
              Company.

Steck, O. H.
    1980   World and Environment [Biblical Encounter Series]. Nashville: Ab-
              ingdon Press.

Terrien, Samuel
    1978   The Elusive Presence. New York: Harper and Row.

Thompson, Thomas L.
    1974   The Historicity of the Patriarchal Narratives. Berlin: Walter de
              Gruyter.

Thompson, Th., and D. Thompson
    1968   "Some legal problems in the book of Ruth." Vetus Testamentum
              18: 79-99.

Trible, Phyllis
1978   *God and the Rhetoric of Sexuality* [Overtures to Biblical Theology].
            Philadelphia: Fortress Press.

Van Seters, John
1975   *Abraham in History and Tradition.* New Haven: Yale University
            Press.

1983   *In search of history: historiography in the ancient world and the
            origins of biblical history.* New Haven: Yale University Press.

Vaux, Roland de
1978   *The Early History of Israel.* Philadelphia: Westminster Press.

Vawter, Bruce
1956   *A Path Through Genesis.* New York: Sheed and Ward.

1977   *On Genesis.* Garden City, N.Y.: Doubleday and Company.

Vogels, Walter
1979   "Lot in his honor restored: a structural analysis of Genesis 13:2-
            18." *Eglise et Theologie* 10: 2-18.

Wallace, Howard N.
1985   *The Eden Narrative.* Atlanta, Ga.: Scholars Press.

Wallon, William
1979   "Biblical Poetry and Homeric Epic." *The Bible in Its Literary Milieu.*
            Edited by J. Maier and V. Toller. Grand Rapids, Mich.: Wm. B.
            Eerdmans.

Wellhausen, Julius
1899   *Die Composition des Hexateuchs und der historischen Bücher des
            Alten Testaments.* Berlin: Georg Reimer.

Wenham, G. J.
1978   "The Coherence of the Flood Narrative." *Vetus Testamentum* 28:
            336-348.

Wesley, John
1975   *Explanatory notes upon the Old Testament, I.* Salem, Ohio:
            Schmul Publishers.

Westermann, Claus
1964   *The Genesis Accounts of Creation.* Translated by N. Wagner.
            [Facet Books, Biblical Series, 7]. Philadelphia: Fortress Press.

1966   *Genesis* [Biblischer Kommentar, Altes Testament, I]. Neukirchen-
            Vluyn: Neukirchener Verlag.

1972   *Beginning and End in the Bible.* Translated by K. Crim. [Facet
            Book, Biblical Series, 31]. Philadelphia: Fortress Press.

1974   *Creation.* Translated by J. Scullion. Philadelphia: Fortress Press.

1978   *Blessing in the Bible and the Life of the Church.* Translated by K.
            Crim. [Overtures to Biblical Theology]. Philadelphia: Fortress Press.

1979   *God's Angels Need No Wings.* Translated by D. Scheidt.
            Philadelphia: Fortress Press.

1980   *Promises to the Fathers.* Translated by D. Green. Philadelphia:
            Fortress Press.

1984   *Genesis 1-11: A Commentary.* Translated by J. Scullion. Min-
            neapolis: Augsburg Publishing House.

1985   *Genesis 12-36: A Commentary.* Translated by J. Scullion. Min-
            neapolis: Augsburg Publishing House.

1986   *Genesis 37-50: A Commentary.* Translated by J. Scullion. Min-
            neapolis: Augsburg Publishing House.

White, Hugh C.
1978   "Direct and Third Person Discourse in the Narrative of the Fall."
            Society of Biblical Literature 1978 Seminar Papers 1: 121-140.
            Missoula, Mont.: Scholars Press.

Wiesel, Elie
1976   *Messengers of God.* New York: Random House.

Williams, James
1980   "Beautiful and barren." *Journal of the Study of the Old Testament*
            17: 107-119.

Williams, R. J.
1956   "The Fable in the Ancient Near East" in *A Stubborn Faith,* pp. 3-
            26. Edited by E. C. Hobbs. Dallas: Southern Methodist University
            Press.

Wilson, Robert R.
1977   *Genealogy and History in the Biblical World.* New Haven: Yale
            University Press.

1980   *Prophecy and Society in Ancient Israel.* Philadelphia: Fortress
            Press.

Wolff, Hans Water
1966   "The Kergyma of the Yahwist." *Interpretation* 20: 131-158.

1974   *Anthropology of the Old Testament.* Translated by M. Kohl.
            Philadelphia: Fortress Press.

Woudstra, M. H.
1970   "The *Toledot* of the Book of Genesis and Their Redemptive-His-
            torical Significance." *Calvin Theological Journal* 5: 184-189.

Wright, George R. H.
1982   "The positioning of Genesis 38." *Zeitschrift für die Alttestamen-
            tliche Wissenschaft* 94: 523-529.

Wyatt, Nicolas
    1981   "Interpreting the Creation and Fall Story in Genesis 2—3."
                Zeitschrift für die Alttestamentliche Wissenschaft 93: 10-21.

Young, E. J.
    1958   *An Introduction to the Old Testament*. Revised Edition. Grand
                Rapids, Mich.: Wm. B. Eerdmans.

Zimmerli, Walther
    1968   *Man and His Hope in the Old Testament* [Studies in Biblical
                Theology, 20]. Naperville, Ill.: Allenson.

    1976   *The Old Testament and the World*. Translated by J. Scullion.
                London: SPCK.

    1978   *Old Testament Theology in Outline*. Translated by D. E. Green. At-
                lanta: John Knox Press.

    1982   *I Am Yahweh*. Translated by D. Stott. Atlanta: John Knox Press.

Selected Reference Books

Brueggemann, Walter. *Genesis.* Atlanta: John Knox Press, 1982. A commentary oriented toward the preaching and teaching of Genesis in the congregation.

Cassuto, U. *A Commentary on the Book of Genesis.* Translated by I. Abraham. Jerusalem: The Magnes Press, 1964. A classic commentary with a conservative perspective on Genesis 1—12.

Coats, George W. *Genesis* [Forms of Old Testament Literature]. Grand Rapids, Mich.: Wm. B. Eerdmans, 1983. Coats emphasizes the literary structure and genre of Genesis in the interpretation of the texts.

Delitzsch, Franz. *A New Commentary on Genesis.* Translated by Sophia Taylor. Edinburgh: T & T Clark, 1899. A classic commentary still valuable because of the author's understanding of Hebrew words and phrases.

Francisca, Clyde T. *Genesis* [The Broadman Bible Commentary]. Revised by C. J. Alen. Nashville: Broadman Press, 1973. A conservative commentary in conversation with a broad range of scholarship.

Gunkel, Hermann. *Genesis.* Goettingen: Vandenhoeck and Ruprecht, 1910. A classic German commentary that calls our attention to the importance of literary form in the interpretation of Genesis.

Luther, Martin. *Luther's Commentary on Genesis*. Translated by J. T. Mueller. Grand Rapids, Mich.: Zondervan Publishing, 1958. Luther was schooled in the Old Testament and with this expansive work launched commentary writing in Protestantism.

Rad, Gerhard von. *Genesis, A Commentary* (Revised Edition) [Old Testament Library]. Philadelphia: Westminster Press, 1973. Still the standard for combining analysis of and reflection on the text of Genesis.

Speiser, E. A. *Genesis* [The Anchor Bible]. Garden City, N.Y.: Doubleday and Co., 1964. Gives special attention to linguistic matters. Concentrates on providing a careful translation.

Trible, Phyllis. *God and the Rhetoric of Sexuality* [Overtures to Biblical Theology]. Philadelphia, Fortress Press, 1978. Opened new doors especially to the interpretation of Genesis 2—3.

Vawter, Bruce. *On Genesis*. Garden City, N.Y.: Doubleday, 1977. Uses the context of the literature of the ancient Near East to enrich our understanding of the Genesis narratives.

Westermann, Claus. *Genesis 1-11: A Commentary, Genesis 12-36: A Commentary,* and *Genesis 37-50: A Commentary*. Translated by J. Scullion. Minneapolis: Augsburg Publishing House, 1984-86. This three-volume set provides an extensive analysis of the history and literature of Genesis.

The Author

Eugene F. Roop is known for his disciplined yet devotional approach to Bible study, his transparent spiritual and prayer life, and his commitment to the Christian faith as understood by the Church of the Brethren. He is active as a teacher and speaker in various congregations within his denomination and beyond.

He is Wieand Professor of Biblical Studies at Bethany Theological Seminary, Oak Brook, Illinois, where he has taught since 1977. He was on the faculty of Earlham School of Religion from 1970 to 1977.

Roop was ordained in the Lincolnshire Church of the Brethren, Fort Wayne, Indiana, 1967 and pastored churches in Indiana, Maryland, and Pennsylvania. He brings to his teaching and writing a deep commitment to the Bible as central to the teaching and preaching ministry of the congregation.

His articles have appeared in such publications as *Brethren Life and Thought, Messenger, Quaker Religious Thought,* and *The Bible Today.* His books include *Living the Biblical Story* (Abingdon Press, 1979) and *The Coming Kingdom: Teacher's Guide* (Brethren Press, 1982).

Roop received the B.S. degree from Manchester College (1964) with high distinction, the M.Div. from Bethany Theological Seminary (1967) *magna cum laude,* and the Ph.D. from Claremont Graduate School (1972). He has done postgraduate study through the Case Study Institute of the Association of Theological Schools. He participated in a joint expedition to the Tel-Hesi archaeological site in Israel in 1975. He has also studied at Fitzwilliam College and Westminster College of Cambridge University in the United Kingdom.

Roop is a member of the Association of Case Teachers, the American Academy of Religion, the Chicago Society of Biblical Research, the Society of Biblical Literature, and has been on the advisory committee for the local school board district 45.

Eugene and Delora Mishler Roop are the parents of Tanya and Frederic. They are members of York Center Church of the Brethren.